Efficient C+·

Efficient C++

Performance Programming Techniques

Dov Bulka
David Mayhew

ADDISON–WESLEY

Boston • San Francisco • New York • Toronto • Montreal
London • Munich • Paris • Madrid
Capetown • Sydney • Tokyo • Singapore • Mexico City

Many of the designations used by manufacturers and sellers to distinguish their products are claimed as trademarks. Where those designations appear in this book and Addison-Wesley was aware of a trademark claim, the designations have been printed in initial caps or all caps.

The authors and publishers have taken care in the preparation of this book, but make no expressed or implied warranty of any kind and assume no responsibility for errors or omissions. No liability is assumed for incidental or consequential damages in connection with or arising out of the use of the information or programs contained herein.

The publisher offers discounts on this book when ordered in quantity for special sales. For more information, please contact:

Pearson Education Corporate Sales Division
201 W. 103rd Street
Indianapolis, IN 46290
(800) 428-5331
corpsales@pearsoned.com

Library of Congress Cataloging-in-Publication Data

Bulka, Dov.
    Efficient C++ : performance programming techniques / Dov Bulka,
David Mayhew.
        p.   m.
    Includes bibliographical references (p.   ).
    ISBN 0-201-37950-3
    1. C++ (Computer program language)   I. Mayhew, David.   II. Title.
QA76.73.C153B85 1999
005.13 ' 3—dc21   99-39175
                                                                    CIP

Text printed on recycled and acid-free paper.
ISBN 0201379503
5 6 7 8 9 10 CRS   06 05 04 03
5th Printing   May 2003

Dedication

To my mother, Rivka Bulka
and to the memory of my father Yacov Bulka,
survivor of the Auschwitz concentration camp.
They could not take away his
kindness, compassion and optimism,
which was his ultimate triumph.
He passed away during the writing of this book.

D.B

To Ruth, the love of my life,
who made time for me to write this.
To the boys, Austin, Alex, and Steve,
who missed their dad for a while.
To my parents, Mom and Dad,
who have always loved and supported me

D.M.

Contents

Preface

If you conducted an informal survey of software developers on the issue of C++ performance, you would undoubtedly find that the vast majority of them view performance issues as the Achilles' heel of an otherwise fine language. We have heard it repeatedly ever since C++ burst on the corporate scene: C++ is a poor choice for implementing performance-critical applications. In the mind of developers, this particular application domain was ruled by plain C and, occasionally, even assembly language.

As part of that software community we had the opportunity to watch that myth develop and gather steam. Years ago, we participated in the wave that embraced C++ with enthusiasm. All around us, many development projects plunged in headfirst. Some time later, software solutions implemented in C++ began rolling out. Their performance was typically less than optimal, to put it gently. Enthusiasm over C++ in performance-critical domains has cooled. We were in the business of supplying networking software whose execution speed was not up for negotiation—speed was top priority. Since networking software is pretty low on the software food-chain, its performance is crucial. Large numbers of applications were going to sit on top of it and depend on it. Poor performance in the low levels ripples all the way up to higher level applications.

Our experience was not unique. All around, early adopters of C++ had difficulties with the resulting performance of their C++ code. Instead of attributing the difficulties to the steep learning curve of the new object-oriented software development paradigm, we blamed it on C++, the dominant language for the expression of the paradigm. Even though C++ compilers were still essentially in their infancy, the language was branded as inherently slow. This belief spread quickly and is now widely accepted as fact. Software organizations that passed on C++ frequently pointed to performance as their key concern. That concern was rooted in the perception that C++ cannot match the performance delivered by its C counterpart. Consequently, C++ has had little success penetrating software domains that view performance as top priority: operating system kernels, device drivers, networking systems (routers, gateways, protocol stacks), and more.

We have spent years dissecting large systems of C and C++ code trying to squeeze every ounce of performance out of them. It is through our experience of slugging it out in the trenches that we have come to appreciate the potential of C++ to produce highly efficient programs. We've seen it done in practice. This book is our attempt to share that experience and document the many lessons we have learned in our own pursuit of C++ efficiency. Writing efficient C++ is not trivial, nor is it rocket science. It takes the understanding of some performance principles, as well as information on C++ performance traps and pitfalls.

The 80-20 rule is an important principle in the world of software construction. We adopt it in the writing of this book as well: 20% of all performance bugs will show up 80% of the time. We therefore chose to concentrate our efforts where it counts the most. We are interested in those performance issues that arise frequently in industrial code and have significant impact. This book is not an exhaustive discussion of the set of all possible performance bugs and their solutions; hence, we will not cover what we consider esoteric and rare performance pitfalls.

Our point of view is undoubtedly biased by our practical experience as programmers of server-side, performance-critical communications software. This bias impacts the book in several ways:

- The profile of performance issues that we encounter in practice may be slightly different in nature than those found in scientific computing, database applications, and other domains. That's not a problem. Generic performance principles transcend distinct domains, and apply equally well in domains other than networking software.

- At times, we invented contrived examples to drive a point home, although we tried to minimize this. We have made enough coding mistakes in the past to have a sizable collection of samples taken from real production-level code that we have worked on. Our expertise was earned the hard way—by learning from our own mistakes as well as those of our colleagues. As much as possible, we illustrated our points with real code samples.

- We do not delve into the asymptotic complexity of algorithms, data structures, and the latest and greatest techniques for accessing, sorting, searching, and compressing data. These are important topics, but they have been extensively covered elsewhere [Knu73, BR95, KP74]. Instead, we focus on simple, practical, everyday coding and design principles that yield large performance improvements. We point out common design and coding practices that lead to poor performance, whether it be through the unwitting use of language features that carry high hidden costs or through violating any number of subtle (and not so subtle) performance principles.

So how do we separate myth from reality? Is C++ performance truly inferior to that of C? It is our contention that the common perception of inferior C++ performance is invalid. We concede that in general, when comparing a C program to a C++ version of what appears to be the same thing, the C program is generally faster. However, we also claim that the apparent similarity of the two programs typically is based on their data handling functionality, not their correctness, robustness, or ease of maintenance. Our contention is that when C programs are brought up to the level of C++ programs in these regards, the speed differences disappear, or the C++ versions are faster.

Thus C++ is inherently neither slower nor faster. It could be either, depending on how it is used and what is required from it. It's the way it is used that matters: If used properly, C++ can yield software systems exhibiting not just acceptable performance, but yield superior software performance.

We would like to thank the many people who contributed to this work. The toughest part was getting started and it was our editor, Marina Lang, who was instrumental in getting this project off the ground. Julia Sime made a significant contribution to the early draft and Yomtov Meged contributed many valuable suggestions as well. He also was the one who pointed out to us the subtle difference between our opinions and the absolute truth. Although those two notions may coincide at times, they are still distinct.

Many thanks to the reviewers hired by Addison-Wesley; their feedback was extremely valuable.

Thanks also to our friends and colleagues who reviewed portions of the manuscript. They are, in no particular order, Cyndy Ross, Art Francis, Scott Snyder, Tricia York, Michael Fraenkel, Carol Jones, Heather Kreger, Kathryn Britton, Ruth Willenborg, David Wisler, Bala Rajaraman, Don "Spike" Washburn, and Nils Brubaker.

Last but not least, we would like to thank our wives, Cynthia Powers Bulka and Ruth Washington Mayhew.

Introduction

In the days of assembler language programming, experienced programmers esti-
mated the execution speed of their source code by counting the number of assembly
language instructions. On some architectures, such as RISC, most assembler instructions executed in one clock cycle each. Other architectures featured wide variations
in instruction to instruction execution speed, but experienced programmers were able
to develop a good feel for average instruction latency. If you knew how many
instructions your code fragment contained, you could estimate with accuracy the
number of clock cycles their execution would consume. The mapping from source
code to assembler was trivially one-to-one. The assembler code *was* the source code.

On the ladder of programming languages, C is one step higher than assembler language.
C source code is not identical to the corresponding compiler-generated assembler code.
It is the compiler's task to bridge the gap from source code to assembler. The mapping
of source-to-assembler code is no longer the one-to-one identity mapping. It remains,
however, a linear relationship: Each source level statement in C corresponds to a small
number of assembler instructions. If you estimate that each C statement translates into
five to eight assembler instructions, chances are you will be in the ballpark.

C++ has shattered this nice linear relationship between the number of source level
statements and compiler-generated assembly statement count. Whereas the cost of C
statements is largely uniform, the cost of C++ statements fluctuates wildly. One C++
statement can generate three assembler instructions, whereas another can generate 300.
Implementing high-performance C++ code has placed a new and unexpected demand
on programmers: the need to navigate through a performance minefield, trying to stay

on a safe three-instruction-per-statement path and to avoid usage of routes that contain 300-instruction land mines. Programmers must identify language constructs likely to generate large overhead and know how to code or design around them. These are considerations that C and assembler language programmers have never had to worry about. The only exception may be the use of macros in C, but those are hardly as frequent as the invocations of constructors and destructors in C++ code.

The C++ compiler might also insert code into the execution flow of your program "behind your back." This is news to the unsuspecting C programmer migrating to C++ (which is where many of us are coming from). The task of writing efficient C++ programs requires C++ developers to acquire new performance skills that are specific to C++ and that transcend the generic software performance principles. In C programming, you are not likely to be blindsided by hidden overhead, so it is possible to stumble upon good performance in a C program. In contrast, this is unlikely to happen in C++: You are not going to achieve good performance accidentally, without knowing the pitfalls lurking about.

To be fair, we have seen many examples of poor performance that were rooted in inefficient object-oriented (OO) design. The ideas of software flexibility and reuse have been promoted aggressively ever since OO moved into the mainstream. However, flexibility and reuse seldom go hand-in-hand with performance and efficiency. In mathematics, it would be painful to reduce every theorem back to basic principles. Mathematicians try to reuse results that have already been proven. Outside mathematics, however, it often makes sense to leverage special circumstances and to take shortcuts. In software design, it is acceptable under some circumstances to place higher priority on performance than reuse. When you implement the `read()` or `write()` function of a device driver, the known performance requirements are generally much more important to your software's success than the possibility that at some point in the future it might be reused. Some performance problems in OO design are due to putting the emphasis on the wrong place at the wrong time. Programmers should focus on solving the problem they have, not on making their current solution amenable to some unidentified set of possible future requirements.

Roots of Software Inefficiency

Silent C++ overhead is not the root of all performance evil. Even eliminating compiler-generated overhead would not always be sufficient. If that were the case, then

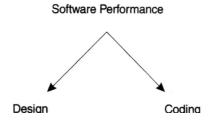

Figure 1. High-level classification of software performance.

every C program would enjoy automatic awesome performance due to the lack of silent overhead. Additional factors affect software performance in general and C++ performance in particular. What are those factors? The first level of performance classification is given in Figure 1.

At the highest level, software efficiency is determined by the efficiency of two main ingredients:

- **Design efficiency**   This involves the program's high-level design. To fix performance problems at that level you must understand the program's big picture. To a large extent, this item is language independent. No amount of coding efficiency can provide shelter for a bad design.

- **Coding efficiency**   Small- to medium-scale implementation issues fall into this category. Fixing performance in this category generally involves local modifications. For example, you do not need to look very far into a code fragment in order to lift a constant expression out of a loop and prevent redundant computations. The code fragment you need to understand is limited in scope to the loop body.

This high-level classification can be broken down further into finer subtopics, as shown in Figure 2.

Design efficiency is broken down further into two items:

- **Algorithms and data structures**   Technically speaking, every program is an algorithm in itself. Referring to "algorithms and data structures" actually refers to the well-known subset of algorithms for accessing, searching, sorting, compressing, and otherwise manipulating large collections of data.

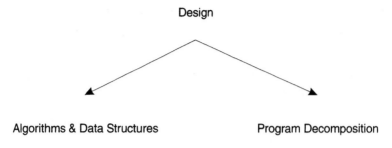

Figure 2. Refinement of the design performance view.

Oftentimes performance automatically is associated with the efficiency of the algorithms and data structures used in a program, as if nothing else matters. To claim that software performance can be reduced to that aspect alone is inaccurate. The efficiency of algorithms and data structures is necessary but not sufficient: By itself, it does not guarantee good overall program efficiency.

- **Program decomposition** This involves decomposition of the overall task into communicating subtasks, object hierarchies, functions, data, and function flow. It is the program's high-level design and includes component design as well as intercomponent communication. Few programs consist of a single component. A typical Web application interacts (via API) with a Web server, TCP sockets, and a database, at the very least. There are efficiency tricks and pitfalls with respect to crossing the API layer with each of those components.

Coding efficiency can also be subdivided, as shown in Figure 3.

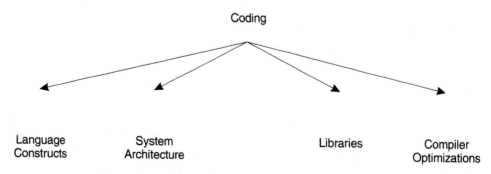

Figure 3. Refinement of the coding performance view.

We split up coding efficiency into four items:

- **Language constructs**   C++ adds power and flexibility to its C ancestor. These added benefits do not come for free—some C++ language constructs may produce overhead in exchange. We will discuss this issue throughout the book. This topic is, by nature, C++ specific.

- **System architecture**   System designers invest considerable effort to present the programmer with an idealistic view of the system: infinite memory, dedicated CPU, parallel thread execution, and uniform-cost memory access. Of course, none of these is true—it just feels that way. Developing software free of system architecture considerations is also convenient. To achieve high performance, however, these architectural issues cannot be ignored since they can impact performance drastically. When it comes to performance we must bear in mind that

  - Memory is not infinite. It is the virtual memory system that makes it appear that way.

  - The cost of memory access is nonuniform. There are orders of magnitude difference among cache, main memory, and disk access.

  - Our program does not have a dedicated CPU. We get a time slice only once in a while.

  - On a uniprocessor machine, parallel threads do not truly execute in parallel—they take turns.

  Awareness of these issues helps software performance.

- **Libraries**   The choice of libraries used by an implementation can also affect performance. For starters, some libraries may perform a task faster than others. Because you typically don't have access to the library's source code, it is hard to tell how library calls implement their services. For example, to convert an integer to a character string, you can choose between

```
sprintf(string, "%d", i);
```

or an integer-to-ASCII function call [KR88],

```
itoa(i, string);
```

Which one is more efficient? Is the difference significant?

There is also the option of rolling your own version even if a particular service is already available in a library. Libraries are often designed with flexibility and reusability in mind. Often, flexibility and reusability trade off with performance. If, for some critical code fragment, you choose to put performance considerations above the other two, it might be reasonable to override a library service with your own home-grown implementation. Applications are so diverse in their specific needs, it is hard to design a library that will be the perfect solution for everybody, everywhere, all the time.

- **Compiler optimizations**   Simply a more descriptive name than "miscellaneous," this category includes all those small coding tricks that don't fit in the other coding categories, such as loop unrolling, lifting constant expressions out of loops, and similar techniques for elimination of computational redundancies. Most compilers will perform many of those optimizations for you. But you cannot count on any specific compiler to perform a specific optimization. One compiler may unroll a loop twice, another will unroll it four times, and yet another compiler will not unroll it at all. For ultimate control, you have to take coding matters into your own hands.

Our Goal

Many books and articles have extolled the virtues of C++ as a language supporting the OO paradigm. C++ is positioned as the latest cure for the software crisis. For those not familiar with the term, the software crisis is our current inability to develop code that is simple enough to be understood, maintained, and extended by a mere mortal, yet powerful enough to provide solutions to complex problems [CE95]. Developers who migrate from other structured languages to C++ have been bombarded with information pertaining to the use of C++ in creating highly flexible and reusable code that will lend itself nicely to easy maintenance and extension. One important issue, however, has received little attention: run-time efficiency. We will examine the relevant performance topics from the perspective of C++ programming. After reading this book you should emerge with a clear understanding of the common C++ performance pitfalls and how to avoid them without compromising the clarity and simplicity of your design. In fact, the high-performance solution is frequently also the simplest solution. This book should also help developers produce

C++ code as efficient as its C counterpart while still benefiting from the extended features of C++ and the inherent superiority of the OO paradigm. A famous physicist once said that an expert is one who has made all possible mistakes in a very narrow field. Although making mistakes is a good way to learn, learning from the mistakes of others (the authors, in this case) is even better.

A secondary goal of this book is to construct a one-stop shop for C++ performance issues. As a C++ developer, the answers to your performance concerns are not readily available. They are scattered over a long list of books and magazine articles that address different pieces of this puzzle. You would have to research this topic and put it all together yourself. Not many developers are going to do that. We are too busy. It will be helpful to have a one-stop shop that focuses entirely on the important topic of C++ performance.

Software Efficiency: Does It Matter?

In an era where processor speed doubles every 18 months (Moore's law), do we really need to worry about software efficiency? The fact is that regardless of phenomenal advances in chip technology, software efficiency is still a prominent concern. In 1971, the Intel 4004 was the first commercial processor to fit on a single chip. It was named a microprocessor. Since then, microprocessor technology has embarked on a 25-year streak of doubling processor speed every 18 months. Today's microprocessors are tens of thousands of times faster than the Intel 4004. If processor speed was the answer to inefficient software, the issue would have been resolved and long forgotten. Yet, software efficiency is still a concern with most development organizations. Why?

Imagine that you are trying to sell your product, say a Web application server, to a Fortune 500 company. They need 600 transactions per second to run their business online. Your application server can support only 60 transactions per second before running out of steam on the latest and greatest server hardware. If the customer is to use your software, they need to string together a cluster of at least 10 servers to reach their 600-transaction per second goal, raising the cost of your solution in terms of hardware, software licenses, network administration, and maintenance. To make matters worse, the customer has invited two of your competitors to pitch their own solutions. If a competitor has a more efficient implementation, they will need less hardware to deliver the required performance, and they will offer a cheaper solution. The speed of the processor is a constant in this situation—the software vendors in this story compete over the same hardware. It is often the case that the most efficient solution wins the bid.

You also must examine how processing speed compares to communication speed. If we can transmit data faster than the computer can generate it, then the computer (processor plus software) is the new bottleneck. The limits imposed by physics might soon put the brakes on the fantastic growth of processor speed [Lew1]. Not so for communication speed. Like processing speed, communication speed has enjoyed phenomenal growth. Back in 1970, 4800 bits per second was considered high-speed communication. Today, hundreds of megabits per second is common. The end of the road for communication speed is nowhere in sight [Lew2].

Optical communication technology does not seem to have show-stopping technological roadblocks that will threaten progress in the near future. Several research labs are already experimenting with 100-gigabit-per-second all-optical networking. The biggest obstacle currently is not of a technical nature; it is the infrastructure. High-speed networking necessitates the rewiring of the information society from copper cables to optical fiber. This campaign is already underway. Communication adapters are already faster than the computing devices attached to them. Emerging network technologies such as 100 Mbps LAN adapters and high-speed ATM switches make computer speed critical. In the past, inefficient software has been masked by slow links. Popular communication protocols such as SNA and TCP/IP could easily overwhelm a 16 Mbps token ring adapter, leaving software performance bottlenecks undetected. Not so with 100 Mbps FDDI or Fast Ethernet. If 1,000 instructions are added to the protocol's send/ receive path, they may not degrade throughput on a token ring connection because the protocol implementation can still pump data faster than the token ring can consume it. But an extra 1,000 instructions show up instantly as degraded throughput on a Fast Ethernet adapter. Today, very few computers are capable of saturating a high-speed link, and it is only going to get more difficult. Optical communication technology is now surpassing the growth rate of microprocessor speed. The computer (processor plus software) is quickly becoming the new bottleneck, and it's going to stay that way.

To make a long story short, software performance is important and always will be. This one is not going away. As processor and communication technology march on, they redefine what "fast" means. They give rise to a new breed of bandwidth- and cycle-hungry applications that push the boundaries of technology. You never have enough horsepower. Software efficiency now becomes even more crucial than before. Whether the growth of processor speed is coming to an end or not, it will definitely trail communication speed. This puts the efficiency burden on the software. Further advances in execution speed will depend heavily on the efficiency of the software, not just the processor.

Terminology

Before moving on, here are a few words to clarify the terminology. "Performance" can stand for various metrics, the most common ones being space efficiency and time efficiency. Space efficiency seeks to minimize the use of memory in a software solution. Likewise, time efficiency seeks to minimize the use of processor cycles. Time efficiency is often represented in terms of response time and throughput. Other metrics include compile time and executable size.

The rapidly falling price of memory has moved the topic of space efficiency for its own sake to the back burner. Desktop PCs with plenty of RAM (Random Access Memory) are common. Corporate customers are not that concerned about space issues these days. In our work with customers we have encountered concerns with run-time efficiency for the most part. Since customers drive requirements, we will adopt their focus on time efficiency. From here on, we will restrict performance to its time-efficiency interpretation. Generally we will look at space considerations only when they interfere with run-time performance, as in caching and paging.

In discussing time efficiency, we will often mention the terms "pathlength" and "instruction count" interchangeably. Both stand for the number of assembler language instructions generated by a fragment of code. In a RISC architecture, if a code fragment exhibits a reasonable "locality of reference" (i.e., cache hits), the ratio between instruction counts and clock cycles will approximate one. On CISC architectures it may average two or more, but in any event, poor instruction counts always indicate poor execution time, regardless of processor architecture. A good instruction count is necessary but not sufficient for high performance. Consequently, it is a crude performance indicator, but still useful. It will be used in conjunction with time measurements to evaluate efficiency.

Organization of This Book

We start the performance tour close to home with a real-life example. Chapter 1 is a war story of C++ code that exhibited atrocious performance, and what we did to resolve it. This example will drive home some performance lessons that might very well apply to diverse scenarios.

Object-oriented design in C++ might harbor a performance cost. This is what we pay for the power of OO support. The significance of this cost, the factors affecting it, and how and when you can get around it are discussed in Chapters 2, 3, and 4.

Chapter 5 is dedicated to temporaries. The creation of temporary objects is a C++ feature that catches new C++ programmers off guard. C programmers are not used to the C compiler generating significant overhead "under the covers." If you aim to write high-efficiency C++, it is essential that you know when temporaries are generated by the C++ compiler and how to avoid them.

Memory management is the subject of Chapters 6 and 7. Allocating and deallocating memory on the fly is expensive. Functions such as `new()` and `delete()` are designed to be flexible and general. They deal with variable-sized memory chunks in a multithreaded environment. As such, their speed is compromised. Oftentimes, you are in a position to make simplifying assumptions about your code that will significantly boost the speed of memory allocation and deallocation. These chapters will discuss several simplifying assumptions that can be made and the efficient memory managers that are designed to leverage them.

Inlining is probably the second most popular performance tip, right after passing objects by reference. It is not as simple as it sounds. The `inline` keyword, just like `register`, is just a hint that the compiler often ignores. Situations in which `inline` is likely to be ignored and other unexpected consequences are discussed in Chapters 8, 9, and 10.

Performance, flexibility, and reuse seldom go hand-in-hand. The Standard Template Library is an attempt to buck that trend and to combine these three into a powerful component. We will examine the performance of the STL in Chapter 11.

Reference counting is a technique often used by experienced C++ programmers. You cannot dedicate a book to C++ performance without coverage of this technique, discussed in Chapter 12.

Software performance cannot always be salvaged by a single "silver bullet" fix. Performance degradation is often a result of many small local inefficiencies, each of which is insignificant by itself. It is the combination that results in a significant degradation. Over the years, while resolving many performance bugs in various C++ products, we have come to identify certain bugs that seem to float to the surface frequently. We divided the list into two sets: coding and design inefficiencies. The coding set contains "low-hanging fruit"—small-scale, local coding optimizations you can perform without needing to understand the overall design. In Chapter 13 we discuss various items of that nature. The second set contains design optimizations that are global in nature. Those optimizations modify code that is spread across the source code, and are the subject of Chapter 14.

Chapter 15 covers scalability issues, unique performance considerations present in a multiprocessor environment that we don't encounter on a uniprocessor. This chapter discusses design and coding issues aimed at exploiting parallelism. This chapter will also provide some help with the terminology and concepts of multithreaded programming and synchronization. We refer to thread synchronization concepts in several other places in the book. If your exposure to those concepts is limited, Chapter 15 should help level the playing field.

Chapter 16 takes a look at the underlying system. Top-notch performance also necessitates a rudimentary understanding of underlying operating systems and processor architectures. Issues such as caching, paging, and threading are discussed here.

1

The Tracing War Story

Every software product we have ever worked on contained tracing functionality in one form or another. Any time your source code exceeds a few thousand lines, tracing becomes essential. It is important for debugging, maintaining, and understanding execution flow of nontrivial software. You would not expect a trace discussion in a performance book but the reality is, on more than one occasion, we have run into severe performance degradation due to poor implementations of tracing. Even slight inefficiencies can have a dramatic effect on performance. The goal of this chapter is not necessarily to teach proper trace implementation, but to use the trace vehicle to deliver some important performance principles that often surface in C++ code. The implementation of trace functionality runs into typical C++ performance obstacles, which makes it a good candidate for performance discussion. It is simple and familiar. We don't have to drown you in a sea of irrelevant details in order to highlight the important issues. Yet, simple or not, trace implementations drive home many performance issues that you are likely to encounter in any random fragment of C++ code.

Many C++ programmers define a simple `Trace` class to print diagnostic information to a log file. Programmers can define a `Trace` object in each function that they want to trace, and the `Trace` class can write a message on function entry and function exit. The `Trace` objects will add extra execution overhead, but they will help a programmer find problems without using a debugger. If your C++ code happens to be embedded as native code in a Java program, using a Java debugger to trace your native code would be a challenge.

The most extreme form of trace performance optimization would be to eliminate the performance cost altogether by embedding trace calls inside `#ifdef` blocks:

```
#ifdef TRACE
Trace t("myFuction"); // Constructor takes a function name argument
t.debug("Some information message");
#endif
```

The weakness of the #ifdef approach is that you must recompile to turn tracing on and off. This is definitely something your customers will not be able to do unless you jump on the free software bandwagon and ship them your source code. Alternatively, you can control tracing dynamically by communicating with the running program. The Trace class implementation could check the trace state prior to logging any trace information:

```
void
Trace::debug(string &msg)
{
    if (traceIsActive) {
      // log message here
      }
}
```

We don't care about performance when tracing is active. It is assumed that tracing will be turned on only during problem determination. During normal operation, tracing would be inactive by default, and we expect our code to exhibit peak performance. For that to happen, the trace overhead must be minimal. A typical trace statement will look something along the lines of

```
t.debug("x = " + itoa(x));   // itoa() converts an int to ascii
```

This typical statement presents a serious performance problem. Even when tracing is off, we still must create the string argument that is passed in to the debug() function. This single statement hides substantial computation:

- Create a temporary string object from "x = "
- Call itoa(x)
- Create a temporary string object from the char pointer returned by itoa()
- Concatenate the preceding string objects to create a third temporary string
- Destroy all three string temporaries after returning from the debug() call

So we go to all this trouble to construct three temporary string objects, and proceed to drop them all over the floor when we find out that trace is inactive. The overhead of creating and destroying those string and Trace objects is at best hundreds of instructions. In typical OO code where functions are short and call frequencies are high, trace overhead could easily degrade performance by an order of magnitude. This is not a farfetched figment of our imagination. We have actually experienced it in a real-life product implementation. It is an educational experience to delve into this particular horror story in more detail. It is the story of an attempt to add tracing capability to a complex product consisting of a half-million lines of C++ code. Our first attempt backfired due to atrocious performance.

Our Initial Trace Implementation

Our intent was to have the trace object log event messages such as entering a function, leaving a function, and possibly other information of interest between those two events.

```
int myFunction(int x)
{
    string name = "myFunction";
    Trace t(name);
    ...
    string moreInfo = "more interesting info";
    t.debug(moreInfo);
    ...
};  // Trace destructor logs exit event to an output stream
```

To enable this usage we started out with the following Trace implementation:

```
class Trace {
public:
    Trace (const string &name);
    ~Trace ();
    void debug (const string &msg);

    static bool traceIsActive;
private:
    string theFunctionName;
};
```

The Trace constructor stores the function's name.

```
inline
Trace::Trace(const string &name) : theFunctionName(name)
{
if (TraceIsActive){
    cout << "Enter function" << name << endl;
    }
}
```

Additional information messages are logged via calls to the **debug()** method.

```
inline
void Trace::debug(const string &msg)
{
if (TraceIsActive){
    cout << msg << endl;
    }
}
inline
Trace::~Trace()
{
    if (traceIsActive) {
      cout << "Exit function " << theFunctionName << endl;
      }
}
```

Once the Trace was designed, coded, and tested, it was deployed and quickly inserted into a large part of the code. Trace objects popped up in most of the functions on the critical execution path. On a subsequent performance test we were shocked to discover that performance plummeted to 20% of its previous level. The insertion of Trace objects has slowed down performance by a factor of five. We are talking about the case when tracing was off and performance was supposed to be unaffected.

What Went Wrong

Programmers may have different views on C++ performance depending on their respective experiences. But there are a few basic principles that we all agree on:

- I/O is expensive.

- Function call overhead is a factor so we should inline short, frequently called functions.

- Copying objects is expensive. Prefer pass-by-reference over pass-by-value.

Our initial `Trace` implementation has adhered to all three of these principles. We avoided I/O if tracing was off, all methods were inlined, and all `string` arguments were passed by reference. We stuck by the rules and yet we got blindsided. Obviously, the collective wisdom of the previous rules fell short of the expertise required to develop high-performance C++.

Our experience suggests that the dominant issue in C++ performance is not covered by these three principles. It is the creation (and eventual destruction) of unnecessary objects that were created in anticipation of being used but are not. The `Trace` implementation is an example of the devastating effect of useless objects on performance, evident even in the simplest use of a `Trace` object. The minimal usage of a `Trace` object is to log function entry and exit:

```
int myFunction(int x)
{
    string name = "myFunction";
    Trace t(name);
    ...
};
```

This minimal trace invokes a sequence of computations:

- Create the `string name` local to `myFunction`.

- Invoke the `Trace` constructor.

- The `Trace` constructor invokes the `string` constructor to create the member `string`.

At the end of the scope, which coincides with the end of the function, the `Trace` and two `string` objects are destroyed:

- Destroy the `string name`.

- Invoke the `Trace` destructor.

- The `Trace` destructor invokes the `string` destructor for the member `string`.

When tracing is off, the `string` member object never gets used. You could also make the case that the `Trace` object itself is not of much use either (when tracing is off). All the computational effort that goes into the creation and destruction of those objects is a pure waste. Keep in mind that this is the cost when tracing is off. This was supposed to be the fast lane.

So how expensive does it get? For a baseline measurement, we timed the execution of a million iterations of the function addOne():

```
int addOne(int x)      // Version 0
{
    return x+1;
}
```

As you can tell, addOne() doesn't do much, which is exactly the point of a baseline. We are trying to isolate the performance factors one at a time. Our main() function invoked addOne() a million times and measured execution time:

```
int main()
{
    Trace::traceIsActive = false;//Turn tracing off
    //...
    GetSystemTime(&t1);    // Start timing

    for (i =0; i < j; i++) {
        y = addOne(i);
        }

    GetSystemTime(&t2);    // Stop timing
    // ...
}
```

Next, we added a Trace object to addOne and measured again to evaluate the performance delta. This is Version 1 (see Figure 1.1):

```
int addOne(int x)      // Version 1. Introducing a Trace object
{
    string name = "addOne";
    Trace t(name);

    return x+1;
}
```

The cost of the for loop has skyrocketed from 55 ms to 3,500 ms. In other words, the speed of addOne has plummeted by a factor of more than 60. This kind of overhead will wreak havoc on the performance of any software. The cost of our tracing implementation was clearly unacceptable. But eliminating the tracing mechanism

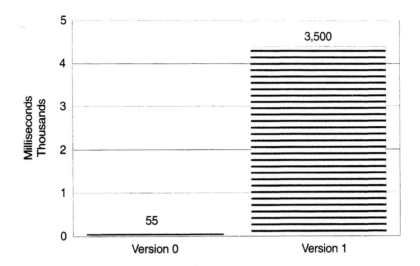

Figure 1.1. The performance cost of the Trace object.

altogether was not an option—we had to have some form of tracing functionality. We had to regroup and come up with a more efficient implementation.

The Recovery Plan

The performance recovery plan was to eliminate objects and computations whose values get dropped when tracing is off. We started with the string argument created by addOne and given to the Trace constructor. We modified the function name argument from a string object to a plain char pointer:

```
int addOne(int x)      // Version 2. Forget the string object.
                       // Use a char pointer instead.
{
    char  *name = "addOne";
    Trace t(name);

    return x+1;
}
```

Along with that modification, we had to modify the Trace constructor itself to take a char pointer argument instead of a string reference:

```
inline
Trace::Trace(const char *name) : theFunctionName(name)// Version 2
{
if (traceIsActive){
    cout << "Enter function" << name << endl;
    }
}
```

Similarly, the `Trace::debug()` method was modified as well to accept a `const *char` as an input argument instead of a `string`. Now we don't have to create the `name` `string` prior to creating the `Trace` object—one less object to worry about. This translated into a performance boost, as was evident in our measurement. Execution time dropped from 3,500 ms to 2,500 ms (see Figure 1.2).

The second step is to eliminate the unconditional creation of the `string` member object contained within the `Trace` object. From a performance perspective we have two equivalent solutions. One is to replace the `string` object with a plain `char` pointer. A `char` pointer gets "constructed" by a simple assignment—that's cheap. The other solution is to use composition instead of aggregation. Instead of embedding a `string` subobject in the `Trace` object, we could replace it with a `string` pointer. The advantage of a `string` pointer over a `string` object is that we can delay creation of the `string` after we have verified that tracing was on. We opted to take that route:

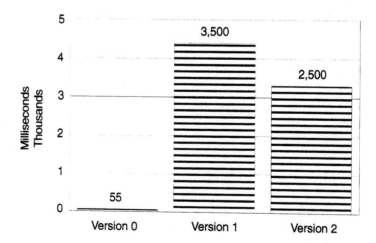

Figure 1.2.   Impact of eliminating one string object.

```
class Trace {// Version 3. Use a string pointer
public:
    Trace (const char *name) : theFunctionName(0)
    {
    if (traceIsActive) {   // Conditional creation
      cout << "Enter function" << name < endl;
      theFunctionName = new string(name);
      }
    }

    ...
private:

    string *theFunctionName;
};
```

The Trace destructor must also be modified to delete the string pointer:

```
inline
Trace::~Trace()
{
    if (traceIsActive) {
      cout << "Exit function " << *theFunctionName << endl;

      delete theFunctionName;
      }

}
```

Another measurement has shown a significant performance improvement. Response time has dropped from 2,500 ms to 185 ms (see Figure 1.3).

So we have arrived. We took the Trace implementation from 3,500 ms down to 185 ms. You may still contend that 185 ms looks pretty bad compared to a 55-ms execution time when addOne had no tracing logic at all. This is more than 3x degradation. So how can we claim victory? The point is that the original addOne function (without trace) did very little. It added one to its input argument and returned immediately. The addition of any code to addOne would have a profound effect on its execution time. If you add four instructions to trace the behavior of only two instructions, you have tripled your execution time. Conversely, if you increase by four instructions an execution path already containing 200, you have only degraded execution time by 2%. If addOne consisted of more complex computations, the addition of Trace would have been closer to being negligible.

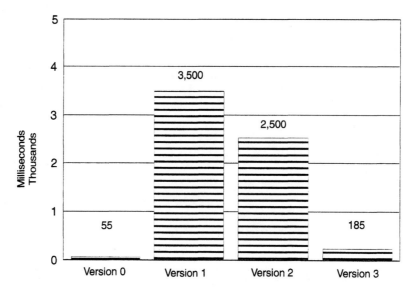

Figure 1.3.   Impact of conditional creation of the string member.

In some ways, this is similar to inlining. The influence of inlining on heavyweight functions is negligible. Inlining plays a major role only for simple functions that are dominated by the call and return overhead. The functions that make excellent candidates for inlining are precisely the ones that are bad candidates for tracing. It follows that Trace objects should not be added to small, frequently executed functions.

Key Points

- Object definitions trigger silent execution in the form of object constructors and destructors. We call it "silent execution" as opposed to "silent overhead" because object construction and destruction are not usually overhead. If the computations performed by the constructor and destructor are always necessary, then they would be considered efficient code (inlining would alleviate the cost of call and return overhead). As we have seen, constructors and destructors do not always have such "pure" characteristics, and they can create significant overhead. In some situations, computations performed by the constructor (and/or destructor) are left unused. We should also point out that this is more of a design issue than a C++ language issue. However, it is seen less often in C because it lacks constructor and destructor support.

- Just because we pass an object by reference does not guarantee good performance. Avoiding object copy helps, but it would be helpful if we didn't have to construct and destroy the object in the first place.

- Don't waste effort on computations whose results are not likely to be used. When tracing is off, the creation of the `string` member is worthless and costly.

- Don't aim for the world record in design flexibility. All you need is a design that's sufficiently flexible for the problem domain. A `char` pointer can sometimes do the simple jobs just as well, and more efficiently, than a `string`.

- Inline. Eliminate the function call overhead that comes with small, frequently invoked function calls. Inlining the `Trace` constructor and destructor makes it easier to digest the `Trace` overhead.

2

Constructors and Destructors

In an ideal world, there would never be a chapter dedicated to the performance implications of constructors and destructors. In that ideal world, constructors and
destructors would have no overhead. They would perform only mandatory initialization and cleanup, and the average compiler would inline them. C code such as

```
{
    struct X x1;
    init(&x1);
    ...
    cleanup(&x1);
}
```

would be accomplished in C++ by:

```
{
    X x1;
    ...
}
```

and the cost would be identical. That's the theory. Down here in the trenches of software development, the reality is a little different. We often encounter inheritance and
composition implementations that are too flexible and too generic for the problem
domain. They may perform computations that are rarely or never required. In practice, it is not surprising to discover performance overhead associated with inheritance
and composition. This is a limited manifestation of a bigger issue—the fundamental
tension between code reuse and performance. Inheritance and composition involve
code reuse. Oftentimes, reusable code will compute things you don't really need in a

specific scenario. Any time you call functions that do more than you really need, you will take a performance hit.

Inheritance

Inheritance and composition are two ways in which classes are tied together in an object-oriented design. In this section we want to examine the connection between inheritance-based designs and the cost of constructors and destructors. We drive this discussion with a practical example: the implementation of thread synchronization constructs.[1] In multithreaded applications, you often need to provide thread synchronization to restrict concurrent access to shared resources. Thread synchronization constructs appear in varied forms. The three most common ones are *semaphore, mutex,* and *critical section.*

A *semaphore* provides restricted concurrency. It allows multiple threads to access a shared resource up to a given maximum. When the maximum number of concurrent threads is set to 1, we end up with a special semaphore called a *mutex* (MUTual EXclusion). A mutex protects shared resources by allowing one and only one thread to operate on the resource at any one time. A shared resource typically is manipulated in separate code fragments spread over the application's code.

Take a shared queue, for example. The number of elements in the queue is manipulated by both `enqueue()` and `dequeue()` routines. Modifying the number of elements should not be done simultaneously by multiple threads for obvious reasons.

```
Type& dequeue()
{
    get_the_lock(queueLock);
    ...
    numberOfElements--;
    ...
    release_the_lock(queueLock);
    ...
}
void enqueue(const Type& value)
{
    get_the_lock(queueLock);
    ...
```

---

[1] Chapter 15 provides more information on the fundamental concepts and terminology of multithreaded programming.

```
    numberOfElements++;
    ...
    release_the_lock(queueLock);
}
```

If both `enqueue()` and `dequeue()` could modify `numberOfElements` concurrently, we easily could end up with `numberOfElements` containing a wrong value. Modifying this variable must be done atomically.

The simplest application of a mutex lock appears in the form of a critical section. A *critical section* is a single fragment of code that should be executed only by one thread at a time. To achieve mutual exclusion, the threads must contend for the lock prior to entering the critical section. The thread that succeeds in getting the lock enters the critical section. Upon exiting the critical section,[2] the thread releases the lock to allow other threads to enter.

```
get_the_lock(CSLock);
{   // Critical section begins
    ... // Protected computation
}   // Critical section ends
release_the_lock(CSLock);
```

In the `dequeue()` example it is pretty easy to inspect the code and verify that every lock operation is matched with a corresponding unlock. In practice we have seen routines that consisted of hundreds of lines of code containing multiple return statements. If a lock was obtained somewhere along the way, we had to release the lock prior to executing any one of the return statements. As you can imagine, this was a maintenance nightmare and a sure bug waiting to surface. Large-scale projects may have scores of people writing code and fixing bugs. If you add a return statement to a 100-line routine, you may overlook the fact that a lock was obtained earlier. That's problem number one. The second one is exceptions: If an exception is thrown while a lock is held, you'll have to catch the exception and manually release the lock. Not very elegant.

---

[2] We must point out that the Win32 definition of critical section is slightly different than ours. In Win32, a critical section consists of one or more distinct code fragments of which one, and only one, can execute at any one time. The difference between a critical section and a mutex in Win32 is that a critical section is confined to a single process, whereas mutex locks can span process boundaries and synchronize threads running in separate processes. The inconsistency between our use of the terminology and that of Win32 will not affect our C++ discussion. We are just pointing it out to avoid confusion.

C++ provides an elegant solution to those two difficulties. When an object reaches the end of the scope for which it was defined, its destructor is called automatically. You can utilize the automatic destruction to solve the lock maintenance problem. Encapsulate the lock in an object and let the constructor obtain the lock. The destructor will release the lock automatically. If such an object is defined in the function scope of a 100-line routine, you no longer have to worry about multiple return statements. The compiler inserts a call to the lock destructor prior to each return statement and the lock is always released.

Using the constructor-destructor pair to acquire and release a shared resource [ES90, Lip96C] leads to lock class implementations such as the following:

```
class Lock {
public:
    Lock(pthread_mutex_t& key)
    : theKey(key) { pthread_mutex_lock(&theKey);
    }

    ~Lock() { pthread_mutex_unlock(&theKey); }
private:
    pthread_mutex_t &theKey;
};
```

A programming environment typically provides multiple flavors of synchronization constructs. The flavors you may encounter will vary according to

- **Concurrency level**   A semaphore allows multiple threads to share a resource up to a given maximum. A mutex allows only one thread to access a shared resource.

- **Nesting**   Some constructs allow a thread to acquire a lock when the thread already holds the lock. Other constructs will deadlock on this lock-nesting.

- **Notify**   When the resource becomes available, some synchronization constructs will notify all waiting threads. This is very inefficient as all but one thread wake up to find out that they were not fast enough and the resource has already been acquired. A more efficient notification scheme will wake up only a single waiting thread.

- **Reader/Writer locks**   Allow many threads to read a protected value but allow only one to modify it.

- **Kernel/User space** Some synchronization mechanisms are available only in kernel space.

- **Inter/Intra process** Typically, synchronization is more efficient among threads of the same process than threads of distinct processes.

Although these synchronization constructs differ significantly in semantics and performance, they all share the same lock/unlock protocol. It is very tempting, therefore, to translate this similarity into an inheritance-based hierarchy of lock classes that are rooted in a unifying base class. In one product we worked on, initially we found an implementation that looked roughly like this:

```
class BaseLock {
public:
    // (The LogSource object will be explained shortly)
    BaseLock(pthread_mutex_t &key, LogSource &lsrc) {};
    virtual ~BaseLock() {};
};
```

The `BaseLock` class, as you can tell, doesn't do much. Its constructor and destructor are empty. The `BaseLock` class was intended as a root class for the various lock classes that were expected to be derived from it. These distinct flavors would naturally be implemented as distinct subclasses of `BaseLock`. One derivation was the `MutexLock`:

```
class MutexLock : public BaseLock {
public:
    MutexLock (pthread_mutex_t &key, LogSource &lsrc);
    ~MutexLock();
private:
    pthread_mutex_t &theKey;
    LogSource &src;
};
```

The `MutexLock` constructor and destructor are implemented as follows:

```
MutexLock::MutexLock(pthread_mutex_t& aKey, const LogSource& source)
    : BaseLock(aKey, source),
      theKey(aKey),
      src(source)
{
    pthread_mutex_lock(&theKey);
```

```
#if defined(DEBUG)
    cout << "MutexLock " << &aKey << " created at " << src.file() <<
    "line" <<src.line() << endl;
#endif
}

MutexLock::~MutexLock() // Destructor
{
    pthread_mutex_unlock(&theKey);

#if defined(DEBUG)
    cout << "MutexLock " << &aKey << " destroyed at " << src.file()<<
    "line" << src.line() << endl;
#endif
}
```

The MutexLock implementation makes use of a LogSource object that has not been discussed yet. The LogSource object is meant to capture the filename and source code line number where the object was constructed. When logging errors and trace information it is often necessary to specify the location of the information source. A C programmer would use a (char *) for the filename and an int for the line number. Our developers chose to encapsulate both in a LogSource object. Again, we had a do-nothing base class followed by a more useful derived class:

```
class BaseLogSource {
public:
    BaseLogSource() {}
    virtual ~BaseLogSource() {}
};

class LogSource : public BaseLogSource {
public:
    LogSource(const char *name, int num) : filename(name),
        lineNum(num) {}
    ~LogSource() {}

    char *file();
    int line();
private:
    char *filename;
    int    lineNum;
};
```

The LogSource object was created and passed as an argument to the MutexLock object constructor. The LogSource object captured the source file and line number at which the lock was fetched. This information may come in handy when debugging deadlocks.

Imagine that `sharedCounter` was an integer variable accessible to multiple threads and needing serialization. We provided mutual exclusion by inserting a lock object into the local scope:

```
{
    MutexLock myLock(theKey, LogSource(__FILE__, __LINE__));
    sharedCounter++;
}
```

The creation of the `MutexLock` and `LogSource` objects triggered the invocations of their respective base classes as well. This short fragment invoked a number of constructors:

- `BaseLogSource`
- `LogSource`
- `BaseLock`
- `MutexLock`

After the `sharedCounter` variable was incremented, we encountered the end of the scope that triggers the four corresponding destructors:

- `MutexLock`
- `BaseLock`
- `LogSource`
- `BaseLogSource`

All told, the protection of the shared resource had cost us eight constructors and destructors. The tension between reuse and performance is a topic that keeps popping up. It would be interesting to find out what the cost would be if we abandoned all these objects and developed a hand-crafted version that would narrow down by doing exactly what we need and nothing else. Namely, it will just lock around the `sharedCounter` update:

```
{
    pthread_mutex_lock(&theKey);
    sharedCounter++;
    pthread_mutex_unlock(&theKey);
}
```

By inspection alone, you can tell that the latter version is more efficient than the former one. Our object-based design had cost us additional instructions. Those instructions were entirely dedicated to construction and destruction of objects. Should we worry about those instructions? That depends on the context; if we are in a performance critical flow, we might. In particular, additional instructions become significant if the total cost of the computation is small and the fragment that executes those instructions is called often enough. It is the ratio of instructions wasted divided by the total instruction count of the overall computation that we care about. The code sample we just described was taken out of a gateway implementation that routed data packets from one communication adapter to another. It was a critical path that consisted of roughly 5,000 instructions. The `MutexLock` object was used a few times on that path. That amounted to enough instruction-overhead to make up 10% of the overall cost, which was significant.

If we are going to use C++ and OO in a performance-critical application, we cannot afford such luxury. Before we present a C++ based fix, we would quickly like to point out an obvious design overkill. If the critical section is as simple as a one-statement integer increment, why do we need all this object machinery? The advantages to using lock objects are

- Maintenance of complex routines containing multiple return points.
- Recovery from exceptions.
- Polymorphism in locking.
- Polymorphism in logging.

All those advantages were not extremely important in our case. The critical section had a clearly defined single exit point and the integer increment operation was not going to throw an exception. The polymorphism in locking and logging was also something we could easily live without. Interestingly, as this code segment reveals, developers are actually doing this in practice, which indicates that the cost of object construction and destruction is seriously overlooked.

So what about a complex routine where the use of the lock object actually makes sense? We would still like to reduce its cost. First let's consider the `LogSource` object. That piece of information had cost us four function calls: base and derived class constructors and destructors. This is a luxury we cannot afford in this context.

Often, when C++ performance is discussed, inlining is offered as a cure. Although inlining could help here, it does not eliminate the problem. In the best-case scenario, inlining will eliminate the function call overhead for all four constructors and destructors. Even then, the LogSource object still imposes some performance overhead. First, it is an extra argument to the MutexLock constructor. Second, there is the assignment of the LogSource pointer member of MutexLock. Furthermore, when the LogSource object is created, some additional instructions are required to set up its virtual table pointer.

In a critical performance path, a common sense trade-off is called for. You trade away marginal functionality for valuable performance. The LogSource object has to go. In a constructor, the assignment of a member data field costs a small number of instructions even in the case of a built-in type. The cost per member data field may not be much but it adds up. It grows with the number of data members that are initialized by the constructor.

The fact that the code using the LogSource object was enclosed in an #ifdef DEBUG bracket provides further evidence that using this object was not essential. The DEBUG compile flag was used only during development test; the code that was shipped to customers was compiled with DEBUG turned off. When executing in a production environment, we paid the price imposed by the LogSource object, but never actually used it. This was pure overhead. The LogSource should have been completely eliminated by careful #ifdef of all remnants of it. That would include elimination of the pointer member of MutexLock as well as the constructor argument. The partial #ifdef of the LogSource object was an example of sloppy development. This is not terribly unusual; it is just that your chances of getting away with sloppy programming in C++ are slim.

The next step is to eliminate the BaseLock root of the lock class hierarchy. In the case of BaseLock, it doesn't contribute any data members and, with the exception of the constructor signature, does not provide any meaningful interface. The contribution of BaseLock to the overall class design is debatable. Even if inlining takes care of the call overhead, the virtual destructor of BaseLock imposes the cost of setting the virtual table pointer in the MutexLock object. Saving a single assignment may not be much, but every little bit helps. Inlining the remaining MutexLock constructor and destructor will eliminate the remaining two function calls.

The combination of eliminating the LogSource class, the BaseLock class, and inlining MutexLock constructor and destructor will significantly cut down the instruction count. It will generate code that is almost as efficient as hand-coded C. The compiler-generated code with the inlined MutexLock will be equivalent to something like the following pseudocode:

```
{
     MutexLock::theKey = key;

     pthread_mutex_lock(&MutexLock::theKey);
     sharedCounter++;
     pthread_mutex_unlock(&MutexLock::theKey);
}
```

The above C++ code fragment is almost identical to hand-coded C, and we assumed it would be just as efficient. If that is the case, then the object lock provides the added power of C++ without loss of efficiency. To validate our assumption, we tested three implementations of mutex locks:

- Direct calls to pthread_mutex_lock() and pthread_mutex_unlock()

- A standalone mutex object that does not inherit from a base class

- A mutex object derived from a base class

In the first test we simply surrounded the shared resource with a pair of pthread_mutex_lock() and pthread_mutex_unlock() calls:

```
int main()// Version 1
{
     ...
     // Start timing here
     for (i = 0; i < 1000000; i++) {
          pthread_mutex_lock(&mutex);
          sharedCounter++;
          pthread_mutex_unlock(&mutex);
          }
     // Stop timing here
     ...
}
```

In Version 2 we used a lock object, SimpleMutex, using the constructor to lock and the destructor to unlock:

```
int main()    // Version 2
{
    ...
    // Start timing here
    for (i = 0; i < 1000000; i++) {
        SimpleMutex m(mutex);
        sharedCounter++;
        }
    // Stop timing here
    ...
}
```

`SimpleMutex` was implemented as follows:

```
class SimpleMutex    // Version two. Standalone lock class.
{
public:
    SimpleMutex(pthread_mutex_t& lock) : myLock(lock) {acquire();}

    ~SimpleMutex() {release();}
private:
    int acquire() {return pthread_mutex_lock(&myLock);}
    int release() {return pthread_mutex_unlock(&myLock);}

    pthread_mutex_t& myLock;
};
```

Inheritance was added in Version 3:

```
class BaseMutex     // Version 3. Base class.
{
public:
    BaseMutex(pthread_mutex_t& lock) {};
    virtual ~BaseMutex() {};
};

class DerivedMutex: public BaseMutex      // Version 3.
{
public:
    DerivedMutex(pthread_mutex_t& lock)
    : BaseMutex(lock), myLock(lock) {acquire();}
    ~DerivedMutex() {release();}
private:
    int acquire() {return pthread_mutex_lock(&myLock);}
    int release() {return pthread_mutex_unlock(&myLock);}

    pthread_mutex_t& myLock;
};
```

In the test loop we replaced SimpleMutex with the DerivedMutex:

```
int main()  // Version 3
{
    ...
    // Start timing here
    for (i = 0; i < 1000000; i++) {
        DerivedMutex m(mutex);
        sharedCounter++;
        }
    // Stop timing here
    ...
}
```

The timing results of running a million iterations of the test loop validated our assumption. Versions 1 and 2 executed in 1.01 seconds. Version 3, however, took 1.62 seconds. In Version 1 we invoked the mutex calls directly—you cannot get more efficient than that. The moral of the story is that using a standalone object did not exact any performance penalty at all. The constructor and destructor were inlined by the compiler and this implementation achieved maximum efficiency. We paid a significant price, however, for inheritance. The inheritance-based lock object (Version 3) degraded performance by roughly 60% (Figure 2.1).

More often than not, the creation and destruction of objects will exact a performance penalty. In an inheritance hierarchy, the creation of an object will trigger the creation of its ancestors. The same goes for object destruction. It follows that the cost associated with an object is directly related to the length and complexity of its derivation chain. The number of objects created (and later destroyed) is proportional to the complexity of the derivation.

This is not to say that inheritance is fundamentally a performance obstacle. We must make a distinction between the overall computational cost, required cost, and computational penalty. The overall computational cost is the set of all instructions executed in a computation. The required cost is that subset of instructions whose results are necessary. This part of the computation is mandatory; computational penalty is the rest. This is the part of the computation that could have been eliminated by an alternative design or implementation. To make the point more concrete, let's look at the SimpleMutex class as an example:

```
class SimpleMutex
{
```

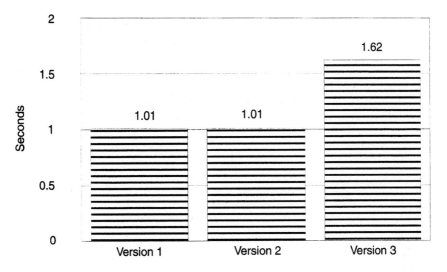

Figure 2.1. The cost of inheritance in this example.

```
public:
    SimpleMutex(pthread_mutex_t& lock) : myLock(lock) {acquire();}

    ~SimpleMutex() {release();}
private:
    int acquire() {return pthread_mutex_lock(&myLock);}
    int release() {return pthread_mutex_unlock(&myLock);}

    pthread_mutex_t& myLock;
};
```

The `SimpleMutex` constructor harbors the following overall computational cost:

- Initialize the `myLock` member

- Call the `acquire()` method

- Invoke `pthread_mutex_lock()` with the `acquire()` method

The third item is the required cost. Regardless of the design options, one way or another, you would have to call `pthread_mutex_lock()` in order to lock the resource. The first item, setting the `myLock` member, is computational penalty. It is our object-based design that forced us to do that. Failing to inline the `acquire()` call would result in additional penalty. In practice, more than likely compilers will eliminate that penalty by inlining.

So we cannot make a blanket statement that complex inheritance designs are necessarily bad, nor do they always carry a performance penalty. All we can say is that overall cost grows with the size of the derivation tree. If all those computations are valuable then it is all required cost. In practice, inheritance hierarchies are not likely to be perfect.[3] In that case, they are likely to impose a computational penalty.

Composition

Like inheritance, object composition raises similar performance concerns with regard to object creation and destruction. When an object is created (destroyed), all its contained member objects must be created (destroyed) as well. For instance, the Trace object discussed in the previous chapter contains a member object of class string.

```
class Trace
{
    ...
    string theFunctionName;
};
```

When you construct an object of type Trace, the constructor invokes the string constructor to initialize the string data member. This behavior is recursive: If class A contains a member of class B and B contains a C, the constructor for A will invoke the construction of a B object which, in turn, will trigger that of a C object. Since at each level in the composition (containment) hierarchy there may be multiple attributes, the composition hierarchy generates a tree, not a simple list. The overall cost of composition is therefore related to the size of this composition tree, which can become quite large. Again, we must emphasize that "cost" does not necessarily mean "overhead." If the program needs the full-blown functionality of the contained object, then there is no overhead. It is just what you have to do. On the other hand, the Trace example (as shown in the previous chapter) is one example where "cost" and "overhead" actually coincided. We did not need the power of a string object to represent the name of the function that is being traced. We never did anything too sophisticated with that object. We easily could have replaced it with a char pointer. A char pointer is much cheaper to construct than a string object. Sadly, there are segments of the C++ programming community that seem to equate failure to use the more complex data types of C++ with a lack of programming sophistication, which results in overkill rather than adherence to

---

[3] In this context, software perfection means you compute what you need, all of what you need, and nothing but what you need.

a prime mantra: "Use a solution that is as simple as possible and no simpler."

You can imagine that in complex hierarchies with large derivation and composition trees, the cost of constructing and destroying an object can skyrocket. This is something to keep in mind during the design phase if there is a good chance that this hierarchy may come to life during a performance-sensitive flow.

The creation and destruction of contained objects is another issue worth consideration. There is no way for you to prevent the creation (destruction) of subobjects when the containing object is created (destroyed). This is automatically imposed by the compiler. Take our earlier `Trace` example:

```
class Trace {
public:
    Trace (const char *name);
    ...
private:
    string theFunctionName;
};
```

The creation of a `Trace` object will create the `string` subobject. The `Trace` destructor will similarly destroy it. It is automatic and you cannot prevent it with this implementation. To gain better control over the creation and destruction of a subobject, we can replace it with a pointer:

```
class Trace {
public:
    Trace (const char *name);
    // ...
private:
    string *theFunctionName;
};
```

Now we are in command of creation and destruction of the `string` object. We still have the option of performing a full-blown initialization. This form will construct a new `string` object and set a pointer to it:

```
Trace::Trace(char *name) : theFunctionName(new string(name))
{
    ...
}
```

We also have the option of a partial initialization. We assign an invalid default value to these pointers indicating that these objects must be constructed prior to being used. Our anticipated usage pattern was such that tracing was normally off and the `Trace` objects created were rarely used. Minimizing the overhead of creation and destruction was therefore critical:

```
Trace::Trace (const char *name) : theFunctionName(0)
{
    if (traceIsActive) {
        theFunctionName = new string(name);
        ...
        }
}
```

The first and second form were very inefficient because of the usage pattern. In the typical scenario tracing would be off and the effort to construct a `string` object is worthless. The third form was best as assigning zero to a pointer is cheaper than constructing a brand-new object. Note that it is the usage pattern that dictates which form is most efficient. If our usage pattern was such that tracing is always on, the first form (containing subobjects, not pointers) would be best. It would be more efficient to embed the `string` object in the `Trace` object since it would consume stack memory as opposed to heap memory. Heap memory is far more expensive to allocate and free. Stack-based memory is allocated at compile time and is freed during the stack cleanup part of a function call return.

Lazy Construction

Performance optimization often has to strike a delicate balance between competing forces. This is perhaps why it is referred to as optimization as opposed to performance maximization. Performance optimization often requires the sacrifice of some other software goal. Important goals such as flexibility, maintainability, cost, and reuse must often give way to the demand for performance. It is unusual when a performance fix, in an otherwise high-quality piece of code, does not compromise any other software development goals. Sometimes we are fortunate when the elimination of simple coding mistakes results in higher performance without any sacrifice. The first optimization we are about to show is one such example. It eliminates the creation (and eventual destruction) of objects from code paths where they are never used.

If you are going to instantiate an object in a performance-critical path, you ought to consider the cost factors. The cheapest object, however, is the one that's never instantiated.

In C, Pascal, and other popular languages, data types must be defined at the beginning of a code block. We get into the habit of defining all the variables needed in a routine right up front at the beginning of that routine:

```
void myFunction()
{
    int i;
    int j;
    ...
    compute(i,j)
    ...
    return;
}
```

In C++, that habit of automatically defining all objects up front could be wasteful—you may construct objects that you end up not using. This happens in practice. In our C++ code we had a class **DataPacket** that allocated and deallocated memory on the fly:

```
class DataPacket
{
public:
    DataPacket(char *data, int sz) : size(sz) {
        buffer = new char[sz];
        ...
        }

    ~DataPacket() {
        delete [] buffer;
        ...
        }
    ... // other public member functions
private:
    char *buffer;
    ... // other private members
};
```

Partly due to memory allocation and deallocation, **DataPacket** was expensive to construct and destroy. Its cost was upwards of 400 instructions, which was significant in our context. It was used in a performance-critical path that routed data from one adapter to another:

```
void routeData(char *data, int size)
{
    DataPacket packet(data, size);
    bool  direction = get_direction();
    ...                    // Some computation
    if (UPSTREAM == direction) {// data going upstream
        computeSomething(packet);
    }
    else {              // data going downstream
        ...             // packet is not used in this scope.
    }
}
```

Object `packet` was used if and only if data was going upstream, which was 50% of the time. When data headed downstream, `packet` was not used at all. Object `packet`, however, was constructed unconditionally at the beginning of the scope. Half the time, this was a perfect waste of computing cycles.

The solution here, as you can imagine, was very easy. Object `packet` should be created if and only if it is actually needed. The definition of `packet` ought to be moved inside the scope that uses it, when data is going upstream:

```
void routeData(char *data, int size)
{
    ...                          // Delete definition of packet
    bool direction = get_direction();
    ...
    if (UPSTREAM == direction) {// data going upstream
        DataPacket packet(data, size); // Add definition of packet
                                 // here...
        computeSomething(packet);
    }
    else  {                 // data going downstream
        ...                 // packet is not used in this scope.
    }
}
```

Although the practice of delaying variable creation until its first usage has been preached by the C++ language experts since the language inception, this coding mistake was detected in real product code. The compatibility between C++ and C has been touted as one of C++'s advantages, but this is an area where that compatibility creates stylistic discontinuity. Adherence to the now obsolete C declaration syntax in C++ can have significant performance costs. Unfortunately, it is a fact that such trivial mistakes often do happen in practice. Part of C++'s being a better C is its ability to delay variable creation.

It is worth noting that the definition of variables at the beginning of any scope are allowed in C as well. It is just that C programmers tend to define all of the variables right at the beginning of the function scope, since there is no run-time cost in a C variable definition. This is not the case with C++ where care must be taken with regard to the placement of object definitions.

Redundant Construction

Along the lines of simple but costly coding mistakes, here's another example of pure overhead. It is the double construction of a contained object [Mey97 item 12], [Lip91].

Class `Person` contains an object of class `string`:

```
class Person {
public:
    Person (const char *s) { name = s; }// Version 0
    ...

private:
    string name;
};
```

Consider the following implementation of the `Person` default constructor:

```
Person (const char *s) { name = s; }
```

The `Person` object must be initialized before the body of the `Person` constructor is executed. The contained `string` object does not appear in the `Person::Person(char*)` initialization list (in this case there was none). Hence, the compiler must insert a call to invoke the `string` default constructor, to initialize the `string` member object properly. The body of the `Person` constructor is then executed. The statement `name = s;` assigns the `char` pointer `s` to the left-hand side object of type `string`. The `string::operator=(const char*)` is invoked to execute that assignment. The computation performed by the assignment operator essentially overwrites the result of the default `string` constructor invoked earlier during initialization. The computational effort contained in the default `string` constructor is thrown away in its entirety.

Many optimizations require some kind of a trade-off. You often trade speed for clarity, simplicity, reusability, or some other metric. But in this example, optimization requires no sacrifice at all. You can rewrite the `Person` constructor implementation, claiming back the lost speed and trading away nothing. You achieve that by specifying an explicit initialization of the `string` member `name`.

```
Person::Person(const char *s) : name(s) {} // Version 1.
```

This constructor will generate the exact same `Person` object with the exception of improved performance. All we get here is a single call to `string::string(const char *)` to initialize `name` with `s`. We tested the performance difference by timing the following loop:

```
for (i = 0; i < MILLION; i++) {
    Person p("Pele");
    }
```

The chart in Figure 2.2 compares the execution time of Version 0 (silent initialization plus explicit assignment) to that of Version 1 (explicit initialization only).

Fortunately, the default string constructor is very cheap, making this inefficiency almost negligible. You are not always going to be that lucky, so don't count on it.

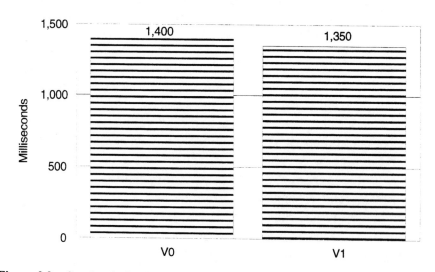

Figure 2.2. Overhead of a silent initialization is negligible in this particular scenario.

Suppose you decided, for some reason, to bypass the standard string implementation and roll your own instead. We'll call it SuperString:

```
class SuperString
{
public:
    SuperString(const char *s = 0);
    SuperString(const SuperString &s);
    SuperString& operator=(const SuperString& s);

    ~SuperString() {delete [] str;}

private:
    char *str;
};

inline
SuperString::SuperString(const char *s)
    : str(0)
{
    if (s != 0) {
        str = new char[strlen(s)+1];
        strcpy(str,s);
        }
}

inline
SuperString::SuperString(const SuperString &s)
    : str(0)
{
    if (s.str) {
        str = new char[strlen(s.str)+1];
        strcpy(str,s.str);
        }
}

SuperString& SuperString::operator=(const SuperString& s)
{
    if (str != s.str) {
        delete [] str;
        if (s.str) {
            str = new char[strlen(s.str)+1];
            strcpy(str,s.str);
            }
        else str = 0;
        }

    return *this;
}
```

Furthermore, you have decided to replace the `string` member with a `Super-String` in your `Person` implementation:

```
class Person {
public:
    Person (const char *s) { name = s; }// Version 2
    ...

private:
    SuperString name;
};
```

Because you did not provide a `SuperString` assignment operator that accepts a `char` pointer argument, the assignment operator demands a `SuperString` object reference as an argument. Consequently, the statement

```
name = s;
```

in the `Person` constructor will trigger the creation of a temporary `SuperString` object. The compiler will convert the `char` pointer `s` to a `SuperString` by invoking the appropriate `SuperString` constructor. Using pseudocode, we have the following transformation of the `Person::Person(char*)` implementation

```
Person::Person(const char *s)
{
    name.SuperString::SuperString();      // Constructor: Initialize
                                          // member "name".

    SuperString _temp;                    // Temporary object.

    _temp.SuperString::SuperString(s);    // Construct a SuperString
                                          // object from "s".

    name.SuperString::operator=(_temp);   // Assign _temp to "name".

    _temp.SuperString::~SuperString();    // Destructor for temporary
                                          // object.
}
```

The content of the temporary `SuperString` object (`temp`) is assigned to member `name` via invocation of the `SuperString` assignment operator. It is then followed by invocation of the `SuperString` destructor to tear down the temporary object.

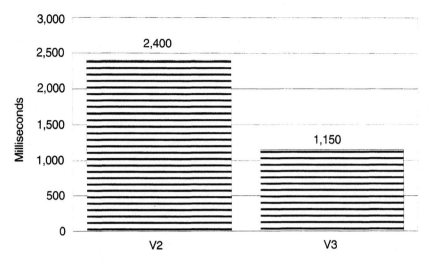

Figure 2.3.   More significant impact of silent initialization.

Overall we get two SuperString constructors, one call to the assignment operator and another to the destructor. The performance damage in this implementation is much more severe (see Figure 2.3). Version 3 fixes it by explicit initialization of the SuperString member:

```
Person::Person(const char *s) : name(s) {}   // Version 3. Explicit
                                             // initialization
```

Version 2 is the one using both silent initialization plus an explicit assignment in the constructor body. Version 3 is the one doing an explicit initialization and no assignment. In the case of our home-grown SuperString, Version 3 is more than twice as fast. The performance damage would have been less severe had an assignment operator been provided that takes a char pointer as an argument. That would have eliminated the need for a temporary SuperString object. It is interesting to note that Version 3 is a little faster than the corresponding version using the compiler string implementation (Version 1). Our home-grown SuperString does not provide anything near the rich functionality of the string class. It is often the case that code runs faster if it does not have to provide much flexibility.

Key Points

- Constructors and destructors may be as efficient as hand-crafted C code. In practice, however, they often contain overhead in the form of superfluous computations.

- The construction (destruction) of an object triggers recursive construction (destruction) of parent and member objects. Watch out for the combinatorial explosion of objects in complex hierarchies. They make construction and destruction more expensive.

- Make sure that your code actually uses all the objects that it creates and the computations that they perform. We would encourage people to peer inside the classes that they use. This advice is not going to be popular with OOP advocates. OOP, after all, preaches the use of classes as encapsulated black-box entities and discourages you from looking inside. How do we balance between those competing pieces of advice? There is no simple answer because it is context sensitive. Although the black-box approach works perfectly well for 80% of your code, it may wreak havoc on the 20% that is performance critical. It is also application dependent. Some application will put a premium on maintainability and flexibility, and others may put performance considerations at the top of the list. As a programmer you are going to have to decide the question of what exactly you are trying to maximize.

- The object life cycle is not free of cost. At the very least, construction and destruction of an object may consume CPU cycles. Don't create an object unless you are going to use it. Typically, you want to defer object construction to the scope in which it is manipulated.

- Compilers must initialize contained member objects prior to entering the constructor body. You ought to use the initialization phase to complete the member object creation. This will save the overhead of calling the assignment operator later in the constructor body. In some cases, it will also avoid the generation of temporary objects.

3

Virtual Functions

The evolution of programming languages tended to make the programming task easier by shifting some burden from the programmer to the compiler, interpreter, assembler, or linker. Programs are becoming easier to develop, maintain, and extend. The problem with this progress is that it is often a zero-sum game where gains in one area mean losses in another. In particular, advances in programming often translate into loss of raw speed. Dynamic binding of function calls is one among many contributions C++ has made to C programming. It shifts the burden of type resolution from the programmer to the compiler, which is good. On the other hand, it can have a negative impact on cost, which is what we intend to examine.

Virtual Function Mechanics

If you really wanted to avoid virtual functions, you could emulate dynamic binding by providing your own type resolution code. Suppose you are maintaining a class hierarchy of zoo animals [Lip91], where ZooAnimal is your base class:

```
class ZooAnimal {
public:
    ...
    virtual void draw();
    int resolveType() { return myType;}
private:
    int myType;
    ...
}
```

The rest of the animals in the zoo are derived from ZooAnimal. The resolveType() method will enable you to distinguish a Bear from a Monkey at run-time.

```
class Bear : public ZooAnimal {
public:
    Bear (const char *name) : myName(name), myType(BEAR) {}
    void draw();
    ...
};
```

Each animal sets its appropriate type in its constructor.

If you wanted to draw all animals in the zoo, you would end up with something along the lines of [Lip91]:

```
void drawAllAnimals (ZooAnimal *pz) // pointer to first animal in the
                                    // list
{
    for (ZooAnimal *p=pz; p ;p = p->next) {
        switch (p->resolveType()) {
        case BEAR:
            ( (Bear *) p)->draw();
            break;
        case MONKEY:
            ((Monkey *) p)->draw();
            break;
        ... // Handle all other animals currently in the zoo.
        }
    }
}
```

This code is a maintenance headache. Any time an animal leaves the zoo, you'll have to remove it from the switch statement, and any time a new animal arrives, you'll have to add it. Dynamic binding of a virtual function allows you to divorce your code from that dependency. Because ZooAnimal::draw() is a virtual function, you can take advantage of dynamic binding at run-time:

```
void drawAllAnimals (ZooAnimal *pz) // pointer to first animal in the
                                    // list
{
    for (ZooAnimal *p=pz; p ;p = p->next) {
        p->draw();
    }
```

This code can still distinguish a `Bear` from `Monkey`. How does it do that? To facilitate late binding we must have a way of resolving a virtual function call at run-time, as opposed to compile-time. If class `X` defines a virtual function or is derived from such class, a virtual function table is generated for class `X` (`vtbl`) by the compiler. The virtual function table holds the pointers to all the virtual functions defined for this particular class. There's one table per class and each object of that class contains a hidden pointer to it—hidden because only the compiler knows the offset of the `vptr` inside the object [Lip96I]. The compiler inserts code into the object constructor to initialize the `vptr` properly.

Virtual functions seem to inflict a performance cost in several ways:

- The `vptr` must be initialized in the constructor.

- A virtual function is invoked via pointer indirection. We must fetch the pointer to the function table and then access the correct function offset.

- Inlining is a compile-time decision. The compiler cannot inline virtual functions whose resolution takes place at run-time.

In fairness to C++, the first two items should not be considered a performance penalty. One way or another, you would have to pay that price even if you bent over backwards to avoid dynamic binding. The cost of setting the `vptr` in the constructor is equivalent to initializing the type member in our `Bear` implementation:

```
class Bear : public ZooAnimal {
    ...
    Bear (const char *name) : myName(name), myType(BEAR) {}
    ...
};
```

The cost of the second item, indirect function invocation, is equivalent to the switch statement logic necessary to distinguish `Bear::draw()` from `Monkey::draw()`.

```
switch (p->resolveType()) {
 case BEAR:
    ( (Bear *) p)->draw();
    break;
 case MONKEY:
    ((Monkey *) p)->draw();
    break;
 ... // Handle all other animals currently in the zoo.
 }
```

The true cost of virtual functions then boils down to the third item only. As Meyers noted in Item 24 of [Mey96], the inability to inline a virtual function is its biggest performance penalty.

In some cases it is possible to resolve a virtual function invocation at compile-time [Lip96I], but this is the exception (this is discussed in more detail in Chapters 8–10). In the majority of virtual function invocations, resolution can happen only at run-time because the type of object whose function is being invoked cannot be determined at compile-time. That inability to resolve at compile-time interacts negatively with inlining. Inlining is a compile-time decision that requires knowledge of the specific function. If you cannot determine what function to invoke at compile-time (as is the case with a typical virtual function), you cannot inline.

Evaluating the performance penalty of a virtual function is equivalent to evaluating the penalty resulting from failure to inline that same function. This penalty does not have a fixed cost. It is dependent on the complexity of the function and the frequency with which it is invoked. On one end of the spectrum are the short functions that are invoked often. Those benefit the most from inlining, and failing to do so will result in a heavy penalty. At the other end of the spectrum are complex functions that are seldom invoked. Inlining and its performance implications are discussed in more detail in Chapters 8–10.

When you throw in multiple inheritance and/or virtual inheritance, object creation involves an additional cost. This additional cost comes from having to set multiple vptrs and added indirection of virtual function invocation. The object layout under multiple and virtual inheritance is an interesting issue, but the performance implications are minor and unlikely to have significant performance impact in typical code. These issues will not be pursued further here. An informative discussion of these issues appears in "Inside the Object Model" [Lip96I].

If a specific virtual function creates a performance problem for you, what are your options? To eliminate a virtual call you must allow the compiler to resolve the function binding at compile-time. You bypass dynamic binding by either hard-coding your class choice or passing it as a template parameter. We will discuss these options next with a concrete example.

Templates and Inheritance

Virtual function calls that can be resolved only at run-time will inhibit inlining. At times, that may pose a performance problem that we must solve. Dynamic binding of a function call is a consequence of inheritance. One way to eliminate dynamic binding is to replace inheritance with a template-based design. Templates are more performance-friendly in the sense that they push the resolution step from run-time to compile-time. Compile-time, as far as we are concerned, is free.

The design space for inheritance and templates has some overlap. We will discuss one such example.

Suppose you wanted to develop a thread-safe string class that may be manipulated safely by concurrent threads in a Win32 environment [BW97]. In that environment you have a choice of multiple synchronization schemes such as critical section, mutex, and semaphores, just to name a few. You would like your thread-safe string to offer the flexibility to use any of those schemes, and at different times you may have a reason to prefer one scheme over another [BW97]. Inheritance would be a reasonable choice to capture the commonality among synchronization mechanisms.

The `Locker` abstract base class will declare the common interface:

```
class Locker {
public:
    Locker() {}
    virtual ~Locker() {}
    virtual void lock() = 0;
    virtual void unlock() = 0;
};
```

`CriticalSectionLock` and `MutexLock` will be derived from the `Locker` base class:

```
class CriticalSectionLock : public Locker { ... };
class MutexLock : public Locker { ... };
```

Because you prefer not to re-invent the wheel, you made the choice to derive the thread-safe string from the existing standard `string`. The remaining design choices are:

- Hard coding. You could derive three distinct classes from `string`: `CriticalSectionString`, `MutexString`, and `SemaphoreString`, each class implementing its implied synchronization mechanism.

- Inheritance. You could derive a single `ThreadSafeString` class that contains a pointer to a `Locker` object. Use polymorphism to select the particular synchronization mechanism at run-time.

- Templates. Create a template-based string class parameterized by the `Locker` type.

We will explore each design option in more detail.

Hard Coding

The standard `string` class will serve as a base class. Each class derived from it makes a commitment to a specific synchronization mechanism. Take the `CriticalSectionString`, for example:

```
class CriticalSectionString : public string {
public:
    ...
    int length();
private:
    CriticalSectionLock cs;
};

int CriticalSectionString::length()
{
    cs.lock()
    int len = string::length();
    cs.unlock();

    return len;
}
```

You are getting the actual string length from the string parent class, but you are wrapping it in a critical section to protect the integrity of the computation. `MutexString` and `SemaphoreString` are implemented similarly using mutex and semaphore, respectively.

This design choice has a performance advantage. Even though the `lock()` and `unlock()` methods are virtual functions, they can be resolved statically by a reasonable compiler. Each of the three thread-safe string classes has committed at compile-time to a particular synchronization class. The compiler, therefore, can bypass the dynamic binding and choose the correct `lock()` or `unlock()` method to use. More importantly, it allows the compiler to inline those calls. The downside to this design choice is that you need to write a separate string class for each synchronization flavor, which results in poor code reuse.

Inheritance

Implementing a separate string class for each synchronization mechanism is a pain. Alternatively, you can factor out the synchronization choice into a constructor argument:

```
class ThreadSafeString : public string {
public:
    ThreadSafeString (const char *s, Locker *lockPtr)
    : string(s), pLock(lockPtr) {}
    ...
    int length();
private:
    Locker *pLock;
};
```

The `length()` method is now implemented as follows:

```
int ThreadSafeString::length()
{
    pLock->lock()
    int len = string::length();
    pLock->unlock();

    return len;
}
```

This class can use all available synchronization schemes depending on the `Locker` pointer given to its constructor. You can use a critical section, as in:

```
{
    CriticalSectionLock cs;
    ThreadSafeString csString("Hello", &cs);
    ...
}
```

or you may elect to go with a mutex lock, as in:

```
{
    MutexLock mtx;
    ThreadSafeString csString("Hello", &mtx);
    ...
}
```

This implementation is more compact than the previous one. It does suffer a performance penalty: The `lock()` and `unlock()` virtual calls can only be resolved at execution time and consequently cannot be inlined.

Templates

The template-based design combines the best of both worlds—reuse and efficiency. The `ThreadSafeString` is implemented as a template parameterized by the `Locker` template argument:

```
template <class LOCKER>
class ThreadSafeString : public string {
public:
    ThreadSafeString(const char *s) : string(s) {}
    ...
    int length();

private:
    LOCKER lock;
};
```

The length method implementation is similar to the previous ones:

```
template <class LOCKER>
inline
int ThreadSafeString<LOCKER>::length()
{
    lock.lock();
    int len = string::length();
    lock.unlock();

    return len;
}
```

If you want critical section protection, you will instantiate the template with a `CriticalSectionLock`:

```
{
    ThreadSafeString <CriticalSectionLock> csString = "hello";
    ...
}
```

or you may go with a mutex:

```
{
    ThreadSafeString <MutexLock> mtxString = "hello";
    ...
}
```

This design also provides a relief from the virtual function calls to `lock()` and `unlock()`. The declaration of a `ThreadSafeString` selects a particular type of synchronization upon template instantiation time. Just like hard coding, this enables the compiler to resolve the virtual calls and inline them.

As you can see, templates can make a positive performance contribution by pushing computations out of the execution-time and into compile-time, enabling inlining in the process. If you think of templates as glorified macros, you will definitely change your mind after reading Todd Veldhuizen's article on expression templates in "C++ Gems" [Lip96C].

Key Points

- The cost of a virtual function stems from the inability to inline calls that are dynamically bound at run-time. The only potential efficiency issue is the speed gained from inlining if there is any. Inlining efficiency is not an issue in the case of functions whose cost is not dominated by call and return overhead.

- Templates are more performance-friendly than inheritance hierarchies. They push type resolution to compile-time, which we consider to be free.

4

The Return Value Optimization

Anytime you can skip the creation and destruction of an object, you are looking at a performance gain. In this chapter we will discuss an optimization often performed by compilers to speed up your source code by transforming it and eliminating object creation. This optimization is referred to as the Return Value Optimization (RVO). Prior to delving into the RVO we need to understand how return-by-value works. We will walk through it with a simple example.

The Mechanics of Return-by-Value

The `Complex` class implements a representation for complex numbers:

```
class Complex
{
    // Complex addition operator
    friend Complex operator+(const Complex&, const Complex&);
public:
    // Default constructor.
    // Value defaults to 0 unless otherwise specified.
    Complex (double r = 0.0, double i = 0.0) : real (r),  imag (i) {}

    // Copy constructor
    Complex (const Complex& c) : real (c.real), imag (c.imag) {}

    // Assignment operator
    Complex& operator= (const Complex& c);

    ~Complex() {}
private:
    double real;
```

```
        double imag;
};
```

The `addition operator` returns a `Complex` object by value, as in:

```
Complex operator+ (const Complex& a,   const Complex& b)
{
    Complex retVal;

    retVal.real = a.real + b.real;
    retVal.imag = a.imag + b.imag;

    return retVal;
}
```

Suppose `c1`, `c2`, and `c3` are `Complex` and we execute

```
c3 = c1 + c2;
```

How do we get the value of `c1  +  c2` into `c3`? One popular technique [Lip96I] used by compilers is to create a temporary `__result` object and pass it into `Complex::operator+()` as a third argument. It is passed by reference. So the compiler rewrites

```
Complex& Complex::operator+ (const complex& c1, const Complex& c2)
{
    . . .
}
```

into a slightly different function:

```
void Complex_Add  (const Complex& __result,
                   const Complex& c1,
                   const Complex& c2)
{
    . . .
}
```

Now the original source statement

```
c3 = c1 + c2;
```

is transformed into (pseudocode):

```
struct Complex __tempResult;      // Storage. No constructor here.
Complex_Add(__tempResult,c1,c2);// All arguments passed by reference.
c3 = __tempResult;                // Feed result back into
                                  // left-hand-side.
```

This return-by-value implementation opens up an optimization opportunity by eliminating the local object RetVal (inside operator+()) and computing the return value directly into the __tempResult temporary object. This is the Return Value Optimization.

The Return Value Optimization

Without any optimization, the compiler-generated (pseudo) code for Complex_Add() is

```
void Complex_Add(const Complex& __tempResult,
                 const Complex& c1,
                 const Complex& c2)
{
    struct Complex retVal;
    retVal.Complex::Complex();             // Construct retVal

    retVal.real = a.real + b.real;
    retVal.imag = a.imag + b.imag;

    __tempResult.Complex::Complex(retVal); // Copy-construct
                                           // __tempResult
    retVal.Complex::~Complex();            // Destroy retVal
    return;
}
```

The compiler can optimize Complex_Add() by eliminating the local object retVal and replacing it with __tempResult. This is the Return Value Optimization:

```
void Complex_Add (const Complex& __tempResult,
                  const Complex& c1,
                  const Complex& c2)
{
    __tempResult.Complex::Complex();   // Construct __tempResult
    __tempResult.real = a.real + b.real;
    __tempResult.imag = a.imag + b.imag;
    return;
}
```

The RVO eliminated the local retVal object and therefore saved us a constructor as well as a destructor computation.

To get a numerical feel for all this efficiency discussion, we measured the impact of RVO on execution speed. We coded two versions of operator+(), one of which was optimized and the other not. The measured code consisted of a million loop iterations:

```
int main ()
{
    Complex a(1,0);
    Complex b(2,0);
    Complex c;

    // Begin timing here
    for (int i = 1000000; i > 0; i--) {
        c = a + b;
    }
    // Stop timing here
}
```

The second version, without RVO, executed in 1.89 seconds. The first version, with RVO applied was much faster—1.30 seconds (Figure 4.1).

Compiler optimizations, naturally, must preserve the correctness of the original computation. In the case of the RVO, this is not always easy. Since the RVO is not mandatory, the compiler will not perform it on complicated functions. For example,

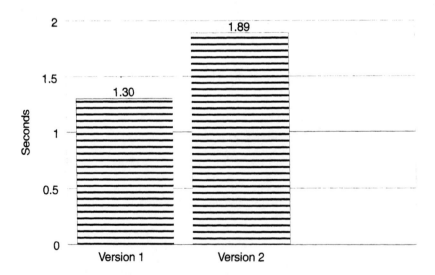

Figure 4.1. The speed-up of RVO.

if the function has multiple `return` statements returning objects of different names, RVO will not be applied. You must return the same named object to have a chance at the RVO.

One compiler we tested refused to apply the RVO to this particular version of `operator+`:

```
Complex operator+ (const Complex& a,   const Complex& b)
// operator+ version 1.
{
    Complex retVal;
    retVal.real = a.real + b.real;
    retVal.imag = a.imag + b.imag;
    return retVal;
}
```

It did, however, apply the RVO to this version:

```
Complex operator+ (const Complex& a, const Complex& b)
// operator+ version 2.
{
    double r = a.real + b.real;
    double i = a.imag + b.imag;

    return Complex (r,i);
}
```

We speculated that the difference may lie in the fact that Version 1 used a named variable (`retVal`) as a return value whereas Version 2 used an unnamed variable. Version 2 used a constructor call in the return statement but never named it. It may be the case that this particular compiler implementation chose to avoid optimizing away named variables.

Our speculation was boosted by some additional evidence. We tested two more versions of `operator+`:

```
Complex operator+ (const Complex& a, const Complex& b) // operator+
                                                       // version 3.
{
    Complex retVal (a.real + b.real, a.imag + b.imag);

    return retVal;
}
```

and

```
Complex operator+ (const Complex& a, const Complex& b) // operator+
                                                       // version 4.
{
    return Complex (a.real + b.real, a.imag + b.imag);
}
```

As speculated, the RVO was applied to Version 4 but not to Version 3.

In addition, you must also define a copy constructor to "turn on" the Return Value Optimization. If the class involved does not have a copy constructor defined, the RVO is quietly turned off.

Computational Constructors

When the compiler fails to apply the RVO, you can give it a gentle nudge in the form of the computational constructor (originally attributed to J. Shopiro [Car92, Lip96I].) Our compiler did not apply the RVO to Version 1:

```
Complex operator+ (const Complex& a,  const Complex& b)
   // operator+ version 1.
{
    Complex retVal;

    retVal.real = a.real + b.real;
    retVal.imag = a.imag + b.imag;

    return retVal;
}
```

This implementation created a default Complex object and deferred setting its member fields. Later it filled in the member data with information supplied by the input objects. The production of the Complex retVal object is spread over multiple distinct steps. The computational constructor collapses these steps into a single call and eliminates the named local variable:

```
Complex operator+ (const Complex& a, const Complex& b) // operator+
                                                       // version 5.
{
return Complex (a, b);
}
```

The computational constructor used in Version 5 constructs a new `Complex` object by adding its two input arguments:

```
Complex::Complex (const Complex& x, const Complex& y)
    : real (x.real+y.real),  imag (x.imag+y.imag)
{
}
```

Now a compiler is more likely to apply the RVO to Version 5 than to Version 1 of the addition operator. If you wanted to apply the same idea to the other arithmetic operators, you would have to add a third argument to distinguish the signatures of the computational constructors for addition, subtraction, multiplication, and division. This is the criticism against the computational constructor: It bends over backwards for the sake of efficiency and introduces "unnatural" constructors. Our take on this debate is that there are times and places where performance issues overwhelm all other issues. This issue is context-sensitive and does not have one right answer.

Key Points

- If you must return an object by value, the Return Value Optimization will help performance by eliminating the need for creation and destruction of a local object.

- The application of the RVO is up to the discretion of the compiler implementation. You need to consult your compiler documentation or experiment to find if and when RVO is applied.

- You will have a better shot at RVO by deploying the computational constructor.

5

Temporaries

In the large collection of performance issues, not all issues are of equal weight. The significance of a performance item is directly proportional to its cost and the frequency with which it appears in a typical program. It is conceivable that you could write highly efficient C++ code without having a clue about the intricacies of virtual inheritance and the (small) influence it has on execution speed. The generation of temporary objects, on the other hand, definitely does not belong in the category of potentially low-impact concepts. The likelihood of writing efficient code is very small unless you understand the origins of temporary objects, their cost, and how to eliminate them when you can.

Temporary objects may come as a surprise to new C++ developers, as the objects are silently generated by the compiler. They do not appear in the source code. It takes a trained eye to detect code fragments that will cause the compiler to insert temporary objects "under the covers."

Next, we enumerate a few examples where temporary objects are likely to pop up in compiler-generated code.

Object Definition

Say that class `Rational` is declared as follows:

```
class Rational
{
friend Rational operator+(const Rational&, const Rational&);
```

```
public:
    Rational (int a = 0, int b = 1 ) : m(a), n(b) {}
private:
    int m;// Numerator
    int n;// Denominator
};
```

We can instantiate objects of type `Rational` in several equivalent ways:

```
Rational r1(100);              // 1
Rational r2 = Rational(100);   // 2
Rational r3 = 100;             // 3
```

Only the first form of initialization is guaranteed, across compiler implementations, not to generate a temporary object. If you use forms 2 or 3, you may end up with a temporary, depending on the compiler implementation. Take form 3 for example:

```
Rational r3 = 100;// 3
```

This form may lead the compiler to use the `Rational::Rational(int, int)` constructor to turn the integer `100` into a temporary object of type `Rational`, and then to use the copy constructor to initialize `r3` from the newly created temporary:

```
{    // C++ pseudo code
    Rational r3;
    Rational _temp;

    _temp.Rational::Rational(100,1);    // Construct the temporary
    r3.Rational::Rational(_temp);       // Copy-construct r3
    _temp.Rational::~Rational();        // Destroy the temporary
    . . .
}
```

The overall cost here is two constructors and one destructor. In the first form,

```
Rational r1(100);      // 1
```

we pay only the cost of one constructor.

In practice, however, most compilers should optimize the temporary away, and the three initialization forms presented here would be equivalent in their efficiency.

Type Mismatch

The previous example is a special case of the more general type mismatch. We tried to initialize an object of type `Rational` with an integer. The generic case of type mismatch is any time an object of type X is expected and some other type is provided. The compiler needs, somehow, to convert the provided type into the expected object of type X. A temporary may get generated in the process. Look at the following:

```
{
    Rational r;
    r = 100;
    ...
}
```

Our `Rational` class did not declare an assignment operator that takes an integer parameter. The compiler, then, expects a `Rational` object on the right-hand side that will be bit-blasted to the left-hand side. The compiler must find a way to convert the integer argument we provided into an object of type `Rational`. Fortunately (or unfortunately for performance), we have a constructor that knows how to do that:

```
class Rational
{
public:
    // If only one integer is provided, the second one will default
    // to 1.
    Rational (int a = 0, int b = 1 ) : m(a), n(b) {}
    ...
};
```

This constructor knows how to create a `Rational` object from an integer argument. The source statement

```
r = 100;
```

is transformed into the following C++ pseudocode:

```
Rational _temp;    // Place holder for temporary

_temp.Rational::Rational(100,1);    // Construct temporary
r.Rational::operator=(_temp);       // Assign temporary to r
_temp.Rational::~Rational();        // Destroy the temporary
```

This liberty taken by the compiler to convert between types is a programming convenience. There are regions in your source code where convenience is overwhelmed by performance considerations. The new C++ standard gives you the ability to restrict the compiler and forbid such conversions. You do that by declaring a constructor `explicit`:

```
class Rational
{
public:
    explicit Rational (int a = 0, int b = 1 ) : m(a), n(b) {}
    ...
};
```

The explicit keyword tells the compiler that you oppose usage of this constructor as a conversion constructor.

Alternatively, this type of temporary object can also be eliminated by overloading the `Rational::operator=()` function to accept an integer as an argument:

```
class Rational {
public:
    ...  // as before
    Rational& operator=(int a) { m=a; n=1; return *this; }
};
```

The same principle can be generalized for all function calls. Let `g()` be an arbitrary function call taking a `string` reference as an argument:

```
void g(const string& s)
{
    ...
}
```

An invocation of g("message") will trigger the creation of a temporary `string` object unless you overload g() to accept a `char *` as an argument:

```
void g(const char* s)
{
    ...
}
```

Cargil [Car92] points out an interesting twist on the type mismatch temporary generation. In the following code fragment the operator+() expects two Complex
objects as arguments. A temporary Complex object gets generated to represent the
constant 1.0:

```
Complex a, b;
...
for (int i; i < 100; i++) {
    a = i*b + 1.0;
    }
```

The problem is that this temporary is generated over and over every iteration through
the loop. Lifting constant expressions out of a loop is a trivial and well-known optimization. The temporary generation in a = b + 1.0; is a computation whose value
is constant from one iteration to the next. In that case, why should we do it over and
over? Let's do it once and for all:

```
Complex one(1.0);

for (int i = 0; i < 100; i++) {
    a = i*b + one;
    }
```

We turned the temporary into a named Complex object. It cost us one construction,
but it still beats a temporary construction for every loop iteration.

Pass by Value

When passing an object by value, the initialization of the formal parameter with the
actual parameter is equivalent to the following form [ES90]:

```
T formalArg = actualArg;
```

where T is the class type. Suppose g() is some function expecting a T argument
when invoked:

```
void g (T formalArg)
{
    ...
}
```

A typical invocation of g() may look like:

```
T t;
g(t);
```

The activation record for g() has a place holder on the stack for its local argument formalArg. The compiler must copy the content of object t into g()'s formalArg on the stack. One popular technique of doing this will generate a temporary [Lip96I].

The compiler will create a temporary object of type T and copy-construct it using t as an input argument. This temporary will then be passed to g() as an actual argument. This newly created temporary object is then passed to g() by reference. In C++ pseudocode, it looks something like:

```
T _temp;

_temp.T::T(t);  // copy construct _temp from t
g(_temp);  // pass _temp by reference
_temp.T::~T();  // Destroy _temp
```

Creating and destroying the temporary object is relatively expensive. If you can, you should pass objects by pointer or reference to avoid temporary generation. Sometimes, however, you have no choice but to pass an object by value. For a convincing argument, see Item 23 in [Mey97].

Return by Value

Another path that leads to temporary object creation is function return value. If you code a function that returns an object by value (as opposed to a reference or pointer), you can easily end up with a temporary. Consider f() as a simple example:

```
string f()
{
    string s;
    ... // Compute "s"
    return s;
}
```

The return value of f() is an object of type string. A temporary is generated to hold that return value. For example:

```
String p;
...
p = f();
```

The temporary object holding f( )'s return value is then assigned to the left-hand side object p. For a more concrete example consider the string operator+. This operator will implement the intuitive interpretation of string "+" operation. It takes two input string objects and returns a new string object representing the result of concatenating the given strings. A possible implementation of this operator may look like this:

```
string operator+ (const string& s, const string& p)
{
    char *buffer = new char[s.length() + p.length() + 1];

    strcpy(buffer,s.str);      // Copy first character string
    strcat(buffer,p.str);      // Add second character string
    string result(buffer);     // Create return object
    delete buffer;

    return result;
}
```

The following code segment is a typical invocation of the string operator+:

```
{
    string s1 = "Hello";
    string s2 = "World";
    string s3;

    s3 = s1 + s2;  // s3 <- "HelloWorld"
    ...
}
```

The statement:

```
s3 = s1 + s2;
```

triggers several function calls:

- operator+(const string &, const string &); ==> String addition operator. This is triggered by s1+ s2.

- `string::string(const char *);==>` Constructor. Execute `string result(buffer)` inside `operator+()`.

- `string::string(const string &);==>` We need a temporary object to hold the return value of `operator+()`. The copy constructor will create this temporary using the returned `result string`.

- `string::~string() ; ==>` Before the `operator+()` function exits, it destroys the `result string` object whose lifetime is limited to the local scope.

- `string::operator=(const string &); ==>` The assignment operator is invoked to assign the temporary produced by `operator+()` to the left-hand side object `s3`.

- `string::~string(); ==>` The temporary object used for the return value is destroyed.

Six function call invocations is a hefty price for one source code statement. Even if most of them are inlined, you still have to execute their logic. The return-value optimization discussed in Chapter 4 can help us eliminate the `result string` object. That takes care of a constructor and destructor call. Can we also eliminate the temporary object? That will eliminate two more function calls.

Why does the statement:

```
s3 = s1 + s2;
```

generate a temporary in the first place? Because we do not have the liberty of clobbering the old contents of `string s3` and overwrite it with the new content of `s1+s2`. The assignment operator is responsible for the transition of `string s3` from old content to new content. The compiler does not have permission to skip `string::operator=()` and hence a temporary is a must. But what if `s3` is a brand new `string` object with no previous content? In this case there is no old content to worry about and the compiler could use the `s3` storage instead of the temporary object. The result of `s1+s2` is copy-constructed directly into the `string s3` object. `s3` has taken the place of the temporary, which is no longer necessary. To make a long story short, the form:

```
{
    string s1 = "Hello";
    string s2 = "World";
    string s3 = s1 + s2;  // No temporary here.
    ...
}
```

is preferable to the form:

```
{
    string s1 = "Hello";
    string s2 = "World";
    string s3;

    s3 = s1 + s2;      // Temporary generated here.
    ...
}
```

Eliminate Temporaries with op=( )

In the previous discussion we have supplied the compiler with an existing object to work with so it will not invent a temporary one. That same idea can get recycled in other situations as well. Suppose that s3 does have a previous value and we are not in position to initialize s3 from scratch with:

```
string s3 = s1 + s2;
```

If we are looking at the case:

```
{
    string s1,s2,s3;
    ...
    s3 = s1 + s2;
    ...
}
```

we can still prevent the creation of a temporary. We can do that by using the string operator+=( ) and rewriting the code to use += instead of +, so

```
s3 = s1 + s2;      // Temporary generated here
```

is rewritten as:

```
s3  = s1;     // operator=(). No temporary.
s3 += s2;     // operator+=(). No temporary.
```

If `string::operator+=()` and `operator+()` are implemented in a consistent fashion (both implementing "addition," as they should) then the two code fragments are semantically equivalent. They differ only in performance. Although both invoke a copy constructor and an operator function, the former creates a temporary object where the latter does not. Hence the latter is more efficient.

As pointed out in [Mey96]:

```
s5 = s1 + s2 + s3 + s4; // Three temporaries generated.
```

is much more elegant than:

```
s5  = s1;
s5 += s2;
s5 += s3;
s5 += s4;
```

But on a performance-critical path you need to forgo elegance in favor of raw performance. The second, "ugly" form is much more efficient. It creates zero temporaries.

Key Points

- A temporary object could penalize performance twice in the form of constructor and destructor computations.

- Declaring a constructor `explicit` will prevent the compiler from using it for type conversion behind your back.

- A temporary object is often created by the compiler to fix a type mismatch. You can avoid it by function overloading.

- Avoid object copy if you can. Pass and return objects by reference.

- You can eliminate temporaries by using `<op>=` operators where `<op>` may be +, -, *, or /.

6

Single-Threaded Memory Pooling

Frequent memory allocation and deallocation can play a significant role in degrading application performance. The performance degradation stems from the fact that the default memory manager is, by nature, general purpose. An application may use memory in a very specific way and pay a performance penalty for functionality it does not need. You could counter that by developing specialized memory managers. The design space for special-purpose memory managers is multidimensional. At least two dimensions easily come to mind: size and concurrency. The size dimension has two distinct points:

- **Fixed-size** Memory managers that allocate memory blocks of a single fixed size.

- **Variable-size** Memory managers that allocate memory blocks of any size. Request size is not known in advance.

Similarly, the concurrent dimension has two points as well:

- **Single-threaded** The memory manager is confined to a single thread. The memory is used by a single thread and does not cross thread boundary. This class is not concerned with multiple threads stepping on one another.

- **Multithreaded** This memory manager is used by multiple threads concurrently. The implementation will have code fragments whose exceution is mutually exclusive. Only one thread can execute in any of these fragments at any point in time.

Right now we already have four distinct flavors of specialized managers: those corresponding to the product of the size dimension, {fixed, variable}, with the concurrent dimension, {single-threaded, multithreaded}. In this chapter we will examine the single-threaded dimension of special-purpose managers and their performance implications. Our goal, of course, is to develop alternative memory managers that are much faster than the default one. At the same time, we don't want to develop too many specialized managers. The ultimate goal is to combine speed with as much flexibility and code reuse as we can.

Version 0: The Global new() and delete()

The default memory manager is, by design, a general-purpose one. This is what you get when you call the global new() and delete(). The implementation of these two functions cannot make any simplifying assumptions. They manage memory in the process context, and since a process may spawn multiple threads, new() and delete() must be able to operate in a multithreaded environment. In addition, the size of memory requests may vary from one request to the next. This flexibility trades off with speed. The more you have to compute, the more cycles it is going to consume.

It is often the case that client code does not need the full power of the global new() and delete(). It may be that client code only (or mostly) needs memory chunks of specific size. It may be that client code operates in a single-threaded environment where the concurrency protection provided by the default new() and delete() is not really necessary. If this is the case, utilizing the full power of those functions is a waste of CPU cycles. You can gain significant efficiency by tailoring a memory allocation scheme to better match your specific requirements.

Say that your code requires frequent allocations and deallocations of objects representing rational numbers:

```
class Rational {
public:
    Rational (int a = 0, int b = 1 ) : n(a), d(b) {}
private:
    int n;    // Numerator
    int d;    // Denominator
};
```

To measure a baseline performance of the global `new()` and `delete()` we executed the following test:

```
int main()
{
    Rational *array[1000];
    ...
    // Start timing here

    for (int j = 0; j < 500; j++)   {
        for (int i = 0; i < 1000; i++)   {
            array[i] = new Rational(i);
            }
        for (i = 0; i < 1000; i++)   {
            delete array[i];
            }
        }

    // Stop timing here

    ...
}
```

Each iteration of the outermost loop executes a thousand allocations and deallocations of `Rational` objects. Five hundred iterations yield a million operations.

The time elapsed for this code fragment was 1,500 milliseconds. What kind of speed can we gain by tailoring a specific `Rational` memory manager? To answer the question we need to roll our own memory manager and overload the `new()` and `delete()` methods for the `Rational` class.

Version 1: Specialized Rational Memory Manager

To avoid frequent hits to the default manager, the `Rational` class will maintain a static linked list of preallocated `Rational` objects, which will serve as the free list of available objects. When we need a new `Rational` object, we will get one from the free list. When we are done with an object, we will return it to the free list for future allocations.

We declare a helper structure to link adjacent elements on the free list.

```
class NextOnFreeList {
public:
    NextOnFreeList *next;
};
```

The free list is declared as a linked list of NextOnFreeList elements.

```
class Rational {
    ...
    static NextOnFreeList *freeList;
};
```

If the free list is a list of NextOnFreeList structures, you may wonder where the Rational objects reside. Although each element on the free list is declared as a NextOnFreeList structure, it is also a Rational object. When we create an element, we allocate it big enough to contain a Rational object. To step from one object to the next, we will use the first few bytes of each Rational object to point to the next object on the free list. We do that by casting the object into a pointer of type NextOnFreeList.

The free list, then, will have a dual role as a sequence of Rational objects as well as a sequence of NextOnFreeList elements (Figure 6.1).

The free list is declared as a static member of the Rational class. The static free list is manipulated by the Rational new() and delete() operators. These operators overload the global ones.

```
class Rational {
public:
    Rational (int a = 0, int b = 1 ) : n(a), d(b) {}

    inline void *operator new(size_t size);
    inline void operator delete(void *doomed, size_t size);

    static void newMemPool() { expandTheFreeList(); }
    static void deleteMemPool();

private:
    static NextOnFreeList *freeList;    // A free list of
                                        // Rational objects.
    static void expandTheFreeList();
    enum { EXPANSION_SIZE = 32};

    int n;    // Numerator
    int d;    // Denominator
};
```

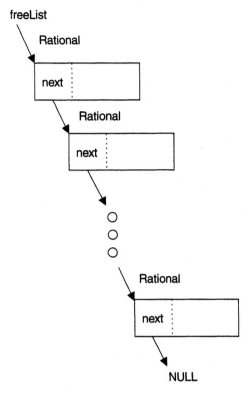

Figure 6.1. A free list of Rational objects.

Operator new( ) allocates a new Rational object from the free list. If the free list is empty, it will get expanded. We pick off the head of the free list and return it after adjusting the free list pointer.

```
inline
void * Rational::operator new(size_t size)
{
    if (0 == freeList) {// If the list is empty, fill it up.
        expandTheFreeList();
        }

    NextOnFreeList *head = freeList;
    freeList = head->next;

    return head;
}
```

Operator delete() returns a Rational object to the free list by simply adding it to the front of the free list.

```
inline
void Rational::operator delete(void *doomed, size_t size)
{
NextOnFreeList *head = static_cast <NextOnFreeList *> doomed;

head->next = freeList;
freeList  = head;
}
```

When the free list is exhausted, we must allocate more Rational objects from the heap. There is a little subtlety here that should be pointed out. Switching between Rational and NextOnFreeList types is slightly dangerous. We need to make sure that the elements of the free list are large enough to serve as either type. When we populate the free list with Rational objects, we have to remember to compare the size of Rational to the size of NextOnFreeList and allocate the larger of the two.

```
void Rational::expandTheFreeList()
{
    // We must allocate an object large enough to contain the next
    // pointer.
    size_t size = (sizeof(Rational) > sizeof(NextOnFreeList *)) ?
        sizeof(Rational) : sizeof(NextOnFreeList *);

    NextOnFreeList *runner =
    static_cast <NextOnFreeList *> new char [size];

    freeList =  runner;
    for (int i = 0; i < EXPANSION_SIZE; i++) {
        runner->next =
              static_cast <NextOnFreeList *> new char [size];
        runner = runner->next;
          }

    runner->next = 0;
}
```

This implementation of expandTheFreeList(), in itself, is not optimal. It invokes operator new multiple times, once per free list element. It would be more efficient to invoke operator new once, get a large block of memory, and slice it ourselves into multiple elements [Mey97]. In isolation, this is a correct observation. In reality, however, we build a memory manager with the idea that expanding and shrinking it will be performed very infrequently, otherwise we must revisit the implementation and fix it. Our implementation is such that the free list never shrinks; it will grow to a steady-state size and stay there. If you want to implement a more efficient version of `expandTheFreeList()`, there is no harm in it, but it is not likely to have an effect on overall performance.

```
void Rational::deleteMemPool()
{
    NextOnFreeList *nextPtr;
    for(nextPtr=freeList; nextPtr!=NULL; nextPtr=freeList){
        freeList = freeList->next;
        delete [] nextPtr;
        }
}
```

We repeated the following performance test, but this time, the use of **new** and **delete** invokes the overloaded operators of the `Rational` class:

```
NextOnFreeList *Rational::freeList = 0;

int main()
{
    ...
    Rational *array[1000];

    Rational::newMemPool();

    // Start timing here

    for (int j = 0; j < 500; j++)    {
        for (int i = 0; i < 1000; i++)   {
            array[i] = new Rational(i);
            }
        for (i = 0; i < 1000; i++)    {
            delete array[i];
            }
        }

    // Stop timing here

    Rational::deleteMemPool();
    ...
}
```

The **new()** and **delete()** calls now result in invocations of the `Rational::oper-ator new()` and `delete()` calls that we implemented. The execution time of the

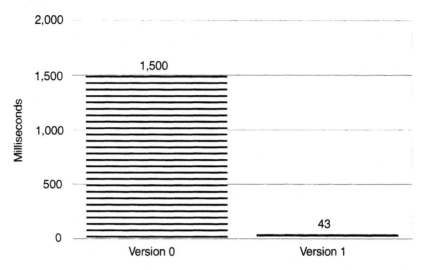

Figure 6.2.   Global `new()` and `delete()` compared to a `Rational` memory pool.

loop dropped from 1,500 milliseconds to 43 milliseconds. This is more than an order-of-magnitude improvement (Figure 6.2).

Where does the speed gain come from? Since we are in a single-threaded environment, our `Rational` memory management routines do not bother with concurrency issues. We do not protect memory manipulation because we don't have any critical sections to worry about. We also take advantage of the fact that all allocations are of fixed size—the size of a `Rational` object. Fixed-size allocations are much simpler; there are a lot less computations to perform (like finding the next available memory chunk big enough to satisfy the request). We simply adjust the free list pointer, and we are done.

Version 2: Fixed-Size Object Memory Pool

Version 1 is limited to managing `Rational` objects only. What if we wanted a memory manager for some other class of a different size? Duplicating the memory management logic for every class will be an unnecessary waste of developer time. If we look at the implementation of the `Rational` memory manager, it becomes apparent that the memory management logic is really independent of the particular `Rational` class. The only dependency is the size of the class object—a good candidate for a template implementation of a memory pool. The memory pool will manage a pool of available objects of a certain type. A template implementation would allow us to vary the specific class that we are managing.

```
template < class T >
class MemoryPool {
public:
    MemoryPool (size_t size = EXPANSION_SIZE);
    ~MemoryPool ();

    // Allocate a T element from the free list.
    inline void* alloc (size_t size);

    // Return a T element to the free list.
    inline void free (void *someElement);
private:
    // next element on the free list.
    MemoryPool<T> *next;

    // If the freeList is empty, expand it by this amount.
    enum { EXPANSION_SIZE = 32};

    // Add free elements to the free list
    void expandTheFreeList(int howMany = EXPANSION_SIZE);
};
```

The `MemoryPool` constructor initializes the free list. The `size` argument specifies the initial length of the free list.

```
template < class T >
MemoryPool < T > :: MemoryPool (size_t size)
{
    expandTheFreeList(size);
}
```

The destructor marches down the free list and deletes all its elements.

```
template < class T >
MemoryPool < T > :: ~MemoryPool ()
{
    MemoryPool<T> *nextPtr = next;
    for (nextPtr = next; nextPtr != NULL; nextPtr = next) {
        next = next->next;
        delete [] nextPtr;
        }
}
```

The `alloc()` member function allocates space large enough for a T element. If the free list has been depleted, we call `expandTheFreeList()` to replenish it.

```
template < class T >
inline
void* MemoryPool < T > :: alloc (size_t)
{
    if (!next) {
       expandTheFreeList();
       }

    MemoryPool<T> *head = next;
    next = head->next;

    return head;
}
```

The `free()` member function deallocates a T element by placing it back on the free list.

```
template < class T >
inline
void MemoryPool < T > :: free (void *doomed)
{
    MemoryPool<T> *head = static_cast <MemoryPool<T> *> doomed;

    head->next = next;
    next  = head;
}
```

`expandTheFreeList()` is used to add new elements to the free list. The new elements are allocated from the heap and stitched together into a linked list. This member function is called when the free list is depleted.

```
template < class T >
void MemoryPool < T > :: expandTheFreeList(int howMany)
{
    // We must allocate an object large enough to contain the
    // next pointer.
    size_t size = (sizeof(T) > sizeof(MemoryPool<T> *)) ?
        sizeof(T) : sizeof(MemoryPool<T> *);

    MemoryPool<T> *runner = static_cast <MemoryPool<T> *> new char
[size];

    next =  runner;
    for (int i = 0; i < howMany ; i++) {
```

```
            runner->next =
                    static_cast <MemoryPool<T> *> new char [size];
            runner = runner->next;
            }
        runner->next = 0;
}
```

The `Rational` class no longer needs to maintain its own free list. This responsibility is delegated to the `MemoryPool` class.

```
class Rational {
public:
    Rational (int a = 0, int b = 1 ) : n(a), d(b) {}

    void *operator new(size_t size) { return memPool->alloc(size); }
    void operator delete(void *doomed,size_t size)
                    { memPool->free(doomed); }

    static void newMemPool() { memPool = new MemoryPool <Rational>; }
    static void deleteMemPool() { delete memPool; }
private:
    int n; // Numerator
    int d; // Denominator

    static MemoryPool <Rational> *memPool;
};
```

We eliminated the static `freeList` member pointer plus its related functions and replaced it with a pointer to a memory pool. In the preceding `Rational` implementation, the template memory pool was specialized in its definition to be a `Rational` memory pool.

Our test loop is almost identical to the previous one:

```
MemoryPool <Rational> *Rational::memPool = 0;

int main()
{
    ...
    Rational *array[1000];

    Rational::newMemPool();

    // Start timing here

    for (int j = 0; j < 500; j++)   {
        for (int i = 0; i < 1000; i++)   {
```

```
                array[i] = new Rational(i);
                }
        for (i = 0; i < 1000; i++)   {
            delete array[i];
            }
    }

    // Stop timing here

    Rational::deleteMemPool();

    . . .
}
```

We expected this measurement to be identical to the previous Rational free list memory manager (Version 1), which executed the loop in 43 milliseconds. For some reason, the template version (Version 2) of the memory pool clocked in at 63 ms (Figure 6.3), a little slower than the previous version. Also, the assembler code generated for Version 2 had some extra instructions. Still, it beats the global new() and delete() by more than an order of magnitude.

So far, we have focused on a single point in the design space of memory allocation. That was the specific problem of fixed-size allocations in a single-threaded environment. We now extend our options by expanding in the size dimension. We stay in the

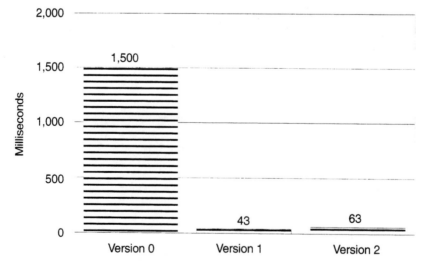

Figure 6.3. Adding a template memory pool for generic objects.

realm of single-threaded memory pools but relax the assumption that all allocations are of the same size.

Version 3: Single-Threaded Variable-Size Memory Manager

Speeding up the allocation and deallocation of fixed-size memory will only take you so far. There is a class of applications that require variable-size memory allocations. A Web server implementation is a perfect example. Typical implementations of a Web server are gigantic string crunchers. If you peek into the code you'll find that the handling of a single HTTP request requires a large number of string surgeries. Many of those calls require space allocation to create new or duplicated strings. Furthermore, you cannot tell in advance how many string allocations would be necessary and of what size. Potentially, strings are unbounded. The nature of string manipulations is dictated by the content of the particular HTTP request. A fixed-size memory manager would fall short of the requirement. Relying on the global new() and delete(), however, is out of the question. The global new() and delete() are expensive. They consume hundreds of instructions and moreover, they contain mutually exclusive critical sections that prevent concurrent thread execution and consequently hurt scalabilty. It would damage the speed and scalability of a Web server. This is a perfect place for a home-grown, variable-size memory manager.

There are many ways to implement a variable-size memory manager [ALG95]. The one we used in our Web server is discussed next.

The MemoryChunk class replaces the NextOnFreeList class we used in earlier versions. It is used to string together chunks of memory of varying sizes into a sequence of chunks.

```
class MemoryChunk {
public:
    MemoryChunk (MemoryChunk *nextChunk, size_t chunkSize);
    ~MemoryChunk() {delete mem; }

    inline void *alloc (size_t size);
    inline void free (void* someElement);

    // Pointer to next memory chunk on the list.
    MemoryChunk *nextMemChunk()    {return next;}

    // How much space do we have left on this memory chunk?
```

```
        size_t spaceAvailable()
                { return chunkSize -    bytesAlreadyAllocated; }

        // this is the default size of a single memory chunk.
        enum { DEFAULT_CHUNK_SIZE = 4096 };
private:
        MemoryChunk *next;
        void        *mem;

        // The size of a single memory chunk.
        size_t chunkSize;

        // This many bytes already allocated on the current memory chunk.
        size_t bytesAlreadyAllocated;
};
```

The MemoryChunk class is a cleaner version of NextOnFreeList. It separates the next pointer from the actual memory used for the allocated object. It uses explicit next and mem pointers, with no need for casting. It is given pictorially in Figure 6.4.

The MemoryChunk constructor first determines the appropriate size of the memory block. It uses this size to allocate its private storage from the heap. The constructor also makes the next member point to the nextChunk input argument. The nextChunk is the previous head of the linked list. Effectively, we are making the newly constructed MemoryChunk the new head of the linked list of MemoryChunk objects. The number of bytes already allocated on this chunk is set to 0 since this is a brand new MemoryChunk:

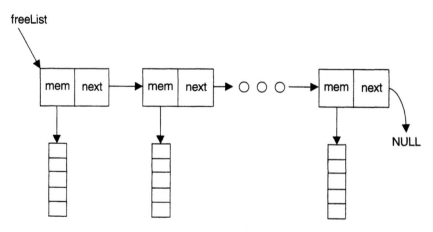

Figure 6.4. Variable-size memory free list.

```
MemoryChunk::MemoryChunk(MemoryChunk *nextChunk, size_t reqSize)
{
    chunkSize = (reqSize > DEFAULT_CHUNK_SIZE) ?
                reqSize : DEFAULT_CHUNK_SIZE;
    next = nextChunk;
    bytesAlreadyAllocated = 0;
    mem = new char [chunkSize];
}
```

The destructor deletes the memory obtained by the constructor:

```
MemoryChunk :: ~MemoryChunk() { delete [] mem; }
```

A memory allocation request is handled by the alloc() method. It returns a pointer to available space in the MemoryChunk private storage pointed to by mem. It keeps track of available space by updating the number of bytes already allocated in this block.

```
void* MemoryChunk :: alloc (size_t requestSize)
{
    void *addr = static_cast <void*>
        (static_cast <size_t> mem + bytesAlreadyAllocated);
    bytesAlreadyAllocated += requestSize;

    return addr;
}
```

In this implementation we do not bother freeing memory fragments on the fly. The whole memory chunk gets deallocated and sent back to the heap when the object is deleted:

```
inline void MemoryChunk :: free (void *doomed) {}
```

The MemoryChunk is just a helper class. It is used by the ByteMemoryPool class to implement a variable-size memory manager:

```
class ByteMemoryPool {
public:
    ByteMemoryPool (size_t initSize =
                    MemoryChunk::DEFAULT_CHUNK_SIZE);
    ~ByteMemoryPool ();

    // Allocate memory from private pool.
    inline void *alloc (size_t size);

    // Free memory previously allocated from the pool
```

```
        inline void free (void* someElement);
private:
        // A list of memory chunks. This is our private storage.
        MemoryChunk *listOfMemoryChunks;

        // Add one memory chunk to our private storage
        void expandStorage(size_t reqSize);
};
```

Although the list of memory chunks may contain more than a single chunk, only the first chunk has memory available for allocation. The rest of the chunks represent memory that has already been allocated. The first element of the list is the only chunk capable of allocating available memory.

The constructor takes an `initSize` argument to specify the size of a single memory chunk. It sets the size of a single memory chunk accordingly. The `expand-Storage()` method sets `listOfMemoryChunks` to point to an allocated `MemoryChunk` object:

```
// Construct the ByteMemoryPool object. Build the private storage.
ByteMemoryPool :: ByteMemoryPool (size_t initSize)
{
        expandStorage(initSize);
}
```

The destructor marches down the list of memory chunks and deletes them:

```
ByteMemoryPool :: ~ByteMemoryPool ()
{
        MemoryChunk *memChunk = listOfMemoryChunks;

        while (memChunk) {
                listOfMemoryChunks = memChunk->nextMemChunk();
                delete memChunk;
                memChunk = listOfMemoryChunks;
                }
}
```

`ByteMemoryPool::alloc()` guarantees that we have sufficient space available, and then delegates the allocation task to the `MemoryChunk` at the top of the list:

```
void* ByteMemoryPool :: alloc (size_t requestSize)
{
        size_t space = listOfMemoryChunks->spaceAvailable();
```

```
      if ( space < requestSize ) {
         expandStorage(requestSize);
         }

      return listOfMemoryChunks->alloc(requestSize);
}
```

The implementation of `ByteMemoryPool::alloc()` is somewhat more complex than our previous equivalent implementations of `MemoryPool<T>::alloc()`, and the `Rational::operator new()`. Take `MemoryPool<T>::alloc()`, for example. We check the state of the free list. If it is empty, we replenish it. Computationally, all we need to do then is to return the element to the top of the free list. That's fast and easy. There's a lot more we need to compute in the case of `Byte-MemoryPool::alloc()`. Since we are dealing with unknown request size, we have to make sure that we have sufficient space available in the `MemoryChunk`. If not, we must call `expandStorage()` to allocate a new `MemoryChunk` and push it on top of the list of chunks. Either way, we are now guaranteed to have enough room to satisfy the request. Next, we call `MemoryChunk::alloc()` to compute the memory address to be returned to the caller and to adjust its bookkeeping to reflect the number of bytes already allocated in that chunk. All these extra computations will degrade performance to some extent. That's the price of extended functionality.

Freeing previously allocated memory is delegated to the `MemoryChunk` on top of the list:

```
inline
void ByteMemoryPool :: free (void *doomed)
{
      listOfMemoryChunks->free(doomed);
}
```

Recall that the `MemoryChunk::free()` method is very simple—it does nothing. Why are we so lazy when it comes to freeing memory? Because this implementation of `ByteMemoryPool` does not reuse memory that was previously allocated. If we need more memory, we will create a new chunk and use it for future allocations. The memory is released back to the heap upon pool destruction. The `ByteMemoryPool` destructor releases all the memory chunks back to the heap.

This is not as wasteful as it sounds. We used this scheme to handle HTTP requests. A `ByteMemoryPool` object was created at the beginning of each request. The memory chunk size was 4,096 bytes and that was good enough for 99% of HTTP requests. So in the typical case, we never had to expand our private storage because a single chunk was sufficient. Since the handling of an HTTP request is a very short-lived task, there is no need to worry about freeing and reusing private memory on the fly. It was much more efficient to unload the whole chunk at once during pool destruction (at the end of a request). This is yet another example of a message that is repeated in various forms throughout the book: Special circumstances allow for simplifying assumptions. Simplifying assumptions, in turn, provide opportunities for significant optimizations. You don't want to use solutions that were meant for bigger problems. Another issue that pops up here is that performance sometimes compromises reuse. To boost performance you sometimes need to tailor niche solutions for special circumstances. Those solutions don't tend to be very flexible or reusable outside of their intended, narrow domain.

In the unlikely case that our storage chunk was exhausted, we expand it by creating a new memory chunk and adding it to the top of the list of memory chunks.

```
void ByteMemoryPool :: expandStorage(size_t reqSize)
{
    listOfMemoryChunks = new MemoryChunk(listOfMemoryChunks, reqSize);
}
```

To test this memory manager, we modified the Rational class implementation by replacing the MemoryPool<Rational> object with a ByteMemoryPool:

```
class Rational {
public:
    Rational (int a = 0, int b = 1 ) : n(a), d(b) {}

    void *operator new(size_t size) {return memPool->alloc(size);}
    void operator delete(void *doomed,size_t size)
                {memPool->free(doomed);}

    static void newMemPool() { memPool = new ByteMemoryPool;}
    static void deleteMemPool() { delete memPool; }
private:
    int n; // Numerator
    int d; // Denominator

    static ByteMemoryPool *memPool;
};
```

With this implementation of the memory pool, we measured our test loop one more time, allocating and deallocating `Rational` objects:

```
MemoryPool <Rational> *Rational::memPool = 0;

int main()
{
    ...
    Rational *array[1000];

    Rational::newMemPool();

    // Start timing here

    for (int j = 0; j < 500; j++)   {
        for (int i = 0; i < 1000; i++)   {
            array[i] = new Rational(i);
            }
        for (i = 0; i < 1000; i++)   {
            delete array[i];
            }
        }

    // Stop timing here

    Rational::deleteMemPool();

    ...
}
```

This loop executed in 140 milliseconds. Figure 6.5 compares the execution speed of the following:

- Version 1, the `Rational` memory manager

- Version 2, a template implementation of an object memory manager

- Version 3, variable-size memory manager

As expected, Version 3 is slower than Versions 1 and 2, due to the increased complexity of the allocation logic. As we march forward to more powerful memory management, we have to give up some speed.

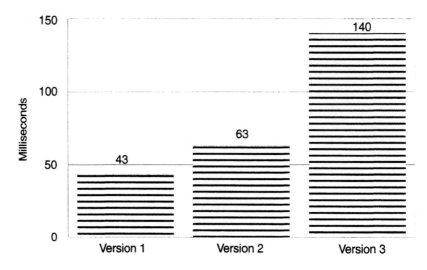

Figure 6.5. A variable-size memory pool is naturally slower than fixed-size.

Key Points

- Flexibility trades off with speed. As the power and flexibility of memory management increases, execution speed decreases.

- The global memory manager (implemented by `new()` and `delete()`) is general purpose and consequently expensive.

- Specialized memory managers can be more than an order of magnitude faster than the global one.

- If you allocate mostly memory blocks of a fixed size, a specialized fixed-size memory manager will provide a significant performance boost.

- A similar boost is available if you allocate mostly memory blocks that are confined to a single thread. A single-threaded memory manager will help by skipping over the concurrency issues that the global `new()` and `delete()` must handle.

7

Multithreaded Memory Pooling

The previous chapter stayed entirely within the realm of a single-threaded environment. The memory pool was owned by a single thread and concurrency issues were absent. We now extend our design to a multithreaded environment. The memory pool will no longer belong to any particular thread; instead it will be shared among all threads in the application process.

The allocators developed for the single-threaded environment will not work properly in a multithreaded environment. To allow multiple threads to allocate and free memory concurrently, we must add mutual exclusion to the allocator methods. We could duplicate the single-threaded implementations and add locking at the right spots, but this brute force mechanism requires that you provide a distinct implementation for each memory pool type and each locking scheme. This is one of those design scenarios that begs for a template implementation. Such an implementation of a multithreaded memory pool could be parameterized by the memory pool type. It would simply decorate the `alloc()` and `free()` calls (developed in the previous chapter) with a lock protection. We can take it a step further by making the lock type a template parameter as well, allowing us to instantiate memory pools with distinct locking schemes. That's another degree of freedom.

Version 4: Implementation

Version 4 implements a multithreaded memory pool. It can handle any pool and lock type that conform to the expected interface:

```
template <class POOLTYPE , class LOCK>
class MTMemoryPool {
public:
    // Allocate an element from the freeList.
    inline void* alloc (size_t size);

    // Return an element to the freeList.
    inline void free (void* someElement);
private:
    POOLTYPE stPool;  // Single-threaded pool.
    LOCK     theLock;
};
```

The `alloc()` method delegates the allocation to the memory pool member, and the locking to the lock member, respectively:

```
template <class M, class L>
inline
void* MTMemoryPool<M,L>::alloc (size_t size)
{
    void * mem;

    theLock.lock();
    mem = stPool.alloc(size);
    theLock.unlock();

    return mem;
}
template <class M, class L>
inline
void MTMemoryPool<M,L>::free (void* doomed)
{
    theLock.lock();
    stPool.free(doomed);
    theLock.unlock();
}
```

To instantiate a `MemPool` template, we'll need to provide a memory pool type plus a lock type. For memory pools, we'll reuse the ones developed in the previous chapter. For lock types, we start with the following:

```
class ABCLock {// Abstract base class
public:
    virtual ~ABCLock() {}
    virtual void lock() = 0;
    virtual void unlock() = 0;
};
```

```
class MutexLock : public ABCLock {
public:
    MutexLock() {pthread_mutex_init(&lock, NULL);}
    ~MutexLock() {pthread_mutex_destroy(&lock);}

    inline void lock() {pthread_mutex_lock(&lock);}
    inline void unlock() {pthread_mutex_unlock(&lock);}
private:
    pthread_mutex_t lock;
};
```

We also need to modify the implementation of `Rational` to instantiate a multi-threaded memory pool. The core memory pool is of type `MemoryPool<Rational>` and the `MutexLock` provides the locking services:

```
class Rational {
public:
    ...
    static void newMemPool() {
        memPool = new MTMemoryPool <MemoryPool <Rational>,
                                    MutexLock>;
    }
private:
    ...
    static MTMemoryPool <MemoryPool<Rational>, MutexLock> *memPool;
};
```

Our test driver remains unchanged. It's the same old loop we used previously to measure allocation and deallocation of `Rational` objects:

```
for (int j = 0; j < 500; j++)   {
    for (int i = 0; i < 1000; i++)   {
        array[i] = new Rational(i);
        }
    for (i = 0; i < 1000; i++)   {
        delete array[i];
        }
    }
```

The last time we measured the execution time of the `MemoryPool`, we clocked in at 63 milliseconds for Version 2. So we were a little surprised to see the execution time of Version 4 increased to 1,300 milliseconds. Figure 7.1 compares the following:

- Version 0. Global `new()` and `delete()`.

- Version 2. `MemoryPool`: A single-threaded template implementation of a fixed object memory manager.

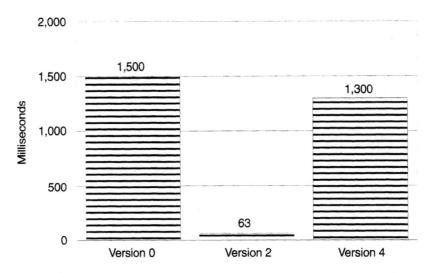

Figure 7.1. Comparing multithreaded to single-threaded memory pooling.

• Version 4. `MTMemoryPool`: Multithreaded `MemoryPool`.

Something has gone wrong with the implementation of Version 4. A quick analysis reveals that execution time is dominated entirely by the pthreads library locking calls. Allocating memory contains a call to `pthread_mutex_lock()` followed by `pthread_mutex_unlock()`. The same holds for deallocating memory. Overall, each iteration of the main loop triggers two calls to `pthread_mutex_lock()` and two more to `pthread_mutex_unlock()`: one pair for allocating an object and another pair for freeing it. Since locking is mandatory in this environment, the only hope we have is a drastic improvement of our locking calls.

Version 5: Faster Locking

What's wrong with our use of the pthreads locking calls? We suggested earlier that sometimes you don't really need the full power and flexibility of the default memory management. We are running into a similar issue with locking. Sometimes, you don't really need the full power of the pthreads library locking services. For example, `pthread_mutex_lock()` must check that the calling thread does not already hold the lock, otherwise we are going to deadlock. `pthread_mutex_unlock()` must check that the calling thread is the one that actually holds the lock. All these little checks and computations consume precious CPU cycles.

Suppose we don't really need all this locking flexibility in Version 4. Suppose that our application's use of the locking services is so simple that we can guarantee that the locking thread does not already hold the lock. Further suppose that we can guarantee that the unlocking thread is the one that locked it in the first place. Now we can get away with a locking scheme that's a lot less sophisticated than the one provided by the pthreads library. What we ought to do is implement a new lock class using faster and more primitive building blocks to provide locking. Along the way we are trading portability for speed. Our next implementation of a lock class is platform-specific. Each platform, however, provides primitive basic blocks that are much faster than the pthreads library. In this case the PrimitiveLock implementation was tailored for AIX.

Version 5 simply replaces the implementation of MutexLock with a faster one called PrimitiveLock:

```
class PrimitiveLock : public ABCLock {
public:
    PrimitiveLock() {
            _clear_lock((static_cast<atomic_p>) &_lock,
                    LOCK_FREE);}
    ~PrimitiveLock() {}

    inline void lock() {// Spin lock
        while (!_check_lock((static_cast<atomic_p>) &_lock,
                    LOCK_FREE, LOCK_BUSY));
        }

    inline void unlock() {
        _clear_lock((static_cast<atomic_p>) &_lock, LOCK_FREE);
        }
private:
    int _lock;
    enum {LOCK_FREE = 0, LOCK_BUSY = 1};
};
```

The implementation of MTMemoryPool remains unchanged. That's the power of a template. We only need to make a slight modification to the Rational class to instantiate an MTMemoryPool template using the PrimitiveLock:

```
class Rational {
public:
    ...
    static void newMemPool() {
        memPool = new MTMempryPool <MemoryPool <Rational>,
                            PrimitiveLock>;
```

```
        }
private:
    ...
    static MTMemoryPool < MemoryPool<Rational>, PrimitiveLock>
        *memPool;
};
```

With this faster locking class, execution time improved significantly to 900 milliseconds (Figure 7.2).

So far we have positioned the MTMemoryPool template as a multithreaded solution. It is actually more flexible than that. You can instantiate it in a single-threaded environment, and it will perform just as well and as fast as the single-threaded solutions. You can achieve that by instantiating MTMemoryPool with a DummyLock class that does nothing:

```
class DummyLock : public ABCLock {
public:
    inline void lock() {}
    inline void unlock() {}
};
```

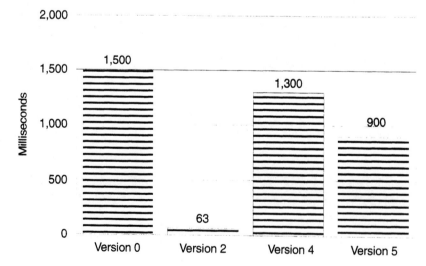

Figure 7.2. Multithreaded memory pool using faster locks.

When you instantiate an MTMemoryPool with a DummyLock as in

MTMemoryPool <MemoryPool<Rational>, DummyLock> myRationalPool;

you essentially get the equivalent of

MemoryPool<Rational> myRationalPool;

The performance of these two forms is identical if inlining is performed by the compiler. Inlining will flatten DummyLock::lock() and DummyLock:unlock() down to zero instructions.

In the previous chapter we developed a single-threaded, variable-size memory allocator named ByteMemoryPool. We can extend ByteMemoryPool into a multithreaded environment in the same way we extended MemoryPool. We simply instantiate the MTMemoryPool template with a ByteMemoryPool parameter. To test it we only need to modify two lines in the Rational implementation:

```
class Rational {
public:
    ...
    static void newMemPool() {
        memPool = new MTMemoryPool <ByteMemoryPool, MutexLock>;
        }
private:
    ...
    static MTMemoryPool <ByteMemoryPool, MutexLock> *memPool;
};
```

Figure 7.3 contrasts the performance numbers of various memory pool classes developed in Chapters 5 and 6:

- Version 0. Global new() and delete().

- Version 2. MemoryPool. A single-threaded template implementation of a fixed object memory manager.

- Version 4. Multithreaded, fixed object memory manager using MemoryPool and pthreads locking.

- Version 5. Essentially Version 4 with faster, platform-dependent locks.

- Version 6. Multithreaded, variable-size memory manager using ByteMemoryPool and fast locks.

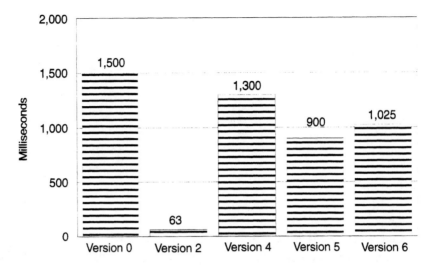

Figure 7.3. Comparing the various flavors of memory pooling.

We presented various memory allocators in Chapters 5 and 6, but they are far from being exhaustive. We have not explored the whole space of memory allocators, just a small subset. Consider the variable-size allocator defined by

```
MemPool <ByteMemoryPool, PrimitiveLock> myPool;
```

This allocator has a serious flaw in SMP environments. It is not scalable. Our implementation of `ByteMemoryPool` manipulates a single `MemoryChunk` to allocate storage. This `MemoryChunk` is a single resource that cannot be accessed concurrently. If two threads are trying to allocate memory, they must be serialized. To break up this scalability bottleneck, we could divide our critical resource into multiple resources. For example, we could have one resource for small allocations (less than 512 bytes) and another one for large (512 bytes or more). Now two requests for 100 and 1,000 bytes could proceed concurrently without getting in each other's way. We will not pursue this particular allocator here. General scalability considerations are discussed in Chapter 15.

Key Points

- The global memory manager (implemented by `new()` and `delete()`) is general-purpose and consequently expensive.

- A significant boost is available if you mostly allocate memory blocks that are confined to a single thread. A single-threaded memory manager is much faster than a multithreaded one.

- If you develop a set of efficient single-threaded allocators, you can easily extend their reach into multithreaded environments by the use of templates.

8

Inlining Basics

This chapter leaves the realm of design and begins a focus on speed mechanisms that are largely design independent. These techniques will improve any program's performance, independent of its overall design quality, However, these mechanistic techniques will not make badly designed programs fast—it will just make them faster than they were. They will not make selection sorts faster than quick sorts, though they can change the data set size of a problem that can be efficiently handled by an otherwise less efficient algorithm. Some of these techniques are free; that is, they are pure performance gains with no negative impacts on other software quality characteristics. Most of these techniques, however, force a designer to trade some aspect of design, like code size, portability, extensibility, or generality, for a needed performance bump. Almost all of these techniques have negative maintenance implications.

What Is Inlining?

Inlining replaces method calls with a macro-like expansion of the called method within the calling method. There are two mechanisms for specifying an intent to inline. One is to prefix the method definition with the reserved word inline, and the other is to define the method within the declaration header. A code sample make this easier to demonstrate:

```
Class GatedInt {
    int x;
public:
    int get () {
        return x;
        }
```

```
        void set (int arg) {
            x = arg;
            }
}
```

`GatedInt::get` and `GeatedInt::set` will both be inlined because they are defined within the declaration. Conversely, the methods to be inlined can be defined outside the class declaration but within the header file or within a file included by the header file.

```
Class GatedInt {
    int x;
public:
    int get();
    void set (int arg) ;
}

inline int GatedInt::get ()
{
    return x;
}

inline void GatedInt::set (int arg)
{
    x = arg;
}
```

Inlined methods are called like any other method, but they do not compile like normal methods. The fact that the code for the inlined method needs to be expanded inline means that any code that calls the inlined method must have access to the definition of the method. The fact that the definition of the inlined method has been incorporated into its calling methods means that any change in the inlined method will require a complete recompilation of every module that uses the method. One of the costs of the potentially significant performance improvement inlining provides is an increase in compile-time. Sometimes the increase will be modest, but in some instances it can be immense, and in the most extreme cases a modification to an inlined method may require a complete recompilation of the entire program. This generally makes it a good idea to wait until the later stages of code development to inline anything.

These methods could be called with a program like this:

```
int main ()
{
    GatedInt gi;
    gi.set(12);
    cout << gi.get();
}
```

A method is represented in a program by a contiguous block of code that contains the operations performed by the method. Using our sample program, get, set, and main would each be represented by independent code blocks that contain the machine language instructions selected by the compiler to perform their respective operations. In our example program, main instantiates an instance of a GatedInt, pushes the literal 12 onto the stack and calls GatedInt::set. It then calls GatedInt::get and pushes the returned value onto the stack so that iostream::operator<< can output the value. GatedInt::get returns the value of the private member variable GatedInt::x, and GatedInt::set assigns the input argument arg to GatedInt::x. Ignoring the work performed by the operating system to get this program loaded and running, an outlined (not inlined) version of this program makes three calls. The first two calls require probably an order of magnitude more effort to perform call and return overhead than to actually execute the code within the called methods.

Conversely, inlined get and set would result in a main program containing a single call to iostream::<<, and the main program logically would look something like this after get and set were inlined and before main was compiled:

```
int main ()
{
    GatedInt gi;
    {
        gi::x = 12;
    }
    int temp = gi::x;
    cout << temp;
}
```

Notice that we said logically; the compiler should do much better than this. An optimization pass on main would reduce it to:

```
int main ()
{
    cout << 12;
}
```

Logically, the procedure used by a compiler to inline a method is as follows: The contiguous code block of the method to be inlined is copied into the invoking method at what would have been its point of call. Any local variables in the inlined method are allocated in block. The inlined method's input arguments and return value are mapped into the invoking method's local variable space. If the inlined method has multiple returns they become branches (the dreaded GOTO) to the end of the inlined block. All vestiges associated with what would have been a call (with the possible exception of an SP modification associated with the creation of a new block) are erased and, along with them, all the performance penalties of the call. However, call avoidance is only half the performance story of inlining. Suppose we had two methods y and build_mask:

```
int x::y (int a)
{
    ...
    int b = 6;
    ...        // b is not modified within this section
    int m = build_mask(b);
    ...        // m is not modified in this section
    int n = m + 1;
    ...
}

inline
int build_mask (int q)
{
    if (q > WORD_SIZE) return -1;
    else if (q > 0) return (1 << q) - 1;
    else return 0;
}
```

The unoptimized result of inlining build_mask into y would be:

```
int x::y (int a)
{
    ...
    int b = 6;
    ...        // b is not modified in this section
    int m;
    {
        int _temp_q = 6;
        int _temp;
        if (_temp_q > WORD_SIZE) _temp = -1;
        else if (_temp_q > 0) _temp = (1 << q) - 1;
        else _temp = 0;
        m = _temp;
```

```
    }
    ...        // m is not modified in this section
    int n = m + 1;
    ...
}
```

However, the optimized result would be:

```
int x::y (int a)
{
    ...
    int b = 6;
    ...        // b is not modified in this section
    int m = 0x3F;
    ...        // m is not modified in this section
    int n = 0x40;
    ...
}
```

Cross-call optimizations are the other half of the inlining performance equation. A good optimizing compiler can make any vestiges of an inlined method's block boundaries unrecognizable. The bulk, and in some instances the entirety, of a method may be optimized out of existence. The compiler may reorder significant amounts of the method. Thus, while logically it is useful to think of inlined methods as maintaining some cohesion, one of the main benefits of inlining is that this is not necessarily the case.

Method Invocation Costs

To understand fully what is involved in the performance benefits of inlining, we must understand what is involved in a method invocation (procedure call) and return. This will help us to understand what we are avoiding and why its avoidance can significantly improve our programs' performance.

Most systems have three or four "housekeeping" registers: an Instruction Pointer (also frequently referred to as a Program Counter in spite of the fact that it does not count programs), a Link Register, a Stack Pointer, a Frame Pointer, and an Argument Pointer, or IP, LR, SP, FP, and AP, respectively. You may have noticed that we listed five registers but said that a system has three or four housekeeping registers. This is because systems tend to mix-and-match combinations of them. We are unaware of any systems that do not use at least three of these registers, but we are also unaware of any systems that use all five.

Following is a brief explanation of each maintenance register's function.

The Instruction Pointer (IP) contains the address of the instruction to be executed next. A method invocation involves a jump to the invoked methods instructions and hence a modification to the IP. But the IP cannot just be overwritten. Its old value must be saved before it is changed, or there would be no way to get back to the invoking method.

A Link Register (LR) contains the address IP of the method that called the current method. This is the location to which the method needs to return after it completes its execution. An LR is typically tied in to the operation of an architecture's call instruction and its value is set automatically as a side effect of executing a call. This is a single register, not a stack of registers. If a method itself calls any other methods, then the LR must be saved to prevent it from being overwritten, as it is difficult to return from a call efficiently if the identity of the caller has been destroyed. The function of an LR is performed in some architectures by automatically or explicitly pushing the calling method's IP on the program's process stack, in which case the architecture will not have an explicit LR.

The local (automatic) variables in a method are allocated on the process' stack. The Stack Pointer (SP) keeps track of how much of the stack has been consumed. Each call consumes stack space and each return releases the previously allocated stack space. Similar to the invoker's IP and LR, after a return, the stack must be restored with possible adjustments to the arguments passed on the stack. This means that the SP must also be saved as part of a method call sequence.

The Argument Pointer (AP) and Frame Pointer (FP) are very system dependent. Some architectures do not have either, some have only one, and some have both. An FP is used to mark the boundary between two areas on the stack: the one where the invoking method saved the registers whose state needed to be preserved, and the other where the invoked method's automatic variables are located. The SP typically has a fair amount of volatility during method execution. An FP is commonly used as a nonvolatile reference point for the method's local variables.

Good call performance necessitates that only those registers that are used by a method be saved. Saving the entire register set on each call would be a needless overhead, but saving only a subset of the registers creates a potentially variable sized memory allocation between the arguments being passed into a method and the memory allocated to the method's automatic variables. If a variable number of register stores are associated with a given method call (that is, the number of register values saved is dependent on the state of the calling method) then an AP is needed to indicate where the arguments (parameters) that are being passed into a method are located in the stack (Figure 8.1).

Some newer processing systems have gone to a caller/callee save paradigm in which some registers are guaranteed by the calling method to be usable by the called method without any action on the called method's part (the called method can over-write their contents without negatively impacting the calling method), and some registers need to be saved by the called method before they can be used. However, not even the most sophisticated call and return mechanism can totally avoid at least some register storage and retrieval per call and return.

A typical call sequence that uses these registers would involve the following.

- The invoking method marshals the arguments to be passed to the invoked method. This typically means pushing the arguments onto the stack, usually in reverse order. When all the arguments have been pushed on the stack, the SP will be pointing to the first argument.

- The address of the instruction to be returned to is then pushed on the stack and the call instruction then branches to the first instruction of the invoked method.

- The invoked method then saves the SP, AP, and FP from the invoking method on the stack and adjusts each of the housekeepers to reflect the context of the invoked method.

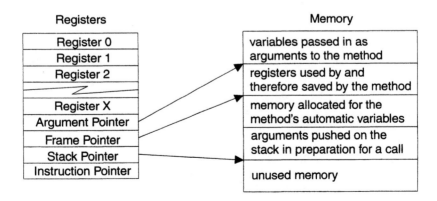

Figure 8.1. Call frame register mapping.

- The invoked method also saves (pushes onto the stack) any other registers that it will be using. (This must be done so that after the method returns, the invoking method's context will be undisturbed. This is typically another three or four registers.)

A typical return sequence to undo the previous call sequence would involve the following.

- If the method returns a value, then the value is usually returned in register 0 and sometimes also in register 1. This typically means that registers 0 and 1 must be scratch pad registers (registers that aren't saved and restored as part of a method call and return). Returning through a register makes it easier to clean up the stack for a return.

- The registers that were saved because they were used by the method are restored from the stack to their original locations.

- The saved values of the caller's FP and AP registers must then be restored from the stack to their corresponding locations.

- The SP must be adjusted such that it points to its position prior to pushing the method's first argument on the stack.

- The return address is then retrieved from the stack and placed in the IP, forcing a return to the point in the method's caller that immediately followed the point of the call.

A simple count of the data movement associated with a method invocation will indicate that six to eight registers (four maintenance registers and two to four registers for use by the method) are saved, four of which are then modified. This generally takes at least a dozen cycles (data movement to or from memory is seldom actually single cycle) and sometimes consumes in excess of 40 cycles. Hence the work associated with a method invocation is very expensive in terms of machine cycles. Unfortunately, this is only half the story. When the method returns, the work done to effect the call must all be undone. The previously saved values must be retrieved from the stack and the machine state must be returned to something approximating its precall state. This means that a method invocation typically requires somewhere between 25 and 100 cycles of overhead, and even this will occasionally be an understatement.

Part of this understatement involves argument preparation and retrieval. The arguments that are pushed on the stack as part of a call prologue frequently could have been directly mapped into the invoked method's view of memory. This is always true of references and sometimes true of pointers and objects. Thus there is additional call overhead associated with pushing arguments on the stack before the call, and then reading them back off the stack within the called method. In some instances these arguments are passed in registers, which provide very good performance (though not free), but the canonical mechanism involves using memory to pass arguments.

If a method returns a value, particularly if it is an object, there can also be the cost of copying the object generated by the invoked method into the storage reserved for the return value in the invoking method. For a large object this can be a significant additional overhead, particularly if complicated copy constructors are employed to perform the task (in which case we get a double dose of call/return overhead: one for the method we explicitly called and one for the copy constructor used to return an object). When all caller/callee communication factors and system maintenance factors are taken into account, the cost of a method invocation is somewhere between 25 and 250 cycles. Typically the larger the invoked method, the larger its overhead, up to the maximum overhead cost of saving and restoring all a processor's registers, passing some large number of arguments, and invoking user-defined methods to effect the construction of a return value.

Exception usage can significantly diminish the full potential of inlined return value optimization. Return value copying is logically an atomic operation performed by a copy-constructor as part of the called method's return. This means that logically, if an exception is thrown prior to execution of the return statement, the value is not returned, and the variable into which the method's value was to be placed will remain unchanged. This essentially necessitates the use of copy semantics for return values in the presence of exceptions. It also becomes a valid reason for avoiding the use of exceptions in some instances. Ideally, for optimization purposes, it would be handy if there were some syntactic marker that would allow return value optimization in the presence of exceptions. Some return value optimization with exceptions is already possible. For example, if the scope of the variable into which the value is being returned is within the same try block as the inlined method, then the return value can be optimized. Unfortunately, while this is relatively easily determined in most cases, it requires cross call optimization, which is expensive and somewhat complicated.

An additional advantage of inlining is that it is not necessary to branch to execute the invoked method. Branching, even unconditional branching, can negatively impact the performance of modern processors. Branching frequently involves a stall in the execution pipeline because the necessary instruction is not in the prefetch buffer. Branches can also require the services of an arithmetic unit to determine the branch target, thus delaying the time until the branch address will be known. Stalling the pipeline means the processor will be idle for the amount of time it takes to redirect the instruction stream. This occurs twice per method invocation, once when the method is called and again when it returns.

There is still one more factor that works against call performance. Compilers are getting reasonably good at optimizing small code windows; that is, compilers can optimize single methods pretty well, but they tend not to optimize across method call boundaries. This means that simple optimizations, like removing the first of two sequential memory writes to the same location, are not realized if there is an intervening call. For example:

```
int x = 10;
x = 20;
```

This looks silly as a single code fragment. Obviously the assignment aspect of the first statement: x = 10, can be ignored (assuming x is not some volatile memory location, like a FIFO). Any good compiler would combine the first and second statement into a simple int x = 20 statement. Unfortunately this sort of code behavior occurs regularly, and goes undetected and unoptimized by the compiler, with a return instruction inserted between the consecutive assignments. For example:

```
int a::b (int& i)
{
    i = 10;
    ...
}

int a::c ()
{
    ...
    int k = 0;
    ret = this->b(k);
    ...
}
```

A change in statement scope from a pair of methods in which one method calls the other to a single method that embodies the functionality of both, though logically uninteresting in terms of the net result, is crucial to a compiler's ability to optimize out inefficiencies. Thus, in some instances the most significant cost of method invocation is the inability to optimize code across method boundaries.

Why Inline?

Inlining is probably the most significant mechanical performance enhancement technique available in C++. The performance of relatively large systems can be transformed rapidly, without rewriting anything. While working on a networking framework, we took a 10,000 line subsystem and improved its performance by more than an order of magnitude. The last step in the transformation involved inlining the working system. This last step took only two days and resulted in a 40% improvement in the system's performance. It took two days to do the inlining because the code was not designed from its inception for inlining. Had we employed what we now know about inlining during the development of this system, we would have been able to perform the same inlining with a quick change to a makefile and a recompilation.

This 40% improvement was not the result of careful profiling and "fast path" analysis but rather was based on a cursory review of the method set and a selection of the obvious candidates for inlined recompilation. Had more performance been required, we would have become more serious about creating a "straight-line fast path," which is the real goal of mechanistic performance techniques.[1]

A program's fast path is the portion of a program that supports the normal, error free, common usage cases of the program's execution. Typically less than 10% of a program's code lies on this fast path. Fast paths containing less than 1% of a program's code are not unusual. Code that exemplifies straight-line execution minimizes the amount of branching (conditional execution, looping, and calling). This characteristic is critical to the realization of highly optimized performance and will be discussed in Chapter 16. Inlining allows us to remove calls from the fast path. On most systems,

---

[1] Sadly, the system on which we were working suffered in the extreme from every performance malady in this book, and it was finally shot to put it out of its misery. We, thankfully, did not design the system, but we did learn a tremendous amount about how not to do OO from our experience with it. The failure of large projects like this one have done a significant amount of damage to OO's reputation. Our contention is that this project did not fail because of OO, but rather it failed because performance was seen as a secondary design consideration. He who fails to design for performance, performs a design failure.

calls are the single most expensive structural entity. In general, no program that relies on lots of small methods as its primary structural component has any hope of reasonable performance unless the proper subset of those methods are identified and inlined.

Inlining Details

The concept of inlining, although relatively simple on its surface, turns out to have its complications. Although we believe that it is important to understand inlining and apply it properly, we also believe that inlining eventually will be a compile- and profile-based optimization that will be performed by compiler/profiler/optimizer tools for you. We also believe that the automatic tools eventually will be able to do a more accurate job of inlining than you will. Unfortunately, the current crop of commercially available compilers lack the sophistication to do anything that even approaches automatic optimized inlining. It therefore falls to you to learn all the subtleties associated with inlining and to deal with the cumbersome syntactic mechanism for achieving inlining. Hopefully in the future you will be able to forget all about inlining, except when you remark to those who follow you, "I remember a time when we had to do code path optimization by hand. Boy, those were the good old days." Hopefully, when you say this you will be thinking, at least with regard to inlining, "Boy, those were the bad old days." The inadvisable preservation of file semantics for C++ integrated development environments operates against the desired level of compiler sophistication.

The reserved word "inline" is a suggestion to the compiler. It tells the compiler that for performance reasons it would be a good idea if the code for a method were expanded inline instead of called. The compiler is under no obligation to grant inlining requests. The compiler can inline or not inline as it wishes or is able. This means that the compiler can inline when it has not explicitly been told to do so (trivial method inlining sometimes occurs as a side effect of optimization) and not inline when it has explicitly been told to do so.

In general, compilers still lack the sophistication to inline a typical method. For example, some compilers will refuse to inline a method that contains a loop, some cannot handle static variables within the inlined method or a method that has been declared to be virtual. On some occasions a compiler may be unable to resolve the mapping of a called method's variable space. In fact, some compilers will inline nothing much more complicated than indirect calls, accessor methods (methods that do little more than set or return the value of an attribute), or methods that contain a couple of lines of simple assignments, possibly with some associated calculations. Thus, in the end, an aggressively inlined program can easily be foiled by a compiler that lacks the ability to satisfy fully, or even largely, the programmer's inlining requests.

Inlining also has some interesting side effects of which you need to be aware. Inlined method definitions are logically part of a class' header file, even though they frequently reside in separate `.inl` files. The header and its logically included `.inl` are then included by the `.c` or `.cpp` files[2] that use them. After a source file is compiled into an object file, there are not necessarily any telltale indications in the object file that it contains an inlined instance of some method. That is, in general, the object has fully resolved the inlined method and does not need to make a record of its existence (there are no linkage requirements). Thus, although the language officially forbids it, one source file could be compiled with one definition of an inlined method and another source file could be compiled with a different version of what is obstensibly the same method. A compiler that was able to detect this would be free to report this as an error, but we are unaware of any compilers that do so.

Inlining Virtual Methods

We previously noted that some compilers will refuse to inline virtual methods. This may have seemed like it should be obvious. After all, a virtual method is one for which the binding is delayed until run-time. Virtual methods are generally considered to be always called indirectly via a function pointer table. Although this view of virtual methods is in general accurate, it is not totally so. Take, for example, the following code fragment:

```
inline
virtual
int x::y (char* a)
{
      ...
}

void z (char* b)
```

---

[2] From here on we will refer to C++ source files containing implementation code as ".cpp" files. If the programming environment with which you are familiar uses the ".c" nomenclature, then please make the appropriate syntactic translation.

```
{
    x_base* x_pointer = new x(some_arguments_maybe);
    x x_instance(maybe_some_more_arguments);
    x_pointer->y(b);
    x_instance.y(b);
}
```

y() is a virtual method, but its binding doesn't always need to be delayed until run-time. In the previous example, y() is invoked against x_pointer and x_instance. Delayed virtual method binding is based on object pointer usage. Any invocation of a virtual method by an object instance will result in a direct call of the virtual method instance associated with the object's type. There will be no delay in the call binding. Such a delay would be counter-productive: The type of the object is known at compile-time, and there is no need or possibility for polymorphism. The additional call overhead of run-time virtual method resolution should be avoided by the compiler whenever possible, and because object instances have no polymorphic characteristics, compilers always create direct calls of virtual methods by object instances.

In some instances, like the previous one, the type of what might potentially be a polymorphic pointer is also known at compile-time and a direct invocation of a virtual method is possible. Object pointers can be polymorphic, but if the creation of the object associated with an object pointer is visible, and there are no intervening assignments to the pointer of objects with unknown actual type, then the compiler can determine at compile-time which of the virtual instances of a method should be invoked, and it can generate a direct call instead of a virtual call. In the case of x_pointer, it trivially determined (the construction of the dynamic object instance is visible, and there are no intervening assignments to x_pointer that might change the type of the object referenced by this base class pointer) the polymorphic resolution of which set of virtual y() methods should be invoked. In reality a large number of virtual method calls are resolvable at compile-time. For example, any invocation of a virtual method against the this pointer from within a virtual method has at least a potential compile-time resolution.

This means that a large number of virtual method calls potentially could be inlined if the compiler were sophisticated enough. Thus, if a profile indicated that some virtual method was accounting for a significant amount of a program's execution time, it may be possible to recover at least some of the method's call overhead by inlining it. It also means that if the compiler can inline virtual methods and you choose to inline one, you are almost guaranteed to have some instances of inlined calls and some instances of virtual calls of the same method.

Performance Gains from Inlining

Consider the effect of inlining a simple access method (a method that provides access to one of an object's attributes):

```
int x::get_y()
{
    return y;
}
```

The method itself probably requires only three or four cycles. If invoked, even this trivial method can generate as much as 20 cycles of overhead. If inlined the method will consume only the one or two cycles (two less than the original instruction count because there are no call and return instructions any more). Thus, inlining can provide as much as a 10x speed up. It should also be remembered that most of those 20 cycles of saved overhead had instructions associated with them. This means that in addition to saving the 20 cycles of overhead, we also decreased our code size by a dozen instructions per static inlined method invocation (number of locations in a program from which the inlined method is called).

Consider the following program:

```
#include <iostream.h>

//inline
int calc (int a, int b)
{
    return a + b;
}

main ()
{
    int x[1000];
    int y[1000];
    int z[1000];

    for (int i = 0; i < 1000; ++i) {
        for (int j = 0; j < 1000; ++j) {
            for (int k = 0; k < 1000; ++k) {
                z[i] = calc(y[j], x[k]);
            }
        }
    }
}
```

This program was run twice to test the effect of inlining on execution speed. The first run, in which the `calc` was inlined, took eight seconds (this is your opportunity to see how much faster your computer is than mine). The second run, in which calc was outlined (not inlined) took 62 seconds. That amounts to an almost 8x performance improvement simply by removing the call overhead. The code size also decreased by 30 bytes for the inlined version, which in this instance *decreased* program size by more than 10%. The result of inlining this method was to make the program significantly faster and somewhat smaller.

Key Points

- Inlining is the replacement of a method call with the code for the method.

- Inlining improves performance by removing call overhead and allowing cross-call optimizations to take place.

- Inlining is primarily an execution-time optimization, though it can also result in smaller executable images as well.

9

Inlining—Performance Considerations

Cross-Call Optimization

As we have already discussed, the performance advantages of avoiding expensive method invocations is only half of the inlining performance story. The other half is cross-call optimizations. Cross-call optimizations allow the compiler to perform source and machine level optimizations to a method based on a more expansive contextual view of its invocation. These optimizations generally take the form of doing things at compile-time to avoid the necessity of doing them at run-time; for example, simple things like converting

```
float x = 90.0;
---                         // nothing that changes x's value
float y = sin(x);
```

to

```
float x = 90.0;
---
float y = 1.0;      // sin(90) = 1
```

This example, perhaps unlikely within the context of a single method, can become quite commonplace within a caller/callee method context, in which a variable is initialized by one method and then sent into another method as an argument. Consider the previous example in a different context:

```
enum TrigFuns {SIN, COS, TAN}

float calc_trig (TRIG_FUNS fun, float val)
{
    switch (fun) {
        case SIN:      return sin(val);
        case COS:      return cos(val);
        case TAN:      return tan(val);
        }
}

TrigFuns get_trig_fun()
{
    return SIN;
}

float get_float()
{
    return 90;
}

void calculator()
{
    ---
    TrigFuns tf = get_trig_fun();
    float value = get_float();
    reg0 = calc_trig(tf, value);
    ---
}
```

If `get_trig_fun`, `get_float` and `calc_trig` were all inlined, the previous code snippet would resolve to a simple `reg0 = 1.0`. Conversely, if not inlined, the compiler would never be able to see the simple optimization because none of the information necessary to carry out the optimization is available within a single method, and only intra-method optimizations are typically possible. This is a simple example of how inlining allows the compiler to perform code optimizations based on what would have required cross-call optimization without the impact of inlining.

The performance gains possible from this sort of cross-call code optimization can improve performance by significantly more than simple call avoidance can. Conversely, the gains from call avoidance are guaranteed and, though not always spectacular, they are regular. Code optimizations are very compiler dependent, and high levels of optimization can take a long time to compile and occasionally actually break the code. Inlined cross-call optimization is the fabled hare and call avoidance is the associated tortoise of inline performance gains.

Unfortunately, optimizers sometimes use assumptions about variable alaising and volatility that run afoul of some source code. Optimizations can break code that uses expected, but not guaranteed, relationships between objects. For example, a program that makes any assumptions about the order in which variables will be stored on a stack can easily be undone by a compiler that chooses to base a variable in a register only and not reserve any stack space for the variable. Fortunately, there are a lot of simple optimizations that do not require that a significant number of assumptions be made. A good text on compiler construction should be consulted if compiler optimizations are of significant interest to you.

Although getting too far into the mechanics of compiler optimization is out of our scope, we can point out the critical role literals play in some of the most effective optimizations. The previous example in which the trigonometric `sin()` function of a literal was resolved at compile time is an excellent example of the sort of leverage that literals provide. This optimization is easily performed if the literal and associated variable are defined and used in the same method. It is impossible if the literal is passed in as an argument.

Let us have a look at another simple example:

```
int i = 100;
---             // nothing that changes i's value
if (i > 10) {
    ===         // 20 instructions
    }
else {
    +++         // 50 more instructions
    }
```

This code snippet is trivially reduced to:

```
int i = 100;
---             // nothing that changes i's value
===             // 20 instructions
```

This reduces code size by a couple hundred bytes and removes a conditional test and branch. In this case it is not a huge win, but it is effective. You may remark that it is stupid to set i to 100 and then turn around and test i, and you would be correct. It is stupid within the context of a single method. Conversely, it is also exactly the sort of thing that happens repeatedly in situations where the variable is initialized in one method and then passed into another method. This is a particularly commonplace occurrence in defensively programed routines that do range checks on input arguments.

Consider the following method containing a case statement:

```
inline
bool is_hex (char c, int& value)
{
    switch (c) {
        case '0' value = 0; break;
        case '1' value = 1; break;
        case '2' value = 2; break;
        case '3' value = 3; break;
        case '4' value = 4; break;
        case '5' value = 5; break;
        case '6' value = 6; break;
        case '7' value = 7; break;
        case '8' value = 8; break;
        case '9' value = 9; break;
        case 'a': value = 10; break;
        case 'A': value = 10; break;
        case 'b': value = 11; break;
        case 'B': value = 11; break;
        case 'c': value = 12; break;
        case 'C': value = 12; break;
        case 'd': value = 13; break;
        case 'D': value = 13; break;
        case 'e': value = 14; break;
        case 'E': value = 14; break;
        case 'f': value = 15; break;
        case 'F': value = 15; break;
        default: return false;
        }
    return true;
}
```

There are jump table mechanisms that actually can make this into a relatively effi-cient method, and certainly the range checked version of the same code would be faster, but this version illustrates an important point. You would generally never inline a routine like this. Depending on the sophistication of the compiler, it has between 10 and 100 instructions, and it just looks big. Even in its smallest incarna-tion, this routine will generate some code expansion. Conversely, examine the impact of a literal input argument on an inlined version of is_hex(). A literal argu-ment allows a compiler to reduce the method to a single assignment. It may seem unlikely to think about this method being called with a literal, but imagine the impact of double depth inlining on the following code.

```
inline
int parse_hex (char* cp)
{
    int ret = 0;
    int temp;
    while (is_hex(*cp, temp)) {
        ret = (ret << 4) + temp;
        ++cp;
        }

    return ret;
}

main()
{
    ---
    char* alpha_number = "12345678";
    ---
    int bin_number = parse_hex(alpha_number);
    ---
}
```

A good compiler could compress the inlined call of `parse_hex()` into a simple assignment of the literal integer `0x12345678`. This use of inlining replaces a couple of hundred run-time instructions with a single run-time immediate assignment. Not only this, but it also allows additional optimizations to be performed based on the now known value of `bin_number`.

A more sophisticated possibility for the optimizations between inlined methods and literals could be demonstrated by passing a literal into a single argument recursive method, like the old standby example used to teach recursion, the Fibonacci number generator. (It pains us to use so hackneyed an example, particularly one so inappropriate to recursive solution, despite its recursive definition. However, its simplicity and general familiarity make it an easy sample target, not to mention the almost unbelievable performance gains from compile-time resolution for literals.)

```
inline
int get_fib (int x)
{
    if (x <= 0) {
        return 0;
        }
    if (x == 1) {
        return 1;
        }
    if (x == 2) {
```

```
            return 1;
            }
        else {
            return get_fib(x - 1) + get_fib(x - 2);
            }
    }
```

An invocation of `get_fib` with a literal argument could be resolved at compile-time. For example: `get_fib(10)`, which would otherwise result in 109 method invocations, could be replaced at compile-time with the literal integer 55. Most compilers currently are unable to provide this level of sophistication with regard to inline method compile-time optimization, but in the longer term, this sort of optimization will become relatively easy to accomplish. In the very long term, this sort of optimization will cease to be associated with inlining at all, and it should simply become a routine, though temporally expensive, cross-call optimization.

Hopefully you are starting to realize that this inlining thing is much more the sort of optimization that a compiler should be doing than a programmer. We agree. Much of the really interesting inlining is selective; that is, methods are only inlined sometimes. The interaction of literals on method inlining is a perfect example. If a compiler can resolve a method's significant input arguments at compile-time, then the compiler is in a position perhaps to make a very cost-effective optimization. Unfortunately, when such optimizations are not universally applicable to all instances of a method's invocation, they transcend C++'s basic inlining protocol. Chapter 10 contains a discussion of programmer-controlled selective inlining. In the near term these techniques can make careful hand-tuning possible, but again, in the long term, we expect that compilers will do this for us.

Why Not Inline?

If inlining is so good, why don't we just inline everything? This simple question has a lot of complicated answers. Let's start the answer with an inlining situation. Suppose we inline a method that, when compiled, contains 550 bytes of source code. Further suppose that 50 bytes of the called method are associated with call prologue and epilogue (method invocation overhead). If our hypothetical method is statically invoked a dozen times (called from a dozen different locations within a program), we have just increased our program size by 5,450 instructions ((550 instructions per inlining— 50 instructions of invocation overhead) * 12)—550 for the otherwise called version), and we have improved the execution performance of each inlined execution of the method say by only 10%. (Assume that the large method has 50 cycles of call over-head and that the method requires 500 cycles to execute. This is pure conjecture; some methods with 500 machine code instructions may have an average execution time of 10 cycles and others may require millions of cycles.) Thus we have a 10x increase in code size of this one method with only marginal per-invocation performance improvement. Code expansions of this magnitude, when extrapolated across all the inlineable methods with a program, will have huge negative secondary performance characteristics, like cache misses and page faults, that will dwarf any supposed primary gains. Put differently, an over-aggressively inlined program will execute fewer instructions, but take longer doing so. Thus, one reason why all methods are not inlined is that the code expansion that inlining creates may not be tolerable.

With disk space and memory sizes growing at the rate they are, some might assume that the size of an executable image is no longer an issue, particularly when virtual memory management mechanisms are employed to facilitate the execution of programs. Code size is not just a storage issue. Multiple instances of a single inlined method means that each instance will have its own address and will therefore consume independent cache storage, thus decreasing the effective cache size and hence its capacity miss rate. For example, suppose an inlined method was called with regularity from four different points in a program. The first time the method was executed, the code cache would fault on the compulsory miss associated with the program's initial call (execution) of the inlined method. When the method was executed again from another inlined code location, the cache would miss again because the inlined code is different each time it is inlined, and even if it were not, the inlined instructions appear at different addresses in the process' code space. In our example of four frequent call points, the inlined method would consume four times as much cache as the same method would if outlined. It will cache fault at least four times more than an outlined version. We say at least four times because of the much higher likelihood that one or more cached instances of the method will be ejected from the cache and need to be reloaded. The single outlined instance would have much higher usage and thus be much less likely to be ejected. The performance improvement associated with call and return overhead may be overshadowed by the cache performance degradation of inlining, particularly when large methods are involved.

Cache fault behavior associated with indiscriminate inlining can become highly degenerative. Suppose the working set for an execution stream just barely fits in a processor's cache; that is, the instruction stream almost never cache faults because the portion of the program's code space that is responsible for the vast majority of the program's execution all fits within the cache. Now suppose we double the size of the working set with indiscriminate inlining. The larger code path will now generate frequent faults because the cache is no longer big enough to hold the working set. This increase in cache faults will impact performance severely, consuming all the gains we might otherwise have achieved by avoiding method calls. So the second reason why all methods are not inlined is that the side effects of code expansion may not be tolerable.

Inline code expansion can sometimes take on another degenerative characteristic. Inlining a method can sometimes create exponential code growth. This can occur when relatively large routines are inlined one within another. Take for example four methods A, B, C, and D, each of which contains 500 bytes of instructions.

```
int D()
{
     ... // 500 code bytes of functionality
}

int C()
{
     D();
     ... // 500 code bytes of functionality
     D();
}

int B()
{
     C();
     ... // 500 code bytes of functionality
     C();
}

int A()
{
     B();
     ... // 500 code bytes of functionality
     B();
}

int main ()
{
     A(); --- A(); --- A();---. A(); --- A(); ---
     A(); --- A(); --- A(); --- A(); --- A();
}
```

A invokes B twice, B invokes C twice, C invokes D twice, and A is invoked 10 times by `main`. Inlining A, B, C, and D will increase the size of the code associated with these four methods by more than 70K bytes, a 37x increase in the size of the code supplying this functionality. Although the previous example was overly simplistic and in general not likely to occur exactly as presented, the reality of overly aggressive inlining can be an explosion in code size. So the third reason all methods are not inlined is that the code expansion will be intolerable.

If you just looked back a couple pages and said to yourself, "Hey, those first three reasons for not inlining are all the same one," then you are correct. If you did not, then you are not paying attention and are perhaps in need of additional caffeine. Code expansion is THE main reason for not inlining everything. This will be even more the case as compiler quality improves and compilers are better able to resolve local static artifacts within inlined methods.

There are some additional reasons for not inlining, particularly on large projects and when using complicated methods. An inlined method creates compilation dependencies on the implementation of a method, not just on its interface. Thus, a method that is expected to be changed often during a program's development is not a particularly good candidate. As a general rule, any inlining that decreases code size is a good one, and any inlining that significantly increases code size is not. A good secondary rule is that a method with any volatility to its implementation should not be inlined.

Another reason for not inlining everything is that some methods cannot be inlined; for example, recursive methods cannot be inlined. Suppose some method A called itself. Any attempt to inline A would result in an infinite loop as the compiler continually attempted to insert A into A. (There are actually some cases in which a very clever compiler could inline a function, particularly if the variable that controls the recursion is passed in as a literal.) Thus, recursive methods generally cannot be inlined (though later we will discuss some mechanisms to achieve a similar net effect). Methods that are indirectly recursive can sometimes be inlined. For example if A calls B and B calls A, then B, although indirectly recursive, can be inlined.

Development and Compile-Time Inlining Considerations

Inlined methods must logically appear in their class' headers. This is necessary to make the code bodies of inlined methods available to their invokers. Unfortunately this also means that any change in the body of an inlined method will necessitate the recompilation of every module that uses it—that is *recompilation,* not just relinking. For large programs this can actually increase a program's development time due to the amount of extra time consumed per compile.

Debugging of inlined code is complicated by the fact that single breakpoints cannot be used to track entry and exit from inlined methods. There are ways of using watchpoints to accomplish the same thing, though doing so hampers the debugger's performance. It is also difficult to track variable names across the source boundaries of the invoking and invoked methods.

Inlined methods do not generally appear in program profiles (tables that indicate a program's execution behavior based on sample executions). "Calls" to inlined methods are sometimes invisible to profilers. Once a method is inlined it must be assumed that the code is executed whenever its enclosing method is executed, though in some instances this it is not necessarily the case. This complicates decisions about extreme performance measures, like rewriting methods in assembly language.

A properly working compiler will not generate errors as a by-product of its inlinings. Conversely, compilers are very sophisticated pieces of software and C++ is a very complicated language. It is unlikely that the ideal error-free C++ compiler will exist any time soon. This creates the possibility that inlining optimizations may generate errors of their own. In terms of inlining, the likelihood of this is relatively low because compilers are free to determine the complexity of an inlining request that they accept. On the other hand, errors induced by inlining are, as a rule, very difficult to find, as are most compiler-induced errors.

Profile-Based Inlining

There are some inlining decisions that seem trivial and some that have guaranteed positive results, and some recursive methods seem to cry out for better performance via call unrolling. The fact is, however, that we could invest a lot of effort into inlining a program, significantly increase its size and compile time, and see very little performance improvement, or even a performance degradation, for our trouble. Conversely, we could inline a couple of important methods and see a significant performance improvement. The difference between spinning our wheels inlining unprofitable methods and significantly improving the speed of our programs is the selection of the right methods for inlining. The best way of finding the right methods is via profiling, which is most effective when a representative data sample can be used for the generation of profile data.

Profiling is a performance-testing technique that relies on a profiling tool (software suite) to instrument a program (insert measurement code) so that its performance can be characterized during sample executions of the program. The quality of the profile is directly dependent on the quality of the sample data used to generate it. Profilers come in many different shapes and sizes and their possible range of output is highly variable, but in general, all profilers will provide at least information about which methods are being executed and how often they are being executed. Most profilers we are familiar with will also provide an execution trace. Using this information, a programmer is in a position to make informed inlining decisions.

Methods have two different sizes: dynamic and static. Static method size is the number of bytes in the compiled machine code for a method. This is the upper bound for the amount of additional code that will be added to a program each time a method is inlined. Dynamic method size is the number of instructions a method executes per invocation, or the amount of execution time it consumes per invocation. This will provide an indication of the ratio of call/return overhead to method execution time. Frequently there is a strong correlation between method size and execution time, though in some cases methods with relatively low instruction counts can have unexpectedly large execution times. Methods with deeply nested loops are an obvious example, but even seemingly simple methods can occasionally have poor execution efficiency because of things like poor cache interaction (methods that interact with uncacheable data are good cases in point).

Static method size is an artifact of compilation; that is, it is fixed at compile-time. Dynamic method size can be significantly impacted by run-time artifacts. It is dependent on the use of good sample data for profile data generation. If the sample executions of a program that are used to generate profile data are representative, then reasonably accurate dynamic method sizes will be generated. Conversely, nonrepresentative sample data may provide erratic results. It is always possible that a profile will provide no data about a method; that is, some methods are seldom if ever executed. Such methods generally will not appear in a profile, or they will have very low call frequencies.

Profilers tend either to count instructions or measure time. Time is a more accurate metric, but instruction counts are easier to generate and they can be used to provide good data with which to make informed inlining decisions. The problem with performance metrics based on instruction counts are

- Even on architectures that claim single instruction execution for most instructions, the reality is that some instructions take longer than others. Loads and stores generally take at least twice as long as logic and arithmetic instructions.

- On architectures with highly variable single-instruction execution-times, instruction counts can be very misleading. Some instructions may execute in a single cycle, and others may require dozens of cycles. Thus, ten fast instructions can consume fewer execution cycles than one slow instruction.

- Instruction counts completely ignore the impact of lower-level architectural structures on performance. This includes things like cache efficiency, branching effects on pipelines, register versus memory utilization, and memory access latencies.

Fortunately, profilers generally will provide a scaled instruction count metric that will take into account variances in instruction timings, and for relatively large numbers of instructions, the variances will tend to average out. Unfortunately, it is frequently the case that inlining decisions are made on small instruction count metrics and interaction with the system's architectural details can easily overshadow raw instruction count metrics.

We are aware of an example in which instruction counts were not particularly effective as a metric. A colleague invented a significantly faster algorithm for calculating TCP/IP checksums, but he encountered stiff resistance to adoption of his new technique because the profiles for the new methodology showed larger instruction counts than the previous method. It was only when the other programmers abandoned their narrow view of performance being equal to instruction counts, and adopted a more informed view of performance being an elapsed time issue, that the larger, but faster, algorithm was adopted, the moral being, even though more than likely you will be provided with instruction count metrics, do not suppose that they tell the entire story.

A simple profile will indicate the number of times a method is invoked and the percentage of total execution time each method consumed. Generally this information is enough to do a reasonably good job of choosing the profiling candidates. Methods with large dynamic size will seldom return much of a performance improvement if inlined, even if they have high invocation rates. The ratio of its call/return overhead to its general execution time will be very low, and the small improvement in performance will be generally unnoticeable. On the other hand, a method with a small dynamic size and a large invocation rate will produce significant performance gains if inlined. Typically small dynamic size and small static size will be highly correlated; however sometimes a small dynamic size will be associated with a method with a large static size. Inlining such methods will result in code expansion, and caution is advised. Sometimes such methods can be rewritten to extract the core functionality into an inlined routine. This technique is presented later.

Table 9.1 provides a reasonable set of inlining guidelines.

A basic program profile will indicate which methods have high execution rates, but they generally do not give you invocation point frequencies; that is, if a method is called 1,000 times, and it has 20 static invocations in the code, a basic profile will probably not tell what percentage of each call was associated with each call point. Inlining decisions about medium size methods with high dynamic and static call frequencies could benefit significantly from this information. If only a small fraction of a method's static occurrences account for the bulk of its dynamic execution, then it may be cost-effective to selectively inline (a mechanism for inlining only some of a method's invocations, discussed in the next chapter) its high-usage cases. If code expansion is not an issue, then general inlining of such methods may be acceptable. Remember, the secondary cache and paging effects of inlining are by-products of code expansion.

Table 9.1. The Inlining Decision Matrix

	Static Size		
Dynamic Frequency	*Large (more than 20 lines of code)*	*Medium (between 5 and 20 lines of code)*	*Small (less than 5 lines of code)*
Low (the bottom 80% of call frequency)	Do not inline	Do not inline	Inline if you have the time and patience
Medium (the top 5–20% of call frequency)	Do not inline	Consider rewriting the method to expose its fast path and then inline	Always inline
High (the top 5% of call frequency)	Consider rewriting the method to expose its fast path and then inline	Selectively inline the high frequency static invocation points	Always inline

Programs tend to have fast paths, as do many large methods. Sometimes methods can be rewritten to expose the important, expected behavior of a method; the extraneous, error correcting portions of the method can be removed to another method. Take the following method, for example:

```
int x::y (int a, int b)
{
    if (/* sanity check on input values for a and b*/) {
        ---          // inline error handling (30 lines)
        }
    ---              // Real work (5 lines)
}
```

Method x::y has roughly 40 statements, making it a relatively large method. If the method has high invocation frequency and a significant number of invocation points, on the surface it may seem that inlining x::y will not be particularly effective. It could have a code image size in excess of 1K, and if it is not a leaf node its inlining could cause some of the combinatorial code size explosion we already talked about. Conversely, there is another method hidden inside x::y that could be very effectively inlined. Consider x::y after it is partitioned into the following two methods:

```
void x::handle_input_error (int& a, int& b)
{
    // error handling (30 lines)
}

inline
int x::new_y (int a, int b)
{
    if (/* sanity check on input values for a and b*/) {
        handle_input_error(a, b);
        }
    ---                      // real work of the method (5 lines)
}
```

The size of new_y() has been reduced to ten lines. Still not small, but much more affordable as an inlined method. This is only effective if erroneous input arguments are infrequent. An indication that this type of rewriting for inlining may be applicable will tend to manifest itself as a method with a small dynamic size but a large static size. Rewriting methods of this type can offer a significant performance boost without significantly increasing code size.

Inlining Rules

There are a few relatively simple rules that we can use to make inlining decisions. Singletons and trivials are always code size, and performance wins. Trivials can be inlined without regard to their frequency of use, and singletons are inlined exactly because of their usage frequency. Frequently these "no brainer" inlinings are enough. When they are not, profiling should indicate the most likely additional candidates. The next chapter presents additional mechanisms for profitably inlining nontrivial methods.

Singletons

A singleton method is a method that has only one point of invocation within a program. This does not mean that it is invoked only once when a program is executed. A singleton can exist within a loop and be called millions of times, but as long as a method has only one invocation point in the program, it is a singleton. Singletons are naturals for inlining. The fact that they have only one call point means that without regard to singleton size or call frequency, the resultant code will be smaller and faster after singleton inlining than before. The amount of improvement may be marginal, though, and not warranted by the effort involved in doing the inlining yourself.

Frequently, singletons are not easily recognized as such. Often a method's singleton nature is temporary and/or circumstantial. Other times, singleton stature is an artifact of design. The latter type should always be explicitly inlined. The former type can be inlined, but its singleton status will then require monitoring to avoid negative consequences.

It would be nice if compilers automatically would recognize and inline all singletons for you. Unfortunately, doing so would require a global analysis of a program's call tree. Global call tree generation is relatively straightforward, but it can be somewhat expensive if a program contains a large number of separately compiled modules. It is certainly not the type of analysis that is performed during code development or debug, but it would be a useful post-production optimization. It should be noted that this type of analysis for a large program can be very processor intensive—bring something to read while you wait (sadly, Tolstoy may be appropriate).

As previously noted, the inlining of complex methods is frequently disallowed by the compiler. This makes routine inlining of singletons more of a theoretical benefit than a real one. A sophisticated compiler that could inline all singletons would always provide some benefit, but given the still relatively unsophisticated state of most compilers, singleton inlining as a standard feature is probably still a long way off.

Trivials

Trivials are small methods with generally less than four simple source level statements that compile into ten or fewer assembly language instructions. These methods are so small that they do not provide any possibility for significant code expansion. The smaller trivials will actually decrease overall code size, and the larger ones will possibly expand it by a fraction. The overall effect of global trivial inlining is to leave code size unaffected. Trivials tend to occur frequently in C++. Accessor methods, indirect calls, and simple operator overloads tend to be small, often one-line methods, but methods that are used frequently. Inlining these methods significantly diminishes the performance penalties associated with maintaining the proper level of object encapsulation.

Some compilers automatically will inline those trivial methods that are visible within the compilation context. This means that methods will be inlined within a separately compiled module if the compiler recognizes it as trivial, but that calls of trivial methods that cross module boundaries will not be inlined. This automatic inlining is a very handy feature, one that would be extended profitably to a global compiler-based inlining of trivial methods. The compiler is in the best position to gauge the actual cost of a call and to see the instruction size of a method. This would allow a compiler always to inline code, size, neutral, or smaller methods. A more sophisticated compiler-based inlining decision could be based on a programmer-supplied metrics of acceptable code expansion, or based on an indication of the relative importance of code size and performance. This capability could be incorporated easily into an automatic singleton inlining pass (concomitantly making it possible to add unabridged Victor Hugo tomes to your reading list).

Care needs to be taken when inlining trivials to ensure that inlined trivials stay trivial. If the scope of what was an inlined trivial method grows, the writer needs to be prepared to demote the method. This is particularly true if the method is not a leaf method (leaf methods contain no method calls, they execute and then return). Unexpected code explosions can result from inlining nonleaf (internal) methods. The code expansion for leaf methods is easily determined by counting the number of static calls to the method in a program and multiplying that times the number of instructions in the method minus the number of instructions necessary to invoke the method. When inlining a nonleaf method, any code expansion created by leaf expansion becomes multiplied.

Key Points

- Literal arguments and inlining, when combined, provide significant opportunities for a compiler to provide significant performance improvements.

- Inlining may backfire, and overly aggressive inlining will almost certainly do so. Inlining can increase code size. Large code size suffers a higher rate of cache misses and page faults than smaller code.

- Nontrivial inlining decisions should be based on sample execution profiles, not gut feelings.

- Consider rewriting high frequency methods with large static size and small dynamic size to extract their significant dynamic characteristic, and then inline the dynamic component.

- Trivial and singleton methods can always be inlined.

10

Inlining Tricks

There are a number of "tricks" that can make inlining more effective. This chapter is dedicated to these tricks. These mechanisms are increasingly available as compiler options and optimizations. Check to see what your compiler will do for you before investing any significant effort in doing them yourself.

Conditional Inlining

The compilation, debugging, and profiling negatives associated with inlining strongly encourage the delay of inlining decisions until late in the development cycle, generally after the bulk of the debugging has been performed. Ideally, inlining decisions will be based on the results of profiling. Most compilers can use compile-line switches to prevent inlining, but in the event yours does not, this is a simple way of building your own compile-line switch.

Sadly, profiling requires a moderate amount of effort on the part of the programmer. It is not the sort of thing where anyone wants to be moving methods back and forth between an inlined state for performance and an outlined state for normal testing. Luckily the preprocessor can be employed to provide an easy migration of methods from inlined to outlined. The basic idea is to use a compile-line argument to pass a macro definition into the compiler. The input argument is used to define a macro called `INLINE`, or it is omitted to leave `INLINE` undefined. This technique depends on the separation of the definitions of all potentially inlined methods from outlined methods. Outlined methods are included in the standard `.c` file, and potentially inlined methods are placed in a `.inl` file. If you want to inline the methods in the

.inl file, then the -D option can be used in the compile statement to define INLINE. Following is an example of how to use this compile-time inlining switch.

File: x.h:

```
#if !defined(_X_H_)
#define _X_H_

class X {
    ...
    int y (int a);
    ...
};

#if defined(INLINE)
#include x.inl
#endif
#endif // _X_H_
```

File: x.inl:

```
#if !defined(INLINE)
#define inline
#endif

inline
int X::y (int a)
{
    ...
}
```

File: x.c:

```
#if !defined(INLINE)
#include x.inl
#endif
```

The .h file is used in its customary fashion. When INLINE is defined, the .h file will include the .inl file and the inline directive that precedes each method will be unaffected. When INLINE is not defined, the .h file will not include the inlined methods, but rather these methods will be included in the .c file, and the inline directive will be stripped from the front of each method. This mechanism provides easy mobility of the inlined methods from inlined to outlined status. This technique is an all-or-nothing approach. Care still needs to be exercised in creating the inlined/outlined partitions.

Selective Inlining

One of the most egregious deficiencies in C++ is the syntax and flexibility of its inlining mechanism. Although generally useful, it is painfully unsophisticated. There is no mechanism for selective inlining; that is, inlining a method in some places and not inlining it in other places. This makes inlining decisions an all or nothing choice, ignoring the reality of fast path optimization. For example, suppose a program's fast path (the typical execution sequence) contains two static invocations of a method that has an additional 20 static invocations outside the fast path. There is no simple mechanism for inlining the method in its two critical call locations and relying on the normal call mechanism for the remaining ones. We will show you how to do it—it is fairly simple and very effective. Unfortunately, it requires a certain level of discipline, and it is hard to strongly recommend the extensive use of this mechanism.

The simplest way to selectively inline a method is to make a copy of the outlined version of the method and place it in the associated `.h` or `.inl` file. Then change the name of the copied version of the method to `inline__whatever_the_original_method_name_was`, add a prototype for the method in the associated `.h` file, and then prefix the instances of the method names you want to conditionally inline with the string `inline_`. This will give you two versions of the method, one that is called as normal and one that is inlined when the original method name is prefixed by `inline_`. This mechanism is clumsy, but effective. It has the obvious drawback that it requires two versions of the same method to be maintained independently. This can be solved by copying another instance of the method to be inlined into the `.inl` file and changing its name to `_whatever_it_was_before`, making it an inlined method, and then replacing the code body of the original version in the `.c` file and the `inline__whatever_the_original_method_name_was` with a call to the now inlined version of the method named `_whatever_it_was_before`. An example will hopefully make this all clear.

Suppose we want to selectively inline the following method:

```
int x::y (int a)
{
    ...
}
```

and it is located in a file called `x.c`. It would be selectively inlined by adding the following code to the indicated files.

File: x.h:

```
class x {

public:  //assuming the original method "y" had public visibility
    ---
    int inline_y (int a);
    int y (int a);      // this should already have been here
    ---
};

#include "x.inl"        // this may already have been here also
```

File: x.inl:

```
inline
int x::inline_y  (int a)
{
    ...                 // original implementation of y
}
```

File: x.c:

```
int x::y  (int a)
{
    return inline_y(a);
}
```

This gives us two versions of y; one that is inlined and named inline_y and one that is outlined, named simply y. We also have a single shared definition of x::y's body, the one in inline_y's definition. This has the added advantage that the single method body also results in a single instance of any static variables within the method.

Recursive Inlining

As already indicated, directly recursive methods cannot be inlined. This can be very problematic for the performance of a number of relatively simple data structures that rely on recursion for insertion, deletion, and searching. These recursive methods typically are directly recursive and fairly small. Performance will suffer greatly if we are forced to execute such methods without the benefits of inlining or some other form of call collapsing. What follows are mechanisms for iterative call collapsing and recursive call unrolling.

Some recursive methods are tail recursive. Tail recursion is evidenced by a method that recursively descends until its base case is reached. At that point some action is taken and the method terminates, possibly returning a value. The significant characteristic of the return sequence associated with tail recursion is that no action is taken after the base case is resolved, except possibly for the return of a value that is identified by the base case resolution. The typical binary tree search is a good example of a tail recursive method:

```
binary_tree* binary_tree::find (int key) {
    if (key == id) {
        return this,
        }
    else if (key > id) {
        if (right) return right.find(key);
        }
    else {
        if (left)  return left.find(key);
        }

    return 0;
}
```

As we can see, no action, other than returning a pointer to the indicated object, is taken after the base case is satisfied. Thus, the context of the recursively generated call stack is unimportant. In fact, if the compiler simply reserved a variable to hold `this`, the method could be executed without generating a new method context. Consider an alternative implementation:

```
binary_tree* binary_tree::find (int key) {
    binary_tree *temp = this;
    while (temp) {
        if (key == temp->id) {
            return this,
            }
        else if (key > id) {
            temp = right;
            }
        else {
            temp = left;
            }
        }

    return 0;
}
```

This alternate implementation demonstrates how a tail recursive method can be transformed into an iterative one. A good compiler will recognize tail recursion and convert it from a recursive method to an iterative one. This sort of compiler optimization makes any further attempts to improve the performance of the method with inlining not particularly interesting. As a general rule, particularly if performance is critical, care should be taken to use iterative solutions instead of recursive ones whenever such solutions are reasonably straightforward.

When iterative solutions are not straightforward and performance is critical, there are some relatively straightforward mechanisms for unrolling recursive method. Suppose we are interested in improving the performance of a nontail recursive method, such as a method that generates an inorder listing of the id fields in a binary tree:

```
void binary_tree::key_out ()
{
    if (left)  left->key_out();
    cout << id << endl;
    if (right) right->key_out();
}
```

The key_out method could trivially be unrolled once with inlining:

```
inline
void binary_tree::UNROLLED_key_out ()
{
    if (left)  left->key_out();
    cout << id << endl;
    if (right) right->key_out();
}

void binary_tree::key_out ()
{
    if (left)  left->UNROLLED_key_out();
    cout << id << endl;
    if (right) right->UNROLLED_key_out();
}
```

The programmer invokes the key_out method, which in turn invokes the UNROLLED_key_out method. The UNROLLED_key_out then indirectly recursively invokes the key_out method. The unrolled version can be inlined within the standard version, which results in the standard version having a couple of versions of itself embedded within itself. The result is roughly twice as big as the original version, but also two to three times faster. This use of inlining results in an easier-to-follow version of something the programmer could have written him- or herself:

```
void binary_tree::key_out ()
{
    if (left) {
        if (left->left)  left->left->key_out();
        cout << left->id << endl;
        if (left->right) left->right->key_out();
        }
    cout << id << endl;
    if (right) {
        if (right->left) right->left->key_out();
        cout << right->id << cout;
        if (right ->right) right->right->key_out();
        }
}
```

Single stage unrolling provides the biggest "bang for the buck," but additional unrolling can be employed if necessary. Following is a four-iteration version of the key_out method:

```
inline
void binary_tree::UNROLLED3_key_out ()
{
    if (left) left->key_out();
    cout << id << endl;
    if (right) right->key_out();
}

inline
void binary_tree::UNROLLED2_key_out ()
{
    if (left)  left->UNROLLED3_key_out();
    cout << id << endl;
    if (right) right->UNROLLED3_key_out();
}

inline
void binary_tree::UNROLLED1_key_out ()
{
    if (left)  left->UNROLLRD2_key_out();
    cout << id << endl;
    if (right) right->UNROLLED2_key_out();
}

void binary_tree::key_out ()
{
    if (left)  left->UNROLLED1_key_out();
    cout << id << endl;
    if (right) right->UNROLLED1_key_out();
}
```

This level of unrolling can provide a significant performance improvement, but four versions of what are essentially the same method makes maintenance of the unrolled recursion error-prone. Use of old style C #define macro expansion can unify the unrolled methods, but it is ugly, and it requires that significant care be taken for maintenance. Following is the macro version of the key_out method.

```
#define KEY_OUT_MACRO(inline_arg, my_label, call_label)        \
                                                               \
inline_arg                                                     \
void binary_tree::UNROLLED##my_label##_key_out ()             \
{                                                              \
    if (left) left->UNROLLED##call_label##_key_out();        \
    cout << id << endl;                                       \
    if (right) right->UNROLLED##call_label##_key_out();      \
}

KEY_OUT_MACRO(inline, 3, 0)
KEY_OUT_MACRO(inline, 2, 3)
KEY_OUT_MACRO(inline, 1, 2)
KEY_OUT_MACRO(\\t   , 0, 1)

inline
void x::key_out()
{
    UNROLLED_key_out();
}
```

Remember: An entry must still be made for key_out() in the binary_tree header file.

This macro mechanism allows additional levels of unrolling without much additional effort. Though you should remember that although the code now looks much smaller in terms of the amount of space it absorbs in the source listing, after the C++ preprocessor expands the macros, and the compiler completes its inlining, there will be just as much code expansion as was true in the earlier case. We have a hard time strongly recommending a mechanism that is as fragile as this sort of macro expansion is, but its benefits (only one copy of the recursive method) generally outweigh its drawbacks when such extreme measures are necessary.

The additional performance improvement that four levels of unrolling provide over just two levels of unrolling is just slightly less than those gained from the first level of unrolling. Eight levels of unrolling will provide an additional two to three times the performance that four provided. However, it should be remembered that extreme levels of unrolling can also result in extreme code expansion. The four-copy version is four times larger than the original. An eight-copy version is 64 times larger. This is a significant expansion, but in some cases the performance advantages may make even this sort of extreme code expansion worthwhile.

Inlining with Static Local Variables

Local static variables can be very problematic for compiler-based inline resolution. Some compilers will refuse to inline any method that contains a static variable declaration. Some compilers will allow statics to be inlined, but then incorrectly create multiple instances of the inlined variable at run-time. There probably are, no doubt, even some compilers that provide the worst of both worlds: they do not inline methods with static variables, but they do create an independent instance of the method within each separately compiled module. Certainly some of this difficulty is the result of a change in the way C++ handles inlined methods. The current language specification requires external linkage of inlined methods and will therefore force a single instance of any local static variables. Unfortunately, not all compilers are up to specification in this regard. Check your compiler. A compiler that has not yet been updated will have the following problem.

The problem with inlining methods that contain static variables is resolving the uniqueness of the static variable and ensuring that it gets initialized. Inlined methods are defined in header files. Inlining such a method requires that all modules that use the header file share a single instance of the static variable. Logically, static local variables are really just global variables with restricted scope. This means that the linker should be intelligent enough to detect the usage of any such static variables, create the variables, reserve space within the global data space, create initialization code for the variable (or otherwise ensure its initialization), and link all inlined references to the static variable to the newly created single instance of it within the global data area. Although conceptually this is not overly difficult, within the realm of separately compiled modules, resolving the location of the shared static has eluded some compiler writers. This will certainly be a short-term problem, but in the interim you need to be aware of the difficulties associated with the use of static variables encapsulated within a method.

It is relatively simple to determine whether your compiler can handle inlining of statics properly. Following is a small program that does just that.

```
z.h:

inline
int test ()
{
    static int i = 0;

    return ++i;
}

y.cpp:

#include "z.h"
void test_a ()
{
    int i = test();
    cout << i;
}

x.cpp:

#include "z.h"
void test_b ()
{
    int i = test();
    cout << i;
}

main.cpp:

int main() {
    test_a();
    test_b();
    cout << endl;
    return 0;
}
```

If your compiler creates the proper code, then separate compilation of the three .cpp files subsequent linking should result in an executable that outputs 12. If you get 11 your compiler has problems with inlining methods with static variables. You also need to pay attention to compiler warnings that indicate that the test method was not inlined at all.

If performance dictates that a method containing a static be inlined, and if your compiler cannot properly resolve this structure, there is an easy work-around. The same net behavior can be achieved by creating a static class attribute (static member variable). This creates a single instance of a variable with limited scope. Unfortunately this mechanism expands the visibility of the static significantly, but with the proper level of documentation this should not generally be a problem.

Architectural Caveat: Multiple Register Sets

Not all architectures have the same call/return performance. Some machines, like the SPARC architecture, exhibit almost no call/return performance penalties within a limited range of call depth. These architectures have the ability to do very fast allocations of new register frames on calls. This obviates the need to store old register contents on calls. Methods return by simply making the previously allocated register set the current register set, thus making register restoration on returns unnecessary. These architectures can pass arguments in the registers (a group of registers are shared by caller and callee), thus making it largely unnecessary to push variables on the system's memory stack prior to a call.

The ability to allocate one new register set per call also significantly decreases pressure on the register allocation mechanism in the compiler. The abundance of registers makes it easy to allocate frequently used atomic variables to registers, where they can be accessed with the lowest cost, both in terms of code size and execution efficiency.

With register storage and retrieval no longer an issue, and variable mapping costs across the call lessened, only the effect of a call on the pipeline, and the inability to optimize across the call boundary, provide any serious hope for a significant benefit from inlining. When the improved cache characteristics of not inlining are taken into effect, along with the reduction of pressure on the register allocator, inlining's performance effectiveness on methods that are not trivials becomes increasingly questionable.

Unfortunately, the effectiveness of these multiple register set architectures is significantly diminished as call depth increases. If a program's call depth exceeds the number of physical register sets in the processor, then these architectures start to experience extreme call costs, typically much worse than those associated with a typical single register set architecture. This is because register set overflow requires that entire register sets be stored to memory and eventually restored from memory. This means that while the direct effects of inlining are negligible, the indirect effect of inlining on call depth could provide a significant performance boost.

This provides the inliner with a dilemma: inlining on nontrivial methods is, in the general case, not nearly as effective. Even in what seem to be obvious wins for inlining, these multiple register sets architectures can make inlining countereffective. On the other hand, inlining does decrease overall call depth and thus decreases the likelihood that register set overflow will occur. There are no good definitive answers. In the general case inlining on such machines will not hurt performance, but it may not do much to improve it either. Our suggestion is that without run-time metric evidence to directly support an inlining decision, inlining of nontrivial methods should be avoided.

Key Points

- Inlining can improve performance. The goal is to find a program's fast path and inline it, though inlining this path may not be trivial.

- Conditional inlining prevents inlining from occuring. This decreases compile-time and simplifies debug during the earlier phases of development.

- Selective inlining is a technique that inlines methods only in some places. It can offset some of the code size explosion potential of inlining a method by inlining method calls only on performance-critical paths.

- Recursive inlining is an ugly but effective technique for improving the performance of recursive methods.

- Care needs to be taken with local static variables.

- Inlining is aimed at call elimination. Be sure of the real cost of calls on your system before using inlining.

11

Standard Template Library

The Standard Template Library (STL) is a powerful combination of containers and generic algorithms. From a performance perspective, a few questions immediately come to mind:

- The STL comes bundled with performance guarantees of the asymptotic complexity of the various containers and algorithms. What does it really mean?

- The STL consists of many containers. Faced with a given computational task, what containers should I use? Are some better than others for a given scenario?

- How good is the performance of the STL? Can I do better by rolling my own home-grown containers and algorithms?

We will address these and other related issues in this chapter.

Even though we often refer to "the STL performance," it should be noted that the STL has various distinct implementations with varying degrees of performance. The measurements provided in this chapter are a reflection of one popular implementation. The observations we make, however, should apply to STL implementations in general.

Asymptotic Complexity

The asymptotic complexity of an algorithm is an approximation of algorithm performance. It is a mapping from the set of algorithms to a special set of performance levels. If you sum up the elements of a vector of N integers, you have to inspect each integer once, and only once, so the complexity is of the order of N, and we call it O(N). Suppose, on the other hand, that you are building a vector of N elements and for some reason you chose to insert them in the front of the vector. Every element insertion at the front of a vector forces the shift of all existing elements by 1. This results in (1+2+3+...+N) overall shifts of vector elements, which is (N/2)(N+1) shifts. Even though we have (N*N/2)+(N/2) shifts we still say the complexity of this algorithm is O(N*N). This is because the set of asymptotic performance levels ignores constant multipliers and low-order factors. Consequently, the complexity of N*N and 7N*N is the same: it is O(N*N). For this reason, asymptotic complexity is a crude approximation. Although perfect for applied mathematicians researching the complexity of algorithms, it is not enough for us programmers. We still care about the constant multipliers. For us, a 2N algorithm is not the same as a 4N algorithm. The former is 100% faster than the latter.

The STL guarantees of the asymptotic complexity of its algorithms is a good start. It tells us that the algorithms used are the best of their breed [MS96]. However, we still must explore the constant multipliers and low-order factors that are ignored by the mathematicians. We will not cover all operations on all containers, but instead will discuss some frequent operations on popular containers, starting with insertion.

Insertion

If your performance-critical path contains code to insert a large number of elements into a container, what container should you use? To gain some insight into that question we will give some containers a workout and discuss the results. The insertion exercise will insert a million random elements into an array, vector, list, and multi-set. Each insertion test takes three parameters:

- A pointer to the target container under test
- A pointer to a data array of elements to be inserted
- The size of the data array

The insertion tests for the various containers are given here:

```
template <class T>
void arrayInsert (T *a, T *collection, int size)
```

```
{
    for (int k =0; k < size; k++) {
        a[k] = collection[k];
        }
}

template <class T>
void vectorInsert (vector<T> *v, T *collection, int size)
{
    for (int k =0; k < size; k++) {
        v->push_back(collection[k]);
        }
}

template <class T>
void listInsert (list<T> *l, T *collection, int size)
{
    for (int k =0; k < size; k++) {
        l->push_back(collection[k]);
        }
}

template <class T>
void multisetInsert (multiset<T> *s, T *collection, int size)
{
    for (int k =0; k < size; k++) {
        s->insert(collection[k]);
        }
}
```

The various insertion tests are given an array (collection) of random elements as input. Those random elements are then inserted into the container under test. In the case of integer data, we generated it using the STL's generate() function:

```
int *genIntData(int size)
{
    int *data = new int[size];

    // generate randon integers and place them in array data
    generate(&data[0], &data[size], rand);

    return data;
}
```

We used these tests to insert a million random integers into each container. The execution speed in milliseconds is shown in Figure 11.1.

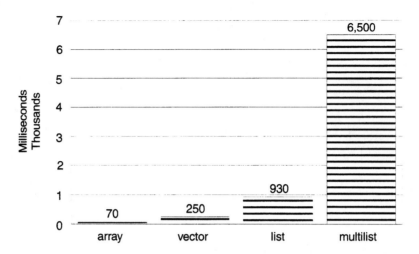

Figure 11.1.   Speed of insertion.

In this scenario, the array beat the other containers by a wide margin. The array had one significant advantage over the other containers: It was large enough, from the start, to contain all million data elements. The vector, on the other hand, did not have an a priori knowledge of how big the collection is going to be. Neither did the list and multiset containers. To make matters worse, the list and multiset had other overhead to contend with. For each data value, the list needed to allocate a list element to hold the data in addition to setting pointers to the list elements before and after. The multiset container maintains its collection in sorted order at all times. For that reason, it finished last in this particular test. We must point out that this particular test we ran does not mean that an array is generally better than the other containers. Each container has particular scenarios in which it will outperform the others. If one container were better than all others in all scenarios, the others would not exist. For example, if you need a collection whose lookup speed is most important, a multiset container would beat the array, vector, and list containers.

The array and vector containers are both sequence containers that occupy a contiguous block of memory. The vector container is more helpful when you cannot determine in advance how big the collection would be. The vector would grow dynamically and free the programmer from collection-size considerations. To better understand the performance difference between a vector and an array, we must first distinguish vector size from vector capacity. The size of a vector is the number of elements it currently holds. The capacity is the maximum number of elements the vector can hold before it must allocate additional memory to accommodate its growth. When you insert the first element into a vector, typical STL implementations will allocate a large block of memory to set the vector capacity beyond its initial size (which is 1). Subsequent insertions will increase the vector size, and capacity remains the same. If the collection continues to grow, eventually vector size will reach its capacity. The next insertion will force the vector implementation to expand its capacity. It must take the following steps [Lip91]:

- Allocate a larger memory block to make room for additional elements.

- Copy the existing collection elements to the newly allocated memory. The copy constructor is invoked for each element in the old collection.

- Destroy the old collection and free its memory. A destructor would be invoked for each element of the old collection copy.

These steps could be expensive. For that reason, we would like to minimize the frequency in which a vector size exceeds its capacity. Allocating and freeing memory is bad enough, but invoking the copy constructor and destructor for each element of the old collection could get particularly expensive. This would be the case when the vector elements involve nontrivial constructor and destructor methods. For example, let's replace our integer collection with a collection of `BigInt` objects.

The `BigInt` class is borrowed from Tom Cargil's "C++ Programming Style" [Car92]. The `BigInt` class represents positive integers as binary coded decimals. For example, the number 123 is internally represented by a 3-byte character array, each byte representing one digit. It allows you to create and manipulate `BigInt` objects as in

```
BigInt a = 123;
BigInt b = "456";
BigInt c = a + b;
```

A subset of the `BigInt` definition is as follows:

```
class BigInt {
public:
    BigInt (const char *);
    BigInt (unsigned = 0);
    BigInt (const BigInt&);
    ~BigInt ();
    ...
```

```
private:
    char     *digits;
    unsigned  ndigits;
    unsigned  size;              // size of allocated string
    ...
};
```

In the course of our discussion we are going to utilize only a subset of the BigInt implementation. That subset consists of constructors and a destructor, presented here:

```
BigInt::BigInt (unsigned u)              // Constructor
{
    unsigned v = u;

    for (ndigits = 1; (v/=10) > 0; ++ndigits) {
        ;                                // Count the number
        }                                // of digits in u

    digits = new char[size=ndigits];

    for ( unsigned i = 0; i < ndigits; ++i) {
        digits[i] = u%10;                // Peel off the
        u /= 10;                         // digits of u
        }
}

BigInt::BigInt(const BigInt& copyFrom)   // Copy constructor
{
    size = ndigits = copyFrom.ndigits;
    digits = new char[size];

    for ( unsigned i = 0; i < ndigits; ++i) {
        digits[i] = copyFrom.digits[i];
        }
}

BigInt::~BigInt()                        // Destructor
{
    delete [] digits;
}
```

To measure the effects of vector capacity growth on performance, we repeated the vector insertion test but replaced the integer elements with BigInt objects. Figure 11.2 compares the insertion time of a million integers to that of a million BigInt objects.

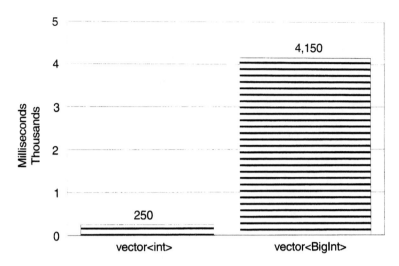

Figure 11.2. Object insertion speed.

The dramatic difference in performance is a reflection of the difference between the cost of copying and destroying plain integers and that of `BigInt` objects. If you find yourself in a situation where the object's copy constructor and destructor are fairly expensive, and vector capacity growth is very likely, you could still circumvent the cost by storing pointers instead of objects. Pointers to objects do not have associated constructors and destructor. The cost of copying a pointer is essentially identical to an integer copy. The vector insertion time of a million `BigInt` pointers was practically the same as the integer case and is given in Figure 11.3.

The list container does not hold its elements in contiguous memory and consequently does not have to contend with capacity issues and their associated performance overhead. As a result, the list container does better than a vector on the `BigInt` insertion test (Figure 11.4).

Figure 11.4 brings up another important point: Each container has its strengths and weaknesses. Although the vector is superior to the list on insertion of a million integers, the list outperforms the vector on a similar test involving `BigInt` objects.

There's one more alternative solution to the performance difficulty posed by vector capacity growth. In many situations, you can estimate the vector capacity that is likely to be sufficient in a particular scenario. In the case where you can make this

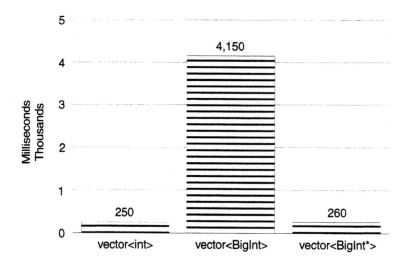

Figure 11.3. Comparing object to pointer insertion.

intelligent guess, you can go ahead and reserve the necessary capacity ahead of time. The vector `reserve(n)` method guarantees that the vector capacity is equal to or greater than n elements. It required a one-line change in our test code:

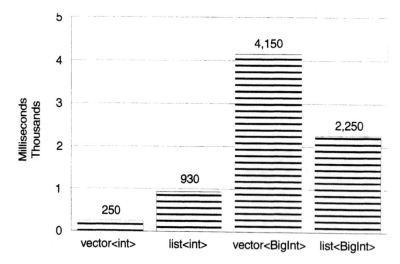

Figure 11.4. Comparing list to vector insertion.

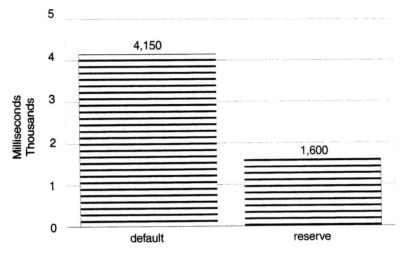

Figure 11.5. Vector insertion with and without capacity reservation.

```
vector<BigInt> *v = new vector<BigInt>;
v->reserve(size);
vectorInsert(v,dataBigInt,size);
```

The reservation of the required capacity has boosted performance by more than a factor of two. Figure 11.5 exhibits the execution time of a million `BigInt` insertions with and without reserved capacity.

So far, we have inserted the elements to the back of the array, vector, and list. The array container performed best in the scenario where the collection size was known in advance. When collection size was unknown, the vector outperformed the list container for integer insertion. What if we need to add elements in the middle or in front of the collection? That may turn the performance story upside down. Next, we compare the performance of the vector and list containers faced with the task of inserting elements to the front of the container. We used the following two functions:

```
template <class T>
void vectorInsertFront (vector<T> *v, T *collection, int size)
{
    for (int k =0; k < size; k++) {
        v->insert(v->begin(),collection[k]);
        }
}
```

```
template <class T>
void listInsertFront (list<T> *l, T *collection, int size)
{
    for (int k =0; k < size; k++) {
        l->push_front(collection[k]);
        }
}
```

The performance of the vector container on front insertions was terrible. It was so bad that we had to limit the collection size to 10,000. Each insertion at the front of the vector forced a shift of all existing elements to make room for the new one. The complexity of such an implementation is O(N*N) where N is the collection size. In other words, making the collection ten times bigger would result in execution time that is 100 times longer. We did not have that much time so we limited the test to 10,000 elements. The list container, on the other hand, takes constant time to insert an element at the front, regardless of collection size. The dramatic difference in execution time is shown in Figure 11.6.

This last test highlights another one of the performance benefits of the STL: The STL design discourages you from doing really silly things like choosing a vector container when you need to insert elements at the front. For that reason the STL does not provide a push_front() method for the vector container. If you really insist on doing something so inefficient, you'll have to do it yourself as we did in the vectorInsertFront() code.

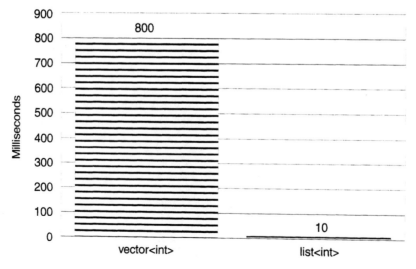

Figure 11.6. Inserting at the front.

Deletion

The deletion performance story is in many ways analogous to insertion. Many of the statements made with regard to insertion efficiency apply equally as well to deletion.[1] For example:

- A vector excels at insertion (deletion) of elements at the back. This is a constant-time operation as it is independent of collection size.

- A vector is a terrible choice for element insertion (deletion) anywhere other than the back. The cost of such insertion (deletion) is proportional to the distance of the insertion (deletion) point and the last element of the vector.

- A deque is efficient (constant-time) at insertion (deletion) at the front and back of a collection. It is inefficient for insertions (deletions) anywhere else.

- A list is efficient (constant-time) for insertion (deletion) anywhere in the collection.

As a sanity check, we tested the deletion of a million elements from a vector and list. For both list and vector, we used the `pop_back()` method provided by the STL. `pop_back()` deletes the last element of a container.

```
template <class T>
void vectorDelete (vector<T> *v)
{
    while (!v->empty()) {
        v->pop_back();
        }
}

template <class T>
void listDelete (list<T> *l)
{
    while (!l->empty()) {
        l->pop_back();
        }
}
```

The execution speed is shown in Figure 11.7.

---

[1] You can find those and many more performance guarantees in [MS96]. It contains complexity guarantees for all containers and generic algorithms.

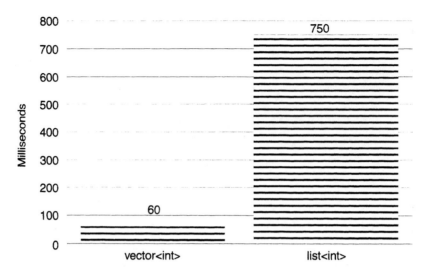

Figure 11.7. Comparing list to vector deletion.

Just like insertion, the vector container outperforms the list when it comes to element deletion at the back of a collection. What about deletion at the front? If it is anything like insertion it should reverse the performance comparison between a vector and a list. The test code is given by:

```
template <class T>
void listDeleteFront (list<T> *l)
{
    while (!l->empty()) {
        l->pop_front();
        }
}

template <class T>
void vectorDeleteFront (vector<T> *v)
{
    while (!v->empty()) {
        v->erase(v->begin());
        }
}
```

Just like insertion at the front, deleting elements at the front of a vector is inefficient. For that reason we had to limit this test to 10,000 elements. The execution times are shown in Figure 11.8.

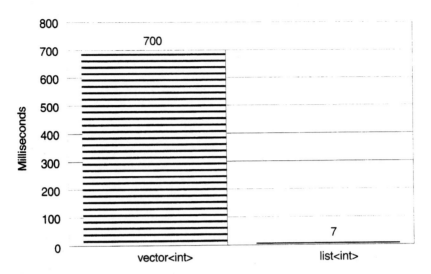

Figure 11.8. Deleting elements at the front.

In this test, the list outperformed the vector by a factor of 100. Notice also how the STL does not provide a `pop_front()` method for the vector container to discourage users from attempting this inefficient manipulation of a vector container.

The deletion performance story told by Figures 11.7 and 11.8 is analogous to the insertion performance revealed by Figures 11.1 and 11.6. It reiterates the statements we made at the beginning of this section: Performance observations made with regard to container insertion will also apply to deletion.

Traversal

We often need to traverse a container one element at a time, performing a computation on each element. We picked the STL's `accumulate()` function to represent container traversal. The `accumulate()` function traverses the container from beginning to end, adding all elements in the process. The containers under test were an array, vector, and list. Each container stored an identical collection of 10,000 random integers. The test code for the various containers is as follows:

```
void vectorTraverse (vector<int> *v, int size)
{
    int sum = accumulate(v->begin(), v->end(),0);
}
```

```
void arrayTraverse (int *a, int size)
{
    int sum = accumulate(&a[0], &a[size],0);
}

void listTraverse (list<int> *l, int size)
{
    int sum = accumulate(l->begin(), l->end(),0);

}
```

The test itself consisted of invoking these traversal functions 100 times each. The execution time of 100 traversals of the various containers is shown in Figure 11.9.

With regard to container traversal, the performance of the vector and array was the same. Both outperformed the list container by a wide margin. The dominant factor in container traversal seemed to be the interaction between the container memory lay-out and the system's cache. Both vector and array hold their collections in contiguous memory. Logically adjacent elements of the collection reside physically next to one another in memory. When a particular element is loaded into the cache, it pulls with it a few more adjacent elements that will be accessed next (the exact number depends on the element size as well as the size of a cache line). This is ideal behavior from a caching perspective. This is not the case with a list container. Logically adjacent list elements are not necessarily adjacent in memory. Moreover, the list elements must

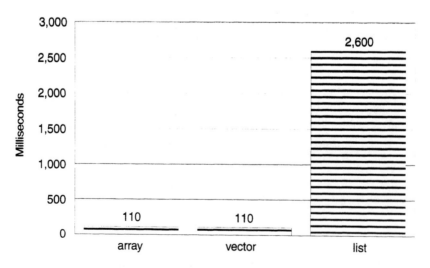

Figure 11.9. Container traversal speed.

store forward and backward pointers in addition to element value, which makes them larger than the corresponding vector elements. Even if some adjacent list elements were placed next to one another in memory, fewer of them would fit on a cache line due to their size. Consequently, traversal of a list container produces far more cache misses than an array or vector traversal.

Find

The previous discussions of insertion, deletion, and traversal provided scenarios in which each of the array, vector, and list containers had a chance to outperform the other containers under test. We now move on to yet another important operation that will allow the multiset container to shine. This is the case where we need to look up a specific element in a collection. The following code uses the STL's find() to perform a lookup on the various containers:

```
void arrayFind (int *a, int *collection, int size)
{
    int const value = collection[size/2];
    int *p = find(&a[0],&a[size],value);
}

void vectorFind (vector<int> *v, int *collection, int size)
{
    int const value = collection[size/2];
    vector<int>::iterator it =
        find(v->begin(), v->end(), value);
}

void listFind (list<int> *l, int *collection, int size)
{
    int const value = collection[size/2];
    list<int>::iterator it =
        find(l->begin(), l->end(), value);
}

// This is using the generic find() which is not the
// best choice when searching a multiset.
void multisetFind (multiset<int> *s, int *collection, int size)
{
    int const value = collection[size/2];
    multiset<int>::iterator it =
        find(s->begin(), s->end(), value);
}
```

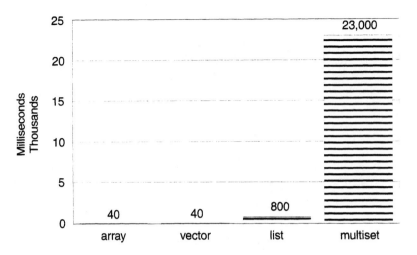

Figure 11.10.   Container search speed.

The performance test consisted of a hundred iterations of a container search. The execution times are shown in Figure 11.10.

Figure 11.10 is misleading in the sense that it seems to indicate that a vector and an array are the best choices for lookup performance. It seems that way only because we have misused the generic find() algorithm on the multiset container. It would be much more efficient to use the find() member method provided by the multiset container. The member find() utilizes the fact that the multiset is a sorted container. The generic find() is oblivious to that fact because it must handle containers that are not sorted. Consequently, the generic find() must perform a sequential search. The following version of the multiset search is using the member find():

```
void multisetFind (multiset<int> *s, int *collection, int size)
{
    int const value = collection[size/2];
    multiset<int>::iterator it =
        s->find(value);
}
```

The member find() outperformed the generic one by orders of magnitude. The generic find() took 23,000 milliseconds to perform a hundred searches through a million element multiset, whereas the member find() performed the same test in 0.06 milliseconds. You can get a visual feel for it in Figure 11.11.

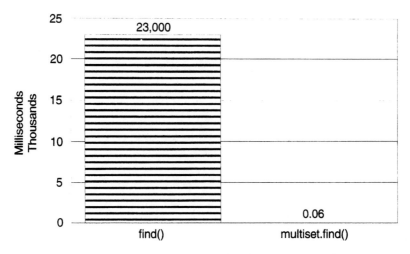

Figure 11.11. Comparing generic find() to member find().

Obviously, using the member find(), the multiset container blew away the rest of the competition when it came to element search. The fact that the multiset is a sorted collection exacted some performance penalty on insertion and deletion. On the other hand, being in sorted order provides the multiset container a large advantage when it comes to searching.

Function Objects

By default, the accumulate() function applies operator+ to all the elements residing in a container and returns the cumulative result of adding all the elements. In the case of an integer collection, if the initial value provided to accumulate() is 0, the result would be the sum of the collection. The accumulate() algorithm is by no means limited to object addition. It is capable of applying any operation to the container elements (given that the operation is supported by the elements) and returning the cumulative result [MS96]:

```
template <class InputIterator, class T>
T accumulate(InputIterator first,
          InputIterator beyondLast,
          T initialValue)
{
    while (first != beyondLast) {
        initialValue = initialValue + *first++;
        }
}
```

In C programming, parameterizing such an operation normally would be achieved by passing a function pointer. The STL can do the same, but in addition, it provides us with a more efficient alternative in the form of function objects.

Suppose that instead of a sum, we would like to compute the product of a set of integers. One option we have is to define a function that returns the product of two integers and passes it as an argument to `accumulate()` [MS96]:

```
int mult(int x, int y) {return x*y;}
...
int a[10] = {1, 2, 3, 5, 7, 11, 13, 17, 19, 23};
int product = accumulate (&a[0],
                          &a[10],
                          1,
                          mult); // Function pointer
```

The second option is to pass a function object as an argument to `accumulate()`. A function object is an instance of a class that overloads `operator()`. For example:

```
class Mult {
public:
     int operator() (int x, int y) const {return x*y;}
};
...
int a[10] = {1, 2, 3, 5, 7, 11, 13, 17, 19, 23};
int product = accumulate (&a[0],
                          &a[10],
                          1,
                          Mult()); // Constructor for a
                                   // function object
```

We really didn't have to reinvent the multiplication wheel as the STL already provides a `times` template class.

The following would be equivalent [MS96]:

```
int product = accumulate (&a[0],
                          &a[10],
                          1,
                          times<int>()); // Constructor for a
                                         // function object
```

We compared the relative performance of `accumulate()` using both function pointers and function objects. The execution times given in Figure 11.12 represent one million calls to the `accumulate()` versions just discussed.

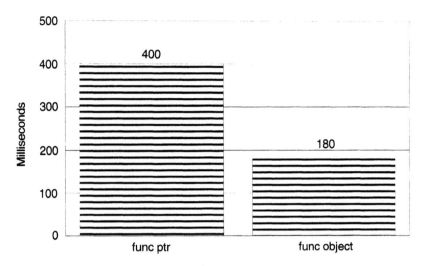

Figure 11.12. Comparing function objects to function pointers.

The version using the function object has significantly outperformed the one using function pointers. This is in line with expectation. Function pointers cannot be resolved until run-time, which prevents them from being inlined. Function objects, however, are determined at compile-time, which gives the compiler the freedom to inline the calls to `operator()` and significantly increase efficiency.

Better than STL?

The STL is regarded by many to have excellent performance. The general trend is to discourage the programmer from even thinking about surpassing the STL performance with home-grown implementations. Although we agree with this notion, for the most part, we would still like to take a closer look at those conceptions. To learn more about it, we will take a few shots at exceeding the STL performance and see how it goes.

We have encountered the `accumulate()` function earlier in this chapter, using it to sum up a collection of integers. Let's see if we can improve upon it with a home-grown implementation:

```
int myIntegerSum(int *a, int size)
{
    int sum = 0;
```

```
        int *begin = &a[0];
        int *end = &a[size];

        for (int *p=begin; p != end; p++) {
            sum += *p;
            }

        return sum;
}
```

The STL-based solution is

```
int stlIntegerSum(int *a, int size)
{
return accumulate (&a[0],&a[size],0);
}
```

The results of a performance comparison test indicated that the execution speed of myIntegerSum() was identical to that of stlIntegerSum(). Our attempt to surpass the STL's speed has come up short. It is reasonable to speculate that this scenario is typical and that, in general, exceeding the STL's performance would be an exception to the rule. An STL implementation has a few things going in its favor:

- STL implementations use best-of-breed algorithms.

- The designers of STL implementations are, more than likely, domain experts.

- Those domain experts were entirely focused on the mission of providing a flexible, powerful, and efficient library. This was their primary task.

For the rest of us, developing reusable containers and generic algorithms is a secondary goal at best. Our primary task is to deliver an application under a tight deadline. In most cases, we are not going to have the time or expertise to match those of the STL designers.

Now that we have done our best to discourage you from trying to compete with the STL, we will shift gears and present some possible exceptions to the rule. For example, suppose our application often needs to reverse a character sequence. Suppose further that our character sequences are of fixed length, say five characters long. Here's a possible STL-based solution:

```
char *s = "abcde";
reverse (&s[0],&s[5]);
```

Alternatively we can roll our own solution, as in:

```
char *s = "abcde";
char temp;

temp = s[4];        // s[0] <-> s[4]
s[4] = s[0];
s[0] = temp;

temp = s[3];        // s[1] <-> s[3]
s[3] = s[1];
s[1] = temp;
```

We executed a million iterations of this string reversal code and recorded the execution times shown in Figure 11.13.

Our brute-force implementation has outperformed the STL solution by a factor of four. The `reverse()` solution was oblivious to the fact that the sequence length was five characters long. It would have worked for any sequence length and is consequently more powerful. Our brute-force approach was not nearly as elegant. It relied heavily on the fact that the sequence was five characters long and would not have worked on any other sequence length. This is a very focused solution to a very specific task.

This example is a bit contrived, but it does make at least three good points with regard to the STL performance:

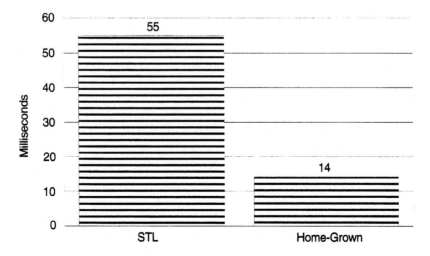

Figure 11.13. Comparing STL speed to home-grown code.

- You have to bend over backwards to concoct scenarios in which a home-grown implementation will outperform the STL.

- Outperforming the STL is possible.

- If you are planning to outperform an STL-based solution, you'd better know something about the domain that the STL doesn't. Otherwise, you'd better invest your time elsewhere.

We can make an even stronger statement with regard to surpassing the STL performance. Our claim is that no matter how good the implementation is, there are always computational scenarios that expose it as suboptimal. It cannot be everything to everybody all the time. Take the list container, for example. Among other things, the list container supports insertion, deletion, and a `size()` member function that returns the number of elements currently stored in the list. When implementing the `size()` member function we basically have two design options [BM97]:

1. We can define a data member field that will keep track of the current list size. This member will eagerly be evaluated and updated for every list insertion or deletion operation. This mandatory update makes the insertion and deletion somewhat slower, but the `size()` function is extremely fast (constant time).

2. Compute the size only when requested. Insertions and deletions will be faster as they will not update the current size, but the `size()` operation will be much slower. The `size()` computation will necessitate a sequential walk to count the number of elements currently on the list.

An STL implementation has to choose between those two design options. No matter what choice is made, there's always a scenario where performance will suffer. A workload dominated by insertions and deletions would benefit from design option 1. On the other hand, a workload that performs frequent `size()` operations on a large list will benefit from option 2. For that reason, the possibility of improving upon the STL performance is always there, in theory.

Key Points

- The STL is an uncommon combination of abstraction, flexibility, and efficiency.

- Depending on your application, some containers are more efficient than others for a particular usage pattern.

- Unless you know something about the problem domain that the STL doesn't, it is unlikely that you will beat the performance of an STL implementation by a wide enough margin to justify the effort.

- It is possible, however, to exceed the performance of an STL implementation in some specific scenarios.

12

Reference Counting

The principle of entropy applies to software just as well as it does to the physical world—all entities tend to disintegrate over time. A software project may start as a small-scale prototype of clear design and simple implementation. Those select few prototypes that make it to the marketplace will often undergo rapid expansion. This is usually in response to an avalanche of customer requests for additional (and sometimes esoteric) new features, as well as defects. New development combined with bug fixes tend to wreak havoc on the original crystal-clear design. Over time, the clarity of the design and implementation evaporates through maintenance and frequent release cycles. Software inevitably tends towards chaos. The only factor separating the good ones from the not-so-good ones is the rate of decay.

One of the major difficulties with chaotic software is memory corruption. Allocated memory flows through the system by way of pointer passing. Pointers are being passed among modules and threads. In a chaotic software system this will result in two major difficulties:

- Memory leaks. This happens when memory is never freed and will, over time, bring the application down when its consumption of memory gets out of hand.

- Premature deletion. When ownership of a memory pointer is not clear, it may result in memory being accessed after it was already deleted, resulting in immediate catastrophic failure.

Fortunately, C++ offers a solution to both problems. C++ allows you to control all points of object creation, destruction, copy, and assignment. You can leverage that control to develop a form of garbage collection called *reference counting*. The basic idea is to transfer the object destruction responsibility from the client code to the object itself. The object keeps track of the current number of references to it and destroys itself when the reference count reaches zero. In other words, the object destroys itself when nobody is using it any longer. With the vast majority of software defects being traced back to memory corruption, reference counting is a very important technique in the C++ arsenal.

Reference counting is also touted as a performance optimization. It is claimed that reference counting can reduce the consumption of memory as well as CPU cycles. Consider an object containing a member pointing at heap storage. What happens when you copy or assign this object? The simplest implementation is to perform a deep copy giving each object an identical private copy of heap storage. For example, take a naive implementation of MyString:

```
class MyString {
public:
    ...
    MyString& operator=(const MyString& rhs);
    ...
private:
    char *pData;
};

MyString& MyString::operator=(const MyString& rhs)
{
    if (this == &rhs) return *this;
    delete [] pdata;
    int length = strlen(rhs.pData) + 1;  // Include the terminating
                                         // null
    pdata = new char[length];            // Make room for the new array
    memcpy(pData, rhs.pData, length);// Copy the characters from the
                                     // right-hand-side object
    return *this;
}
```

When you assign one MyString object to another, as in

```
MyString p,s;
p = s = "TWO";
```

you end up with the picture in Figure 12.1.

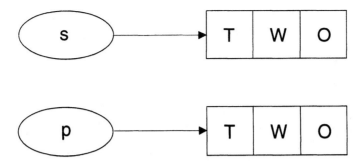

Figure 12.1. Duplicating resources.

This seems wasteful both in terms of memory utilization as well as the CPU cycles it takes to allocate heap memory and copy the string content. In theory, it would be cheaper if we utilized reference counting to have both objects point to the same memory resource.

There is no doubt that reference counting is always a winner in reducing memory usage. It is not clear, however, that it is always an execution speed winner. This is the topic of this chapter: When does reference counting help execution speed and under what circumstances does it actually hurt?

An intelligent discussion of reference counting performance requires a rudimentary grasp of the implementation details, which we cover next.

Implementation Details

Implementing reference counting is a delicate, nontrivial task. The same goes for explaining it. Instead of re-inventing the wheel, we chose to base our performance discussion on the reference counting implementation developed by Meyers in item 29 of "More Effective C++" [Mey96], for several reasons:

- It is an efficient implementation, given what it set out to accomplish.

- It is explained very well in [Mey96]. You may refer to it for more details than we provide here.

- Many people may already be familiar with this particular implementation.

Let's start with a `Widget` class and evolve it into a reference-counted one. The `Widget` class contains a member pointing to heap memory (Meyers uses a `String` class in his initial demonstration of the concept):

```
class Widget {
public:
    Widget(int size);
    Widget(const Widget& rhs);
    ~Widget();

    Widget& operator=(const Widget& rhs);

    void doThis();
    int showThat() const;
private:
    char *somePtr;
};
```

The first step towards reference counting is adding a counter member to `Widget`. The counter will keep track of the number of references to a particular `Widget` object:

```
class Widget {
    ...  // As before
private:
    char *somePtr;
    int refCount;
};
```

The `Widget` object will destroy itself when its `refCount` reaches 0. The next step introduces the reference-counted `Widget` class:

```
class RCWidget {  // Reference-counted Widget class
public:
    RCWidget(int size) : value(new Widget(size)) {}

    void doThis() { value->doThis(); }
    int showThat() const {return value->showThat();}
private:
    Widget *value;
};
```

`RCWidget` acts as a `Widget` proxy. It exposes an identical interface and simply forwards the real work to the `Widget` object to which it points. This is the basic idea, shown in Figure 12.2.

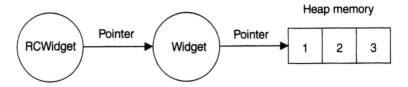

Figure 12.2. A simple design for a reference-counted Widget class.

The discussion so far was an over-simplification. Meyers' implementation is more sophisticated. He embedded a smart pointer (see item 28 in [Mey96]) in RCWidget instead of a dumb pointer, which we showed. He also had the Widget publicly derived from an RCObject class, which is a base class for all reference-counted classes. RCObject encapsulates the manipulation of the reference count variable. Meyers' implementation looks like Figure 12.3.

This was the high-level view of the reference-counting design. We now proceed to the implementation details. First, we replace the Widget with a more concrete example that is easier to relate to. The BigInt class is borrowed from Tom Cargil's "C++ Programming Style" [Car92]. The BigInt class represents positive integers as binary-coded decimals. For example, the number 123 is internally represented by a 3-byte character array, each byte representing one digit. It allows you to create and manipulate BigInt objects as in the following code.

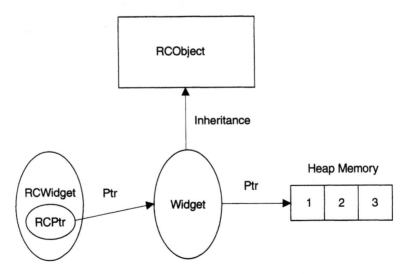

Figure 12.3. Adding inheritance and smart pointer to the reference-counting design.

```
BigInt a = 123;
BigInt b = "456";
BigInt c = a + b;
```

`BigInt` is a good candidate for a reference counting discussion since it uses heap memory to store its digits. The implementation of `BigInt` follows and is almost identical to the original [Car92]:

```
class BigInt {
friend BigInt operator+ (const BigInt&, const BigInt&);
public:
    BigInt (const char *);
    BigInt(unsigned = 0);
    BigInt (const BigInt&);
    BigInt& operator= (const BigInt&);
    BigInt& operator+= (const BigInt&);
    ~BigInt();

    char *getDigits() const { return digits; }
    unsigned getNdigits() const { return ndigits; }
private:
    char *digits;
    unsigned ndigits;
    unsigned size;                        // size of allocated string
    BigInt (const BigInt&, const BigInt&);// operational ctor
    char fetch(unsigned i) const;
};
```

In the course of our reference counting discussion we are going to utilize only a subset of the `BigInt` implementation. That subset consists of one constructor, destructor, and an assignment operator. It will suffice to familiarize yourself with these three.

```
BigInt::BigInt (unsigned u)
{
    unsigned v = u;

    for (ndigits = 1; (v/=10) > 0; ++ndigits) {
        ;
        }

    digits = new char[size=ndigits];

    for ( unsigned i = 0; i < ndigits; ++i) {
        digits[i] = u%10;
        u /= 10;
        }
}
```

```
BigInt::~BigInt()
{
    delete [] digits;
}

BigInt& BigInt::operator= (const BigInt& rhs)
{
    if (this == &rhs) return *this;
    ndigits = rhs.ndigits;
    if (ndigits > size) {
        delete [] digits;
        digits = new char[size = ndigits];
        }

    for (unsigned i = 0; i < ndigits; ++i) {
        digits[i] = rhs.digits[i];
        }

    return *this;
}
```

The rest of the BigInt implementation will not play a role in our discussion. It is given here for the sake of completeness:

```
BigInt::BigInt (const char *s)
{
    if (s[0] == '\0') {
        s = "0";
        }

    size = ndigits = strlen(s);
    digits = new char[size];
    for ( unsigned i = 0; i < ndigits; ++i) {
        digits[i] = s[ndigits-1-i] - '0';
        }
}

BigInt::BigInt(const BigInt& copyFrom)    // Copy constructor
{
    size = ndigits = copyFrom.ndigits;
    digits = new char[size];

    for ( unsigned i = 0; i < ndigits; ++i) {
        digits[i] = copyFrom.digits[i];
        }
}

// Operational constructor: BigInt = left + right
BigInt::BigInt (const BigInt& left, const BigInt& right)
```

```
    {
        size = 1 + (left.ndigits > right.ndigits ?
            left.ndigits : right.ndigits);
        digits = new char[size];
        ndigits = left.ndigits;
        for (unsigned i = 0; i < ndigits; ++i) {
            digits[i] = left.digits[i];
            }

        *this += right;
    }

inline
char BigInt::fetch(unsigned i) const
{
    return i < ndigits ? digits[i] : 0;
}

BigInt& BigInt::operator+= (const BigInt& rhs)
{
    unsigned max = 1 + (rhs.ndigits > ndigits ?
        rhs.ndigits : ndigits);

    if (size < max) {
        char *d = new char[size=max];
        for (unsigned i = 0; i < ndigits; ++i) {
          d[i] = digits[i];
            }
        delete [] digits;
        digits = d;
        }

    while (ndigits < max) {
        digits[ndigits++] = 0;
        }

    for (unsigned i = 0; i < ndigits; ++i) {
        digits[i] += rhs.fetch(i);
        if ( digits[i] >= 10) {
          digits[i] -= 10;
          digits[i+1] += 1;
          }
        }

    if (digits[ndigits-1] == 0) {
        --ndigits;
        }

    return *this;
}
```

```
ostream& operator<< (ostream& os, BigInt& bi)
{
    char c;

    const char *d = bi.getDigits();

    for (int i = bi.getNdigits() -1; i >= 0; i--) {
        c = d[i]+'0';
        os << c;
    }
    os << endl;

    return os;
}

inline
BigInt operator+ (const BigInt& left, const BigInt& right)
{
    return BigInt(left,right);
}
```

To facilitate reference counting we need to associate a reference count with every BigInt object. We can do that by either adding a refCount member directly to BigInt or inheriting it from a base class. Meyers chose the latter approach, and we will follow his lead. The RCObject class is a base class for reference-counted objects and encapsulates the reference count variable and its manipulations.

```
class RCObject {
public:
    void addReference() { ++refCount;}
    void removeReference() {if (--refCount == 0) delete this;}

    void markUnshareable() { shareable = false;}
    bool isShareable() const { return shareable; }

    bool isShared() const { return refCount > 1; }

protected:
    RCObject() : refCount(0), shareable(true) {}
    RCObject(const RCObject& rhs) : refCount(0), shareable(true) {}
    RCObject& operator=(const RCObject& rhs) {return *this;}
    virtual ~RCObject() {}

private:
    int refCount;
    bool shareable;
};
```

The `BigInt` class must now be modified to inherit from the `RCObject` class:

```
class BigInt : public RCObject {
    // Same as before
};
```

We are working our way toward `RCBigInt`, which is the reference-counted implementation of `BigInt`. Somehow, it needs to point at the real `BigInt` object. You can
achieve that with a real (dumb) pointer or a smart pointer. Meyers elected to go with
a smart pointer. (A smart pointer is an object encapsulating a dumb pointer by overloading the "->" and "*" operators. See [Mey96] item 28.) This particular smart
pointer is responsible for the reference count bookkeeping:

```
template <class T>
class RCPtr {
public:
    RCPtr(T *realPtr = 0) : pointee(realPtr) { init();}
    RCPtr(const RCPtr& rhs) : pointee(rhs.pointee) { init();}
    ~RCPtr() { if (pointee) pointee->removeReference();}

    RCPtr& operator=(const RCPtr& rhs);

    T* operator->() const { return pointee; }
    T& operator*() const { return *pointee; }
private:
    T *pointee;
    void init();
};

template <class T>
void RCPtr<T>::init()
{
    if (0 == pointee) return;

    if (false == pointee->isShareable() ) {
        pointee = new T(*pointee);
        }

    pointee->addReference();
}

template <class T>
RCPtr<T>& RCPtr<T>::operator=(const RCPtr& rhs)
{
    if (pointee != rhs.pointee) {
        if (pointee) pointee->removeReference();
```

```
        pointee = rhs.pointee;
        init();
        }

    return *this;
}
```

Finally, we have all the required fragments to assemble a reference counted `BigInt`, which we are calling `RCBigInt`. `RCBigInt` is pretty straightforward. The hard work has already been done in `RCPtr` and `RCObject`:

```
class RCBigInt {
friend RCBigInt operator+ (const RCBigInt&, const RCBigInt&);
public:
    RCBigInt (const char *p) : value (new BigInt(p)) {}
    RCBigInt (unsigned u= 0) : value (new BigInt(u)) {}
    RCBigInt (const BigInt& bi) : value (new BigInt(bi)) {}

    void print() const { value->print(); }

private:
    RCPtr<BigInt> value;
};

inline
RCBigInt operator+ (const RCBigInt& left, const RCBigInt& right)
{
    return RCBigInt(*(left.value) + *(right.value));
}
```

In performance testing, `RCBigInt` should shine in workloads dominated by frequent assignments and copies of `RCBigInt` objects. On the other hand, new `RCBigInt` objects that create a first reference to a new `BigInt` object have become more expensive in comparison to working with plain `BigInt`. Whenever an `RCBigInt` object gives rise to a first `BigInt` reference, it creates a `BigInt` object on the heap and points to it. This is one cost you don't have to pay with a stack-based (local variable) plain `BigInt` object. A similar argument applies to the removal of the last `BigInt` reference. The underlying `BigInt` object is freed back to the heap. To quantify those performance gains and losses we developed assignment and creation test cases and applied them to both `BigInt` and `RCBigInt`. The first test measured the creation and destruction time of `BigInt` objects:

```
void testBigIntCreate(int n)
{
```

```
    . . .
    GetSystemTime(&t1);

    for ( i = 0; i < n; ++i) {
        BigInt a = i;
        BigInt b = i+1;
        BigInt c = i+2;
        BigInt d = i+3;
        }

    GetSystemTime(&t2);
    . . .
}
```

The equivalent test for RCBigInt construction is almost identical to the BigInt test. We simply replaced the BigInt objects with RCBigInt ones. It is important to note that the following RCBigInt test will be very busy creating first references and then destroying them:

```
void testRCBigIntCreate(int n)
{
    . . .
    GetSystemTime(&t1);

    for ( i = 0; i < n; ++i) {
        RCBigInt a = i;
        RCBigInt b = i+1;
        RCBigInt c = i+2;
        RCBigInt d = i+3;
        }

    GetSystemTime(&t2);
    . . .
}
```

Similarly, we have two corresponding assignment test cases. We show only the first one for BigInt. The one for RCBigInt is almost identical:

```
void testBigIntAssign(int n)
{
    . . .
    BigInt a,b,c;
    BigInt d = 1;

    GetSystemTime(&t1);

    for ( i = 0; i < n; ++i) {
        a = b = c = d;
```

```
        }
    GetSystemTime(&t2);
        ...
}
```

We measured a million iterations of the loop in each of our four test cases. The execution time (in ms) is given in Figures 12.4 and 12.5.

As expected, the assignment of RCBigInt objects was very efficient, almost twice as fast as the one for BigInt objects. We have the reverse story on object creation and destruction. Creating and destroying BigInt objects was significantly faster than doing the same to RCBigInt objects. This should serve as a reminder that reference counting is not synonymous with performance gains. This was our first encounter with a scenario in which reference counting inflicted a performance penalty. On the other hand, we also have a scenario (the assignment test) where reference counting has boosted performance. The natural question here is, how do you tell one set from the other? The relationship between reference counting and execution speed is context-sensitive. It depends on a few factors:

- What is the magnitude of resource consumption by the target object? If the target object uses gigantic amounts of memory, for example, a failure to conserve

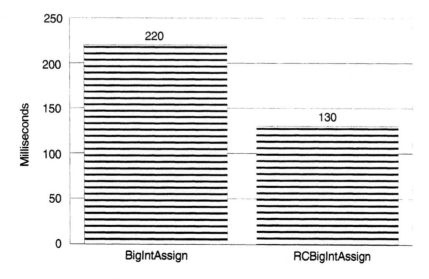

Figure 12.4. BigInt assignment speed.

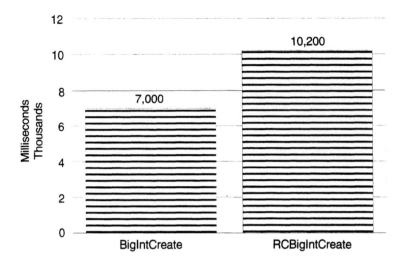

Figure 12.5. `BigInt` creation speed.

memory will push the limits on available memory and lead to dramatic performance loss in the form of cache misses and page-faults.

- How expensive is it to allocate (and deallocate) the resource used by the target object? This is different from the previous factor. An object such as `BigInt` will typically consume a small amount of storage and is unlikely to deplete available memory. However, allocating even one byte from the heap will cost you hundreds of instructions. The same goes for deallocating a single byte.

- How many objects are likely to share a single instance of the target object? Sharing is increased by the use of the assignment operator and copy constructor.

- How often do we create (destroy) first (last) references to the target object? Creating a brand-new reference-counted object using a constructor other than the copy constructor will create a first reference to the target object. This is expensive. It has more overhead in comparison to creating the target object. The same argument applies to the removal of a last reference.

On one extreme we may have a situation in which we have many reference-counted instances sharing a small number of target objects (via the copy constructor and assignment operator), but creation and destruction of first and last references is limited. The target object is a large consumer of a limited resource, which in itself is expensive to acquire and unload. This would be the poster-child for a reference-counted performance boost. On the other extreme, you may have a scenario in which many target objects are created but their reference counts rarely exceed one or two (indicating little to no sharing). The target object is a negligible resource consumer, and the resource itself is cheap to obtain and release. In this case, reference counting is an execution-time loser.

What makes the judgement call so cloudy is that most scenarios will fall between these two extremes. Even in our `BigInt` example, we could tilt the scales further against reference counting by providing a memory pool to allocate the storage consumed by the `BigInt` internal buffer. In that case, the cost of duplicating `BigInt` objects would be significantly reduced, making the case for reference counting even less appealing from a performance standpoint. The next section provides another implementation variant that affects the performance balance between a reference-counted and a plain object.

Preexisting Classes

Our previous implementation of a reference-counted `BigInt` class involved some modifications to the original `BigInt` implementation. That required, of course, that we had the liberty to modify the `BigInt` source code. This option is not always available. The target class could come from a library whose source code is not given. We can still implement reference counting for such preexisting, hands-off target classes, but we need to make some design changes.

Previously, with access to the source code, we added the reference counter to `Big-Int` by making `BigInt` inherit from `RCObject`. Now that we cannot touch the `BigInt` implementation, we must introduce a separate class to hold the reference count and manipulate it. Meyers calls this class the `CountHolder`. The modified design is given visually in Figure 12.6.

Other than divorcing the reference count from the `BigInt` class, we also have the `RCPtr` object (previously embedded in `RCBigInt`) replaced by an `RCIPtr` object. `RCIPtr` is a smart pointer just like `RCPtr`, but it points at `BigInt` indirectly via a pointer to `CountHolder`. `RCPtr` used to point directly at `BigInt`. From an implementation standpoint we have three issues to consider. First, the `BigInt` class reverts

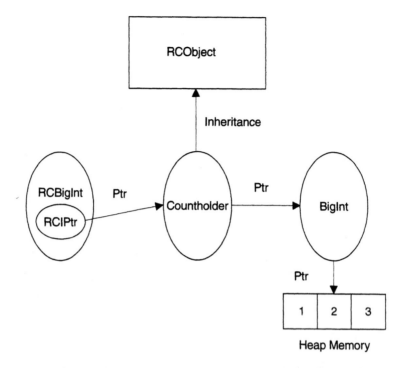

Figure 12.6. Reference-counting a pre-existing BigInt.

back to its original form and no longer inherits from RCObject. Second, the RCBig-Int class now has an RCIPtr member instead of RCPtr:

```
class RCBigInt {
    ...                      // The same as before
private:
    RCIPtr<BigInt> value;    // RCIPtr not RCPtr
};
```

Third, we have to present an implementation of RCIPtr. The RCIPtr implementation also introduces the CountHolder as a nested class:

```
template < class T>
class RCIPtr {
public:
    RCIPtr(T *realPtr = 0);
    RCIPtr(const RCIPtr& rhs);
    ~RCIPtr();
```

```
    RCIPtr& operator=(const RCIPtr& rhs);

    T* operator->() const { return counter->pointee; }
    T& operator*() const { return *(counter->pointee); }
private:
    struct CountHolder : public RCObject {
        ~CountHolder() { delete pointee; }
        T *pointee;
    };

    RCIPtr<T>::CountHolder *counter;
    void init();
};


template <class T>
void RCIPtr<T>::init()
{
    if (0 == counter) return;

    if (false == counter->isShareable() ) {
        counter = new CountHolder;
        counter->pointee = new T(*counter->pointee);
        }

    counter->addReference();
}

template <class T>
RCIPtr<T>::RCIPtr(T *realPtr)
    : counter(new CountHolder)
{
    counter->pointee = realPtr;
    init();
}

template <class T>
RCIPtr<T>::RCIPtr(const RCIPtr& rhs) : counter(rhs.counter)
{
    init();
}

template <class T>
RCIPtr<T>::~RCIPtr()
{
    if (counter) counter->removeReference();
}

template <class T>
RCIPtr<T>& RCIPtr<T>::operator=(const RCIPtr& rhs)
{
```

```
    if (counter != rhs.counter) {
        if (counter) counter->removeReference();

        counter = rhs.counter;
        init();
    }

    return *this;
}
```

The implementation of RCIPtr<T>::operator= is similar in cost to the corresponding implementation of RCPtr. Consequently, the execution speed of the assignment test (testRCBigIntAssign) has remained the same for both versions of RCBigInt. This is not the case with the creation test (testRCBigIntCreate). This test creates first references to new BigInt objects and then turns around and destroys them. The migration from RCPtr to RCIPtr has made the creation of a first BigInt reference, and its destruction, more expensive. Not only do we need to allocate a new heap-based BigInt object, we also have to allocate a new CountHolder object, and we have to delete them upon destruction. The performance gap between BigInt and RCBigInt has gotten bigger in this scenario. The new execution speed of our test is given in Figure 12.7.

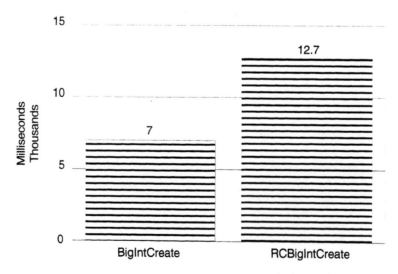

Figure 12.7. BigInt creation speed.

Concurrent Reference Counting

We have already investigated two versions of reference counting and established that one (using RCPtr) was faster than the other (using RCIPtr). There's one more important twist on reference counting that we need to evaluate. The third implementation variant handles reference-counted objects in a multithreaded execution environment. In that case, multiple threads may access a reference-counted object concurrently. Therefore, the variable holding the reference count must be protected so that updates are atomic. Atomic updates require a locking mechanism. We have discussed locking classes in Chapter 7, and we reproduce the relevant code subset here:

```
class MutexLock {
public:
    MutexLock() {mutex = CreateMutex(NULL, FALSE,NULL);}
    virtual ~MutexLock() {CloseHandle(mutex);}
    void lock() {WaitForSingleObject(mutex, INFINITE);}
    void unlock() {ReleaseMutex(mutex);}
private:
    HANDLE mutex;
};
```

Adding concurrency-control to RCBigInt requires a one-line change to its class declaration. We are adding a MutexLock template argument to the RCIPtr smart pointer:

```
class RCBigInt {
    ... // Same as before
private:
    RCIPtr<BigInt, MutexLock> value;// Add MutexLock
};
```

The task of handling concurrent access has been given to the RCIPtr class. We have expanded its template declaration to allow an additional lock class argument. That lock is used to serialize access to variables requiring atomic updates:

```
template < class T, class LOCK>
class RCIPtr {
public:
    ...
private:
    struct CountHolder : public RCObject {
            ~CountHolder() { delete pointee; }
            T *pointee;
            LOCK key;
```

```
    };

    RCIPtr<T,LOCK>::CountHolder *counter;
    void init();
};
```

The `init()` method does not bother with concurrency and is unchanged. Atomic access, if necessary, is going to be handled by the callers of `init()`:

```
template <class T, class L>
void RCIPtr<T,L>::init()
{
    if (0 == counter) return;

    if (false == counter->isShareable() ) {
        T *p = counter->pointee;
        counter = new CountHolder;
        counter->pointee = new T(*p);
        }

    counter->addReference();
}
```

The rest of the methods will manipulate the lock explicitly. The implementation is straightforward—all operations that require serialization are surrounded by a pair of `lock()` and `unlock()` calls:

```
template <class T, class L>
RCIPtr<T,L>::RCIPtr(T *realPtr)
: counter(new CountHolder)
{
    counter->pointee = realPtr;
    init();
}

template <class T, class L>
RCIPtr<T, L>::RCIPtr(const RCIPtr& rhs)
: counter(rhs.counter)
{
    if (rhs.counter) rhs.counter->key.lock();
    init();
    if (rhs.counter) rhs.counter->key.unlock();
}

template <class T, class L>
RCIPtr<T, L>::~RCIPtr()
{
    if (counter) {
        if (counter->isShared() {
```

```
                counter->key.lock();
                counter->removeReference();
                counter->key.unlock();
        }
        else
            counter->removeReference();
        }
}

template <class T, class L>
RCIPtr<T, L>& RCIPtr<T,L>::operator=(const RCIPtr& rhs)
{
    if (counter != rhs.counter) {
        if (counter) {
            if (counter->isShared() {
                counter->key.lock();
                counter->removeReference();
                counter->key.unlock();
            }
            else
                counter->removeReference();
            }
    }

        counter = rhs.counter;
        if (rhs.counter) rhs.counter->key.lock();
        init();
        if (rhs.counter) rhs.counter->key.unlock();
        }

    return *this;
}
```

The additional computations required to provide atomic updates have slightly raised the cost of RCBigInt assignment. The execution-time of our test (testRCBigInt-Assign) has gone up from 130 to 150 ms. Still, assigning RCBigInt objects is cheaper than BigInt, and reference counting is still a winner in this case, as shown in Figure 12.8.

The migration to multithreaded environment did not have a huge impact on object assignment. It did, however, have a dramatic effect on reference creation and destruction. The creation (destruction) of a BigInt reference was already expensive because we had to create (destroy) a BigInt and CountHolder objects on the heap. On top of that, we now have to add the cost of creating (destroying) a MutexLock object. In this scenario, the performance gap between a plain BigInt and reference-counted one has blown up into a factor of (almost) 9x in favor of a plain BigInt object, as shown in Figure 12.9.

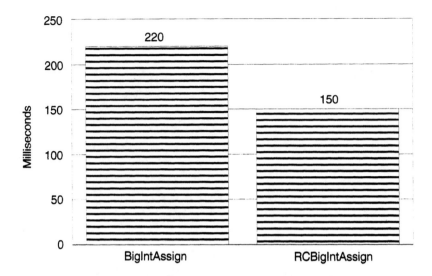

Figure 12.8. Multithreaded `BigInt` assignment speed.

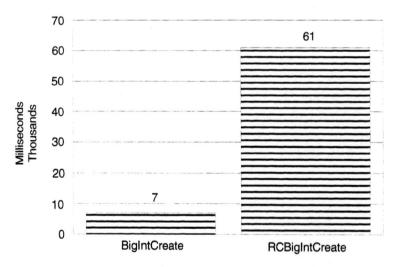

Figure 12.9. Multithreaded `BigInt` creation speed.

Key Points

Reference counting is not an automatic performance winner. Reference counting, execution speed, and resource conservation form a delicate interaction that must be evaluated carefully if performance is an important consideration. Reference counting may help or hurt performance depending on the usage pattern. The case in favor of reference counting is strengthened by any one of the following items:

- The target object is a large resource consumer

- The resource in question is expensive to allocate and free

- A high degree of sharing; the reference count is likely to be high due to the use of the assignment operator and copy constructor

- The creation or destruction of a reference is relatively cheap

If you reverse these items, you start leaning towards skipping reference counting in favor of the plain uncounted object.

13

Coding Optimizations

If our discussion centered around domain- or application-specific issues, it would be of very little use for most people. It would benefit only programmers working in that specific domain or a related application. To appeal to a larger audience we must address the performance issues that spread across programming domains and are likely to appear in a random application, without making any assumptions about the problem domain.

Although manifestations of performance issues are infinite, they may be classified into a finite set of types. Each type represents a set of equivalent performance bugs. They may look different on the surface, but they are essentially the same. As an example, take redundant computations, which can take many forms. Consider a loop-invariant computation:

```
for (i = 0; i < 100; i++) {
    a[i] = m*n;
    }
```

The value of m*n is computed every iteration. By moving loop-invariant computations outside the loop, we avoid redundant computations:

```
int k = m*n;
for (i = 0; i < 100; i++) {
    a[i] = k;
    }
```

Computational waste takes other forms as well. In the following example each routine needs to access information that is private to the current thread. `pthread_getspecific()` returns a pointer to a thread-private data structure. Both functions `f()` and `g()` need access to that data so each calls `pthread_getspecific()`:

```
static pthread_key_t global_key;

void f()
{
    void *x = pthread_getspecific(global_key);
    g();
    ...
}

void g()
{
    void *y = pthread_getspecific(global_key);
    ...
}
```

Since `f()` calls `g()` on the same thread of execution, calling `pthread_getspecific()` twice on the same flow is a waste. It is made worse by the fact that `pthread_getspecific()` is a fairly expensive call. We should eliminate the second call to `pthread_getspecific()` by passing its result to `g()`:

```
static pthread_key_t global_key;

void f()
{
    void *x = pthread_getspecific(global_key);

    g(x); // Pass a pointer to thread-private data as a parameter
    ...
}

void g(void *y)
{
        ...
}
```

Both examples are distinct manifestations of the same inefficiency: redundant computations. We are recomputing something we already know: the value of (m*n) in the first example and the return value of `pthread_getspecific()` in the second.

This chapter focuses on performance problems that are introduced in the application coding phase. We will not cover all instances as they are infinite. We will cover what we perceive as the dominant types. Those types are often small-scale issues; their resolution does not necessitate looking any further than a few lines of code. Lifting invariants outside the loop is an example of such coding optimization. You really don't have to understand the overall program design. Understanding the `for` loop is sufficient.

Performance coding issues are easier to fix than deep design problems. When we first joined the Web server development team we were not in position to make far-reaching design optimizations. We did not understand the overall server design well enough, at that point, to perform invasive surgery on it. But we immediately spotted the `pthread_getspecific()` inefficiency we just described. This call was made at least a hundred times during HTTP request handling. By passing the return value to those routines that needed it, we gained an easy 10% on server throughput.

Caching

Caching is often associated with data and instruction caching on modern processors. But, caching opportunities appear in much wider contexts, including application-level coding and design. Caching is about remembering the results of frequent and costly computations, so that you will not have to perform those computations over and over again.

Caching opportunities are easier to detect and implement in the coding arena. Evaluating constant expressions inside a loop is a well known performance inefficiency. For example:

```
for(... ;!done;... ) {
   done = patternMatch(pat1, pat2, isCaseSensitive());
   }
```

The `patternMatch()` function takes two string patterns to match and a third argument indicating whether a case-sensitive match is required. The decision itself is generated by a function call, `isCaseSensitive()`. This function simply distinguishes the case sensitive UNIX platforms from the nonsensitive PC platforms. This decision is fixed. It is independent of the loop and will not change from one iteration to the next. It should, therefore, be called outside the loop:

```
int isSensitive = isCaseSensitive();

for(... ;!done;... ) {
    done = patternMatch(pat1, pat2, isSensitive);
    }
```

Now you compute case-sensitivity once, cache it in a local variable, and reuse it.

Precompute

Precomputing is a close relative of caching. When you cache a result, you pay the price of computing it once in the performance-critical path. When you precompute, you don't even pay the first time. You perform the precomputation outside the performance-critical path (say, initialization-time) and never pay the price of performing a costly computation inside the performance-critical path.

Back to the Web server implementation for an example: A Web server spends a significant portion of its time manipulating character strings. If you can speed up string manipulation, performance will rise significantly. One string manipulation task we often encountered was uppercasing strings and characters. If the browser sends us an "Accept:" request header, the server must recognize it regardless of case. We should not distinguish among "accept:", "AcCePt:" or any other combination of lower- and uppercase letters. (The accept header tells the server what document types are acceptable to the browser—text/html, image/gif, ...)

Since memcmp(header, "ACCEPT:", 7) is case sensitive, we need to uppercase the header string prior to calling memcmp(). We may do the following:

```
for (char *p = header; *p ; p++) {        // Uppercase the header
    *p = toupper(*p);
    }

if (0 == memcmp(header, "ACCEPT:", 7)) {
    ...
    }
```

In a performance-critical path, you may find the cost of repeated **toupper()** calls to be unacceptable. Even if **toupper()** was implemented as an inline function, it would still contain a conditional statement of the form:

```
return (c >='a' && c<='z') ? c - ('a'-'A') : c;
```

This is the ASCII implementation. It gets even more complex with the EBCDIC character set (the EBCDIC alphabet sequence is not contiguous).

We didn't want to pay the price of a possible library call or even an inlined conditional statement. We chose to precompute the corresponding uppercase value of each possible character:

```
void initLookupTable()
{
    for (int i = 0; i < 256; i++) {
        uppercaseTable[i] = toupper(i);
        }
}
```

It doesn't matter how expensive `islower()` and `toupper()` are since the `uppercaseTable` is initialized at start-up time and performance is not an issue.

Now we can uppercase a character consuming two instructions only. This significantly speeds up our string manipulation:

```
for (char *p = header; *p ; p++) {
    *p = uppercaseTable[*p];
    }
if (0 == memcmp(header, "ACCEPT:", 7)) {
    ...
    }
```

While we were at it, we precomputed a table lookup of other character functions that were required in the performance critical path: `islower()`, `isspace()`, `isdigit()`, and others.

Reduce Flexibility

As a domain expert you are often in position to make simplifying assumptions that boost performance.

Often, a Web server needs to know the IP address of the client where the request originated. An IP address is a dotted decimal expression like 9.37.37.205. Initially, for every request, our code allocated heap storage large enough to hold the client IP address. That storage was deallocated at the end of the request handling. Calling `new()` and `delete()` for heap memory is expensive. This is particularly bad since you do it for every request. Using memory pools can alleviate the burden, but it is still not as good as eliminating the `new()` and `delete()` calls altogether.

If an IP address was potentially unbounded in length, we would have had no choice but to allocate memory on-the-fly. However, we are TCP/IP domain experts, and we know that currently an IP address cannot be longer than 15 bytes. The longest address would be

```
xxx.xxx.xxx.xxx
```

If you add a terminating NULL, you get 16 bytes. The next generation IP address (IPv6) will be longer, but still bounded. Since the string length is bounded, it is more efficient to store the IP address on the stack as a local variable:

```
char clientIPAddr[256];
```

This is good enough for our domain for many years to come. Although 32 bytes would be more than enough, we chose 256 to be on the safe side. This bounded character array eliminates expensive calls to both `new()` and `delete()`. We traded flexibility that we never needed for higher performance.

80-20 Rule: Speed Up the Common Path

The 80-20 rule has many applications: 80% of the execution scenarios will traverse only 20% of your source code, and 80% of the elapsed time will be spent in 20% of the functions encountered on the execution path. The 80-20 rule is the dominating force driving the argument that premature tuning is a sin. If you randomly tune everything you can think of, not only do you waste 80% of the effort, you will also hack the design beyond repair.

The HTTP specification is a 100-page document that describes all possible HTTP requests that a Web server must handle. Most of the HTTP requests that traverse the Web these days are very simple. They contain only a small subset of the possible HTTP headers that a request could potentially contain. Finding out what these typical request headers look like is fairly simple: Since Microsoft and Netscape have a dominating share of the browser market, all you need to do is peek at the request headers sent by these two browsers. This is yet another manifestation of the 80-20 rule—20% of your possible inputs will occur 80% of the time.

HTTP request headers determine the request type and will often traverse separate execution paths. An efficient use of programmer resources is to tune those 20% of the request types that appear 80% of the time.

There's another point to the 80-20 idea. Not only do you need to focus on the typical execution path, you should take advantage of the fact that most of your input data is going to come from a narrow range of the whole input space. Some examples follow.

The HTTP `Accept` header is part of an HTTP request. It specifies what document formats are acceptable to the browser. The HTTP specification allows for the `Accept` header to have any combination of upper- and lowercase. When you read a string token and want to determine if it is the `Accept` header, it is not enough to perform

```
memcmp("Accept:", header, 7)
```

We need to perform a case-sensitive string compare. We implemented a home-grown version for a case-sensitive string-compare:

```
int memCaseCmp(char*,char*, int) {...}
```

To be HTTP compliant, the correct action should be

```
if ( 0 == memCaseCmp("accept:", header, 7) ) {
   // This is the Accept header
   }
```

However, `memCaseCmp()` is not cheap. It needs to uppercase both strings and then call `memcmp()`. This is where our domain expertise must come into play. Like we said, Microsoft and Netscape have a commanding share of the browser market. The `Accept` header they send happens to be `"Accept:"`. This is only one of the many upper- and lowercase combination that HTTP allows, but it is the one we are going to receive 95% of the time, so it is the one we care about. The following test tries to take advantage of that:

```
if ( (0 == memcmp("Accept:", header,7)) ||    // An intelligent
                                               // gamble...
     (0 == memCaseCmp("accept:", header, 7)))  {

   // This is the Accept header
   }
```

In 95% of the inputs, the `memcmp()` test is going to succeed, and we will never call the more expensive `memCaseCmp()`.

The last code sample leads us right into another 80-20 issue of evaluation order. It is often the case that conditional expressions are built as a logical combination of sub-expressions. When we examine expressions of the form

```
if (e1 || e2) {...}
```

or

```
if (e1 && e2) {...}
```

the order of evaluation has performance implications. Take the former `if` statement as an example:

```
if (e1 || e2) {...}
```

If (e1 || e2) evaluates to FALSE, we lose. Both subexpressions, e1 and e2, must be evaluated. However, in the case where (e1 || e2) is TRUE, if e1 is TRUE, e2 will not be evaluated and the overall cost of the expression is reduced. In the following discussion, we narrow our attention to the case where (e1 || e2) is TRUE.

If e1 and e2 are equally likely to evaluate to TRUE, then the subexpression with the smaller computational cost should be placed first in the evaluation order. If, on the other hand, e1 and e2 are of equal computational cost, then the one most likely to evaluate to TRUE should appear first. In a more general situation, let

> p1 = The conditional probability that e1 is TRUE given that (e1 || e2) is TRUE.
>
> c1 = The computational cost of evaluating e1.

We are trying to minimize the expected cost of computing (e1 || e2):

cost = C1+(1-p1)*C2

Our example only dealt with two subexpressions, but this easily extends to any number of subexpressions in a logical OR expression.

Previously we encountered a conditional statement checking for an `Accept` HTTP header:

```
if ( (0 == memcmp("Accept:", str,7)) ||
     (0 == memCaseCmp("accept:", str, 7)))  {

   // This is the Accept header
   }
```

In this case,

$$e1 \text{ is } (0 == \text{memcmp("Accept:", str, 7)})$$

$$e2 \text{ is } (0 == \text{memCaseCmp("accept:", str, 7)})$$

In the case where the `if` statement is TRUE, `e2` will evaluate to TRUE 100% of the time since it is a case-sensitive string compare. So $p_2 = 1.0$. The subexpression `e1` will evaluate to TRUE only 90% of the time. So $p_1 = 0.9$. The computational cost is roughly given by:

$$c_1 = 10 \text{ instructions}$$

$$c_2 = 100 \text{ instructions}$$

Our expected cost is

$$\text{cost} = 10 + 0.1 * 100 = 20$$

If we flipped the order of `e1` and `e2`, our expected cost would be

$$\text{cost} = c_2 + (1 - p_2) * c_1 = 100 + 0 * 10 = 100$$

Therefore,

```
if (e1 || e2)
```

is a better choice than

```
if (e2 || e1)
```

There's similar logic for logical AND expressions like

```
if (e1 && e2)
```

Given the case where the whole expression evaluates to FALSE, we would like it to fail as early as possible without having to evaluate all subexpressions. The definition of the probability in this case is slightly different:

> p1 = The conditional probability that e1 is FALSE given that (e1 && e2) is FALSE.

You can easily encounter such decisions in practice; for example, when the specifications require an implementation to check and handle some rare combination of events like:

```
if ( rareCondition_1() && rareCondition_2() ) {
  // Handle it
  }
```

Since this combination is rare, this condition will fail most of the time. We'd like for it to fail quickly on the first subexpression. This is, by the way, the reason why HTTP 1.1-compliant servers are somewhat slower than HTTP 1.0 implementations. The HTTP 1.1 specifications are much more complex, and force the server to perform many checks for all kinds of esoteric scenarios that rarely happen. But you still have to perform the test to be HTTP 1.1-compliant. For example, an HTTP 1.1-compliant browser may ask for a portion of a large document instead of the complete document. In practice, the browsers ask for complete documents in the vast majority of requests. The server, however, must still check for a partial document request and handle it properly.

Lazy Evaluation

Paying a performance penalty for a computation you ultimately may not need is a bad idea. It happens way too often in complex code. You should not perform costly computations "just in case." Costly computations should be performed only if necessary. That often means deferring computations until they are actually needed, hence the name Lazy Evaluation [Mey96, ES90].

Back in the days of pure C programming we were in the habit of defining all of our variables up front, at the beginning of each routine. In C++, object definitions trigger constructors and destructors and that may be expensive. It leads to eager evaluation—

something we want to avoid. The Lazy Evaluation principle suggests that we ought to delay object definition to the scope where it is being used. There is no sense paying for object construction and destruction if we are not going to use it. This sounds silly, but it happens in practice.

In a C++ gateway application we had a performance-critical piece of code that ran in the AIX kernel. That code routed messages between downstream and upstream communication adapters. One of the objects we used was very expensive to construct and destroy:

```
int route(Message *msg)
{
    ExpensiveClass upstream(msg);

    if (goingUpstream) {
        ...    // do something with the expensive object
        }

    // upstream object not used here.

    return SUCCESS;
}
```

The `upstream` object was very expensive. In the original code it was eagerly constructed at the top of the function. It was used only half the time when a message was routed upstream. The `upstream` object was not used at all when a message was routed downstream (50% of the time). In the event of a downstream message, the evaluation of the `upstream` object was pure waste. A better solution would define the expensive `upstream` object in the scope where it is actually necessary:

```
int route(Message *msg)
{

    if (goingUpstream) {
        ExpensiveClass upstream(msg);

        // do something with the expensive object
        }

    // upstream object not used here.

    return SUCCESS;
}
```

In item 32 of [Mey97] Meyers makes another important observation on Lazy Evaluation. Not only should you defer object creation to the correct scope, you should also delay that construction until you have all the necessary ingredients for an efficient construction. For example:

```
void f()
{
    string s;              // 1
    ...
    char *p = "Message";   // 2
    ...
    s = p;                 // 3
    ...
}
```

In statement 1, we construct the `String` object `s` using the default `String::String()` constructor. Later, in statement 3, we pour some real content into `s`. Object `s` is really not complete until statement 3 has been performed. As such, this is an inefficient construction. It entails

- The default `string` constructor, statement 1

- The assignment operator, statement 3.

The Lazy Evaluation principle can reduce this to a single constructor call. We do that by deferring construction of `string s` until we have the necessary parts:

```
void f()
{
    char *p = "Message";
    string s(p);           // invoke String::String(char*)
    ...
}
```

By deferring the creation of `s` we managed a single-step construction—definitely more efficient.

Useless Computations

Lazy Evaluation is about computations that are not always necessary, depending on execution flow. Useless computations are about those computations that are never necessary. These are entirely pointless computations whose results are never used regardless of execution flow.

A subtle example of a useless computation is the wasted initialization of a member object.

```
class Student {
public:
    Student(char *nm);
        ...
private:
    string name;
};
```

The Student constructor turns the input character pointer into a string object representing the student's name:

```
Student::Student(char *nm)
{
    name = nm;
    ...
}
```

C++ guarantees that all member objects have already been constructed before the body of the Student constructor is executed. In our case it is the string name object. Since we did not tell the compiler explicitly how to do this, it silently inserts a call to the string default constructor. That call is invoked prior to executing the body of the Student constructor. The constructor body follows with an invocation of:

```
name = nm;
```

which essentially wipes away the previous contents of the name object. We never used the results of the compiler-generated call to the string default constructor. We can eliminate this pointless computation by specifying an explicit string constructor on the Student constructor initialization list:

```
Student::Student(char *nm) : name(nm) // explicit string constructor
{
    ...
}
```

Since we explicitly told the compiler what string constructor to use, the compiler does not generate the hidden call to the string default constructor [Mey97]. Thus, we have achieved a single-step creation of the member string object.

System Architecture

The cost of memory access is far from being uniform. On one particular RISC architecture, data access takes one CPU cycle if it resides in the data cache, 8 cycles if the data resides in main memory (cache miss), and 400,000 cycles if the data is on disk (page fault). Although the exact number of cycles may vary, the general picture is the same across processor architectures: The speed difference between a cache hit, cache miss, and page fault is measured in orders of magnitude.

The data cache is the first place that is searched when data is accessed. If the data is not in the cache, a cache miss is generated by the hardware. The cache miss results in this data being loaded from RAM or disk into the cache. The cache is loaded in units of cache lines that are typically larger then the size of the specific data item we are after. A cache miss on a 4-byte integer may result in a cache line of 128 bytes loaded into cache. That's helpful because related data items tend to lie in close proximity in memory. If a subsequent instruction tries to access another data item on the same cache line, we will benefit from a cache hit the very first time we ask for that data. In as much as we can, we ought to help our code exhibit such locality of reference.

Take the class X for example:

```
class X {
public:
    X() : a(1), c(2) {}
    ...
private:
    int a;
    char b[4096]; // buffer
    int c;
};
```

The X::X() constructor initializes members a and c. A standard-conforming compiler will lay out object X in the declaration order: members a and c will be separated by 4096 bytes of member b, and will not reside on the same cache line. The X::X() constructor is likely to suffer a cache miss when it accesses c.

Since a and c are accessed by neighboring instructions, we could be more cache-friendly by placing them next to one another:

```
class X {
    ...
private:
    int a;
    int c;
    char b[4096]; // buffer
};
```

a and c are more likely now to reside on the same cache line. Since a is accessed prior to c, c is almost guaranteed to reside in the data cache when we need it.

Memory Management

Allocating and deallocating heap memory on the fly is expensive. From a performance perspective, it is cheaper to work with memory that does not necessitate explicit management. An object defined as a local variable resides on the stack. Stack memory occupied by this object is part of the stack memory set aside for the function in whose scope the object is defined. The alternative to a local object is using new( ) and delete( ) to acquire and release heap memory:

```
void f()
{
    X *xPtr = new X;
    ...
    delete xPtr;
}
```

A better performance choice would be to define a local object of type X:

```
void f()
{
    X x;
    ...
} // no need to delete x.
```

In the latter implementation, object x is on the stack. There's no need to allocate it up front, or to deallocate it upon exit. The stack memory is reclaimed automatically when f( ) returns. We have saved the nontrivial cost of calling new( ) and delete( ).

A similar issue exists with member data. This time it is not heap vs stack memory; it is the choice of embedding a pointer or a whole object in a containing object:

```
class Z {
public:
    Z() : xPtr (new X) { ... }
    ~Z() {delete xPtr; ... }

 private:
    X *xPtr;
        ...
};
```

The cost of a Z object is significantly increased by the overhead of calling new() in the constructor and delete() in the destructor. We could eliminate the cost of memory management by embedding the X object within Z:

```
class Z {
public:
    Z() { ... }
    ~Z() { ... }

private:
    X x;
        ...
};
```

By replacing an X pointer with an X object, we have traded away the option of using this member polymorphically. If you really need that flexibility then this optimization is not available to you. Once again, performance is about trade-offs.

Library and System Calls

The evolution of computer languages steadily has simplified the task of designing and coding solutions to complex problems. As languages moved forward in expressive power, we used them to tackle problems of higher complexity. Theoretically, a Turing Machine with its primitive syntax is as powerful as any programming language we have today. By powerful we mean you can code any algorithm using a Turing Machine. It is just a very difficult environment in which to program. The same goes for assembly language. The reason we don't develop Web servers in assembly is of a practical nature: It is too difficult and time-consuming to develop software solutions to complex problems using low-level languages.

If we want to add two integers, it is very simple in a language such as C++:

```
k = i + j;
```

If we tried it in assembly language, there would be minute details we would have to handle ourselves:

- Load integer i to register X
- Load integer j to register Y.
- Add contents of registers X and Y.
- Store the result in memory address of integer k

In a higher level language, all those little details are handled by the compiler, and we normally ignore it. This simplicity leads to higher productivity and the ability to take on programming tasks of higher complexity.

There are several ways to hide complexity: We can hide it in hardware and in software. Software hiding is accomplished by the compiler transforming our source code to assembly instructions. We could also perform it ourselves: We can encapsulate complexity away in system calls, libraries, and class implementations.

Take the case of concatenating two strings. We need to allocate memory large enough to contain both strings plus a terminating null:

```
{
    char s0;
    char *s1 = "Hello";
    char *s2 = "World";

    s0 = (char *) malloc ( strlen(s1) + strlen(s2) + 1 );
    strcpy(s0,s1);   // Copy first string
    strcat(s0,s2);   // Concatenate the second
    ...
}
```

In C++, all these details are encapsulated in a `string` class implementation. The overloaded "+" operator for `string` would simplify our client code to this:

```
{
    string s1 = "Hello";
    string s2 = "World";

    string s0 = s1 + s2;
    ...
}
```

As we move to higher levels of programming simplicity, the detailed work does not vanish; it is done elsewhere. From a performance standpoint we cannot ignore the work that is done under the covers. That's where the performance engineer differs from the rest of the developers, whose only concern is to put together the necessary functionality rapidly and ship it. The performance developer must be aware of hidden costs as they may have a profound impact on system performance.

For concrete examples we peek into the implementation of the `pthreads` library. This library provides the user with a simple interface to thread services on UNIX platforms. The `pthread_mutex_lock()` and `pthread_mutex_unlock()` calls provide mutual exclusion. If you lock a resource, you have exclusive access to it until you unlock it. What you don't see is that the `pthreads` library implementation checks that your thread does not already own the lock when `pthread_mutex_lock()` is called. That prevents deadlocks. When you call `pthread_mutex_unlock()` a check is performed to see that the caller actually holds the lock. A thread cannot unlock a resource unless it is the one that locked it previously. All these necessary error checks increase the pathlength of execution and slow down performance.

In many situations, your application's use of locks may be simple enough, where all this overhead is a waste. The design of your code may already guarantee the preconditions: that the locking thread does not presently hold the lock and that the unlocking thread is the one that has it locked. In that case, you can build a simple locking scheme that builds upon primitive building blocks supplied by the native operating system. That will be significantly more efficient. If you are not aware of the details of a library implementation, you may not know that you are paying a performance cost for functionality you don't really need.

We stay in the realm of the `pthreads` library for a related example. You can associate each thread with a private data area where thread globals may be stored [NBF96]. If you need access to thread private data you need a pointer to that thread-specific area in memory. You can get that pointer by calling `pthread_getspecific()`. The `pthreads` library performs this magic by keeping an association between current threads and their private data. Since threads can come and go, this association is dynamic. Access to this collection must be serialized. As a result, a call to `pthread_getspecific()` hides an internal serialization code. We must lock the collection while retrieving the data associated with the given thread. This is something you may need to know if you are concerned with scalability. If multiple threads perform frequent calls to `pthread_getspecific()`, the serialization logic will cause a scalability logjam as the threads lock each other out.

Once you are aware of the internals of `pthread_getspecific()` you may opt to use other methods to pass thread-specific data around. Instead of making a data item a thread global, you could just pass it around as a function call parameter. If you truly need frequent access to thread global variables, you could perform the `pthread_getspecific()` call once and then pass the pointer around as a function call parameter.

Compiler Optimization

There are quite a few important optimizations that a decent compiler can apply on your behalf without requiring any source code intervention on your part. The first optimization that comes to mind is register allocation. Loading and storing a variable is fastest when that variable resides in a register. Otherwise, we are going to have to spend a few cycles fetching this variable from elsewhere. If an update is performed, we will also need to store it back where it came from. In that case, it gets even worse if the variable is not in the cache. A single memory access on modern architecture is upwards of five cycles. All this is avoided if the variable resides in a register. Register allocation is an important optimization because its application is available on many of the methods along the execution path. This is particularly significant when it comes to loop index variables. Those variables are accessed and updated at every iteration of the loop.

A second dominant optimization that we strongly care about is inlining. Chapters 8, 9, and 10 already stressed the point that inlining could significantly help performance of many C++ applications. Another optimization of interest to C++ programmers is the return value optimization discussed in Chapter 4. The list goes on. For a more exhaustive enumeration of various compiler optimizations see [O98]. The point we are trying to make is not necessarily to list all possible optimizations but to raise awareness to the fact that you cannot take them for granted.

It is often the case that by default the compiler does not perform any optimization at all. That means that these important speed optimizations will not take place—not even if you place the `register` and `inline` keywords in your code. The compiler is free to ignore them, and it often does. To enhance your chance at those optimizations you have to turn on compiler optimization manually by adding a switch to the command line (-O on UNIX flavors) or selecting the speed optimization option on your GUI interface.

It's hard to quantify the effect of compiler optimizations precisely since it varies from one application to another. In our experience we have seen a 20–40% speedup on various applications. This is significant "low hanging fruit."

Key Points

Coding optimizations are local in scope and do not necessitate understanding of overall program design. This is a good place to start when you join an ongoing project whose design you don't yet understand.

The fastest code is the one that's never executed. Try the following to bail out of a costly computation:

- Are you ever going to use the result? It sounds silly, but it happens. At times we perform computation and never use the results.

- Do you need the results now? Defer a computation to the point where it is actually needed. Premature computations may never be used on some execution flows.

- Do you know the result already? We have seen costly computations performed even though their results were available two lines above. If you already computed it earlier in the execution flow, make the result available for reuse.

Sometimes you cannot bail out, and you just have to perform the computation. The challenge now is to speed it up:

- Is the computation overly generic? You only need to be as flexible as the domain requires, not more. Take advantage of simplifying assumptions. Reduced flexibility increases speed.

- Some flexibility is hidden in library calls. You may gain speed by rolling your own version of specific library calls that are called often enough to justify the effort. Familiarize yourself with the hidden cost of those library and system calls that you use.

- Minimize memory management calls. They are relatively expensive on most compilers.

- If you consider the set of all possible input data, 20% of it shows up 80% of the time. Speed up the processing of typical input at the expense of other scenarios.

- The speed differential among cache, RAM, and disk access is significant. Write cache-friendly code.

14

Design Optimizations

Performance optimizations can roughly be divided into two major categories: coding and design. We define a coding optimization as one that does not necessitate overall understanding of the problem domain or the application's execution flow. Coding optimizations are by definition localized and well isolated from the surrounding code. Design optimizations are what's left, everything but the "low hanging fruit." These optimizations are systemic—they have dependencies on other components and remote parts of the code. A design optimization will often leave its fingerprints throughout the code. This is not exactly a precise mathematical definition, and some optimizations will fall in the gray area created by this imprecise definition. The overall idea should become clearer with the examples provided in this chapter.

Design Flexibility

In the last ten years we have encountered quite a few C++ projects that fell far short of their required performance. At the heart of those performance failures was a design and an implementation geared for extreme flexibility and reusability. The obsession with reusable code has produced software that, due to the lack of efficiency, was not even usable, not to mention reusable. C++ ushered OO programming into the mainstream and paved the way for the enthusiastic adoption of OO by the wide programming community. The OO education machinery has transformed C programmers into a new generation whose main focus was the creation of generic, flexible, and reusable software. The problem is that performance and flexibility are often enemies. It is not an artifact of poor design or of implementation. We are talking about a fundamental tension between two forces that are pushing in opposite directions. In mathematics, if the product of X*Y is a constant, then as X becomes larger, Y must become smaller. Period. Generally speaking, there's a similar relationship between performance and flexibility.

If you try making the counterpoint that performance and flexibility could actually coexist in peace, you'd probably throw in the STL (Standard Template Library) as evidence. The STL is powerful, generic, flexible, and extendible. The STL, in some cases, generates code whose performance can rival that of hand-coded C. It seems to defeat our proposition. Let's take a closer look.

Take the STL's `accumulate()` template function; it is capable of adding an arbitrary collection of objects. It takes three parameters:

- An iterator pointing to the start of the collection
- An iterator indicating the end of the collection
- An initial value

The `accumulate()` function will iterate from start to finish adding objects to its initial value. It is capable of adding a diverse set of objects: integers, floats, characters, strings, and even user-defined types. It does not care if the collection is an array, list, vector, or any other collection. All it cares about is that you pass in the two required iterators to control the start and finish of the iteration. Furthermore, `accumulate()` is also capable of performing other binary operations, not just additions. You can specify the binary operator as an optional argument.

Obviously, this is a fine piece of code. It is highly flexible and generic. At times, `accumulate()` will even exhibit superb performance. It can add an array of integers such as

```
sum = accumulate(&x[0], &x[100], 0);
```

just as fast as your home-grown version:

```
int sum = 0;
for (int i = 0; i < 100; i++) {
    sum += x[i];
    }
```

This is pretty good. The implementation of the `accumulate()` function is something along the lines of [MS96]:

```
template <class InputIterator, class T>
T accumulate(InputIterator first,
             InputIterator beyondLast,
             T initialValue)
{
    while (first != beyondLast) {
        initialValue = initialValue + *first++;
        }
}
```

The strength of the `accumulate()` implementation stems from the fact that it makes very few assumptions about the collection and the objects contained in it. It knows only two things:

- Starting from the `first` iterator, it will advance sequentially, eventually running into the `beyondLast` iterator.

- The objects contained in the collection are acceptable arguments to the + operator.

These two minimal assumptions allow `accumulate()` its extreme flexibility. They could also become its performance weakness. Those assumptions may suffice for high-performance integer addition, but other classes with richer structure will have to forgo the benefit of their class-specific knowledge. Take `string` for example. Suppose you wanted to concatenate a collection of strings such as:

```
vector<string> vectorx;

for (i = 0; i < 100; i++) {
    vectorx.push_back("abcd");
    }
```

Using `accumulate()` should be your first choice. You don't want to reinvent the wheel unless you have a compelling reason to do so:

```
string empty;     // initial value for result string.

result = accumulate(vectorx.begin(), vectorx.end(), empty);
```

This would do it, but how fast is it? We timed 100,000 iterations of this code as follows:

```
string empty;     // initial value for result string.

for (i = 0; i < 100000; i++) {
    result = accumulate(vectorx.begin(), vectorx.end(), empty);
    }
```

This code snippet elapsed in 29 seconds. Can we beat the STL by crafting a home-grown solution? We tried the following:

```
void stringSum1(vector<string> vs, string& result)
{
    int i=0;
    int totalInputLength = 0;
    int vectorSize = vs.size();
    int *stringSizes = new int[vectorSize];

    for (i = 0; i < vectorSize; i++) {
        stringSizes[i] = vs[i].length();
        totalInputLength += stringSizes[i];
        }

    char* s = new char [totalInputLength+1];

    int sp = 0;
    for (i = 0; i < vectorSize; i++) {
        memcpy(&s[sp], vs[i].c_str(), stringSizes[i]);
        sp += stringSizes[i];
        }

    delete stringSizes;
    result = s;

    return;
}
```

We timed this solution as well:

```
string result;   // initial value for result string.

for (i = 0; i < 100000; i++) {
    stringSum1(vectorx, result);
    }
```

Our home-grown solution was much faster—only five seconds. We got better than a 5x speedup. We have beaten accumulate() by a wide margin because we chose to sacrifice generality for improved performance. Our stringSum1() implementation makes the following string-specific assumptions:

- We know that the only objects we are adding here are strings.

- We know that `string` additions will require memory allocations to contain the evolving `string` result.

- We know that each `string` object can tell us what size it is by invoking `string::length()`.

We use these assumptions to figure out in advance how big the result `string` is going to be. We use that knowledge to allocate, in a single step, a memory buffer large enough to contain it. This is the primary reason why our implementation is so much faster than `accumulate()`. The `accumulate()` function has to make multiple calls to allocate additional memory buffers on-the-fly. It does not know in advance how big a buffer it really needs. Worse yet, every time `accumulate()` runs out of buffer space, it needs to copy the content of the old buffer to the newly acquired larger one.

This is a good example of how reduction in flexibility leads to increased efficiency. Our `stringSum1()` is nowhere near the flexibility and power of `accumulate()`. We cannot add anything other than `string` objects. This is the difference between a 60W lightbulb and a laser beam. The laser beam does not pack more energy than a lightbulb—it is just a narrowly focused light beam. Although we cannot use a laser beam to illuminate the room, we could use it to drill a hole in a brick wall.

Our purpose is not to criticize the STL. Far from it. You should only consider replacement of STL code on performance hot spots. Since these hot spots are hard to predict, you should use the STL, by default, everywhere in the early phases of software development. The point of this discussion is to highlight a principle that has been pushed aside in the mad dash to create reusable software: There is a fundamental trade-off between software performance and flexibility. Special circumstances and simplifying assumptions are commonplace in typical applications. Software libraries are general-purpose, but applications are not. The ability to narrow the focus of a code fragment leads to higher efficiency.

Caching

We have discussed caching optimizations in Chapter 13 with respect to coding. But caching opportunities are abundant in the design arena as well. In this section we describe three design optimizations representing this set.

Web Server Timestamps

There are multiple times during the service of an HTTP request that the server must take a timestamp to record the current time. For example, right after a TCP connection is established between the server and browser, the server starts a timer for this particular connection. If the timer pops before the request has arrived on the connection, the connection is terminated. These time-outs prevent attackers from flooding the server with connections that never submit any request. These dead connections tie up server resources (such as threads) and hang the server. Server termination of dead connections is designed specifically to address this type of attack on the server.

A Web server also generates a log entry for every request. It is very useful to know how popular your site is, who is visiting it, and what particular information on your site is in hot demand. The request log contains a timestamp indicating when the request was serviced.

The last time we counted, each request handling triggered seven timestamps. Since the life of a request lasts only a few milliseconds, and the necessary timing granularity is measured in seconds, it would be more efficient to generate a single timestamp per request and reuse it. On some platforms, timestamp generation is expensive. On one particular platform the computational cost of a typical request was 120,000 instructions. Each timestamp call cost 1,500 instructions, and the seven calls we had totalled about 10,500 instructions. By caching the result of the first timestamp, we eliminated six timestamp computations and saved 9,000 instructions. That's roughly 8% improvement in the speed of request handling.

We stashed away the result of the first timestamp computation, and passed it along to the other six functions as a function call argument. This is an example of caching a result on the call stack. This particular value was never stored in memory.

Data Expansion

There are many different ways to cache previous results. One of them is in the object itself as a data member. If you find yourself using an object over and over to derive a related result, it may be better to stash that result as an object data member and reuse it in future computations.

A web server spends a significant amount of time manipulating character strings. It is often the case that we compute the length of the same string multiple times as the string travels through the code. In a naive `string` class implementation, you'll find yourselves doing redundant `strlen()` calls:

```
class string {
public:
    ...
    int length() const {return strlen(str);}
private:
    char *str;
};
```

It would be more efficient to add a data member that stores the string length:

```
class string {
public:
    ...
    int length() const {return strLen;}
private:
    char *str;
    int    strLen;
};
```

The member `strLen` is computed when the `string` object is created or modified. Subsequent calls to compute the length of the string will return the already computed length and avoid a costly `strlen()` call.

There's another advantage to remembering the length of a string: The family of `mem*()` calls (`memcpy()`, `memcmp()`, etc.) is more efficient than the `str*()` family (`strcpy()`, `strcmp()`, etc.). The added efficiency of the `mem*()` family stems from the fact that those functions don't have to inspect every byte for a possible null termination. The `mem*()` family requires the length of the string as a parameter. If you stash away the length of the `string` object, you'll be able to use the `mem*()` family of calls to achieve higher efficiency.

The Common Code Trap

Typical Web server implementations provide support for multiple closely related protocols. Most implementations support both HTTP as well as SSL. (Secure Socket Layer provides a secure connection for Web documents. It is essentially a secure, encrypted HTTP.) Naturally, most of the code that implements Web connections is common between HTTP and SSL. This is great for reuse but care must be taken to protect performance. In an early implementation of our Web server, we maximized reuse and paid a performance penalty. There were many decision points along the execution path of request handling where the SSL code branched off the HTTP code. Every such branch point necessitated a conditional statement of the form

```
bool HTHandle(StreamSocket& mySocket)
{
    ...
    if (mySocket->SSL()) {
        requestHandler->perform_the_SSL_action();
        }
    else {
        requestHandler->perform_the_HTTP_action();
        }
    ...
}
```

This repeated computation was a burden on execution speed. If we performed this check 20 times in the life of a request, that's 19 too many. The caller of HTHandle() already knew the request type (SSL or HTTP), and we failed to hold on to this knowledge and reuse it.

Since most of those checks were clustered in a small number of routines, one possible approach to resolve this redundancy was to duplicate each routine: say, split the routine HTHandle() into HTHandle_HTTP() and HTHandle_SSL(). Now each routine "knows" what type of connection it is dealing with and can avoid the HTTP/ SSL decision.

A better solution is to derive an SSLRequestHandler and HTTPRequestHandler from a base RequestHandler class. Now HTHandle() becomes a virtual function and the HTTP/SSL decision is resolved once via virtual function resolution. The code simply calls

```
RequestHandler->HTHandle(mySocket)
```

and HTHandle() will be resolved to the correct routine. The advantage of the virtual call solution is that it takes a single decision point to separate SSL from HTTP. That's more efficient than revisiting this decision multiple times inside of a combined SSL/HTTP HTHandle() implementation.

Actually, our server implementation was even more complex than this description. Our server was not only an HTTP and SSL server, it was also a proxy server and an FTP server. It is a real design challenge to avoid having to make the HTTP/SSL/FTP/proxy decision over and over, hundreds of times.

A similar issue exists with current TCP/IP implementations. The current dominating IP implementation is Version 4. The emerging next generation IP implementation is Version 6, also known as IPNG (IP Next Generation). In recent years, TCP/IP vendors have rushed to add V6 support to their existing V4 TCP/IP implementations. Since both V4 and V6 are closely related, they will execute lots of common code. It is probably very tempting to use a single V4 base code with V6 branches where necessary. This will produce code littered with conditional statements of the form:

```
if (V4) {
    do_one_thing();
    }
else { // V6
    do_something_else();
    }
```

With such implementation, the performance of bothV4 and V6 will be slightly degraded. A more efficient design is necessary to eliminate those multiple decision points. Once the execution flow determines whether it is V4 or V6, it should retain this knowledge and reuse it.

Efficient Data Structures

Software performance is often equated with the efficiency of the algorithms and data structures used by the implementation. It is sometimes suggested that algorithm and data structure efficiency is the most important factor in software performance. Whether it is or it isn't, there is no question that the use of efficient algorithms is a necessary condition for software efficiency. No amount of microtuning will help if you choose inefficient algorithms. You can stuff all variables into registers, inline every function, and unroll every loop. Still, your bubble-sort program is not going to be anywhere near as fast as a sloppy implementation of quick-sort.

A detailed discussion of this important topic is beyond the scope of this book. Efficient algorithms and data structures have been the focus of intense research, and many books have been dedicated entirely to this subject [AHU74, Knu73].

As important as they are, efficient algorithms are necessary but not sufficient to guarantee application efficiency. It is our experience that software performance is a combination of several necessary factors. You cannot single out any one of them as the most important one. The human heart is definitely an important organ, but you also need a liver to survive. Focusing on algorithms as the only performance issue is just plain wrong.

Lazy Evaluation

Many performance optimizations gain speed by taking a computation and performing it in a more efficient manner. Some of the big performance wins in the optimization game are achieved not by merely speeding up a computation but by eliminating it altogether.

Issues of lazy evaluation are more likely to present themselves on large-scale code. If you are coding a solution for, say, the Traveling Salesman Problem (TSP), the problem description fits in one paragraph and the implementation is less than 100 lines of code. The TSP problem description and implementation can fully be comprehended by a single developer. That's typical of small scale projects. In such circumstances you are highly unlikely to find costly computations that are utterly useless and which could be easily avoided. Optimizations on such small-scale code are often tricky by nature [Ben82].

When you move on to large-scale programming projects, you often find yourself swamped. Large-scale projects could contain hundreds of thousands lines of code. The problem description no longer fits in one short paragraph. It's more like the 100 pages that make up the HTTP protocol specification. The problem specification is more often then not a moving target. It changes from one release to the next, influenced by market trends and customer requirements.

The added complexity leads to a situation where no single individual in the organization has a deep and comprehensive view of the whole implementation landscape. Development organizations are split into smaller teams that specialize in particular aspects of the whole solution.

The loss of the big implementation picture leads to plenty of significant performance coding and design errors. It is in this complex environment that lazy evaluation shows up as a tuning weapon.

getpeername()

A TCP/IP socket connection is a communication pipe between remote and local sockets. `getpeername()` computes the socket IP address of the remote socket. Your application can then proceed to convert it into dotted decimal notation, such as 9.37.37.205. In a Web server, the typical log record generated per request contains the IP address of the remote client. This is very interesting information for business Web sites that are eager to know who browses their site and what are they looking for. So imagine that you are a member of the HTTP logging team and your task is to add the client IP address to the log. You need to call `getpeername()` but where exactly do you insert the call? You don't know the full blown details of the whole server implementation but you suspect that the client's IP address may come in handy in other parts of the application. It sounds like a good idea to perform the `getpeername()` at the beginning of each request, right after the `accept()` call establishes a new socket connection. If any part of the server ever needs the client's IP address, it will already be available.

A similar issue existed with `getsockname()`. Similar to `getpeername()`, `getsockname()` computes the IP address of the local socket. Why do we need the local socket address? So we can host multiple Web sites on a single physical server. When you are hosting both www.lotus.com and www.tivoli.com on the same physical server, how do you route requests to the correct site? How do you know if the request for index.html is for the Lotus site or the Tivoli site? One way to tell them apart is to host each site on a separate IP address; then you can tell Web sites apart by the IP address on which the request has arrived. That's where `getsockname()` comes in. It tells us the IP address associated with the local socket.

`getpeername()` and `getsockname()` are expensive system calls. Furthermore, if you spend some time studying the internal server design you'll find out that these calls are not always necessary. If the system administrator has chosen to turn off logging, then `getpeername()` is no longer necessary. If your server hosts only a single Web site, you may not need to call `getsockname()` either. By electing to place these calls at the start of every request, you have inflicted a performance penalty on all requests, whether they truly need those values or not.

Paying a performance penalty for a computation you ultimately may not need is a bad idea. It happens way too often in complex code. Costly computations should be performed only if necessary. That often means deferring computations until they are actually needed, hence the name Lazy Evaluation. There are plenty other examples of Lazy Evaluation aside from the ones we discussed here [Mey96, ES90].

Here's the idea. Say you have a class X containing a data member pointing to data of type Z whose computation is prohibitively expensive:

```
class X {
public:
    X();
    ~X();

    Z      *get_veryExpensive();
    void    set_veryExpensive();
private:
    Z   *veryExpensive;
    ...
};
```

If the data member veryExpensive is essential to the usage of class X objects, then it may need to be computed in the X object constructor. However, we are talking Lazy Evaluation so we assume that this is not the case here, that some manipulations of X objects make perfect sense even when veryExpensive is not available. For example, a socket is still useful even if we don't know its IP address. We can still send and receive data. In that case, the X constructor ought to set veryExpensive to some default value indicating that it has not been computed yet:

```
X::X()
{
    veryExpensive = 0; // Lazy evaluation.
    ...
}
```

If you ever need the value of veryExpensive you can call the following method:

```
Z *get_veryExpensive()
{
    if (0 == veryExpensive) {
        set_veryExpensive();  // Compute it.
        }

    return veryExpensive;
}
```

The `get_veryExpensive()` method checks first to see if the requested value has already been computed. If not, it performs the computation. In any event, you get back the requested value. This implementation guarantees that the costly computation is deferred until you explicitly request it. Now if you request it way before it is actually needed, you are on your own.

Let's step back to a more concrete example of socket addresses.

```
class StreamSocket {
public:
    StreamSocket(int listenSocket);
    ...
    struct sockaddr *get_peername();
    void            set_peername();
private:
    int              sockfd;    // Socket descriptor
    struct sockaddr  remoteSockAddr;
    struct sockaddr *peername; // Will point to remoteSockAddr
    ...
};
```

The constructor will set the peer name to a default value indicating unavailability:

```
StreamSocket::StreamSocket(int listenSock)
{
    ...
    peername = 0; // Not computed, yet.
}
```

`get_peername()` will compute the `peername` if necessary:

```
int StreamSocket::get_peername()
{
    if (0 == peername) {
        set_peername();
        }

    return peername;
}
```

Even though network programming is not our topic, we need to set the record straight on `getpeername()`. In reality, the `getpeername()` call may not be necessary at all. You may avoid the call even if you need the socket address of the remote socket.

On the server side, you must call accept(int sockfd, struct sockaddr *remoteAddr, int addrLen) to establish the connection. The accept call computes the IP address of the remote socket and stores it in its second argument: struct sockaddr *remoteAddr.

```
StreamSocket::StreamSocket(int listenSock)
{
    int addrLen;

    accept(listenSock, &remoteSockAddr, &addrLen);
    peername = &remoteSockAddr;     // Now it's available.
    ...
}
```

You must perform the accept() to create a new connection, so you might as well get the peer name right then as a free by-product of the accept() call.

Useless Computations

One programming habit you may encounter in practice is to zero out large data structures automatically. You can do that by calling calloc() to allocate a zero-filled memory block, or you can do it yourself by invoking memset(void *block, 0, int blockLen).

In the Web server we used a buffered socket object to store incoming requests:

```
class BufferedStreamSocket {
private:
    int    sockfd;              // Socket descriptor
    char   inputBuffer[4096];
    ...
};
```

The BufferedStreamSocket constructor automatically zeros out the input buffer:

```
BufferedStreamSocket::BufferedStreamSocket(...)
{
    memset(buffer,0,4096);
    ...
}
```

We are not generally opposed to the `memset()` call. It has its place. We are opposed to it only when it achieves nothing.

A close inspection of our source code revealed that nowhere did we use the fact that the input buffer was zeroed out. We never assumed it and never took advantage of it. Apparently, the buffer was `memset()` "just in case." When you read data from a socket the data is copied into a user-supplied buffer, and you also get back the number of bytes read. That's all you need. The number of bytes read tells you where the logical end of your data buffer is. This is not a null-terminated string. Since we never used it, the constructor call to `memset()` was a pure waste of time.

Examples of useless computations often look silly, and you may think that you would never do something like that. We, however, have encountered such computations on numerous occasions in practice. You are more likely to see it in complex, large-scale code.

Obsolete Code

This is another one of those tips that sounds silly but actually happens in practice quite often. We are talking about code that no longer serves a purpose but still remains on the execution path. This is not likely to happen on a school programming assignment or a small prototype. It happens on large-scale programming efforts. The requirements that drive a software implementation are a moving target, tending to evolve from one release to the next. New features are added and support for old features may be dropped. The implementation itself keeps shifting underneath your feet with bug fixes and enhancements. This constant movement of requirements and implementation creates bubbles of dead (never executed) and obsolete (executed but not necessary) code. Let's go back to the trenches of one HTTP server for a concrete example.

The initial crop of Web servers supported both HTTP and the Secure-HTTP (S-HTTP) protocols. Shortly thereafter SSL emerged as a replacement for S-HTTP. For a while we supported all three. Then, SSL took off and knocked S-HTTP into oblivion. Naturally, we followed the market trend and dropped support for S-HTTP.

In the early days of the WWW craze, product release cycles had been reduced from 1–2 years to 2–3 months. Consequently, even though S-HTTP support was disabled, nobody bothered to go and clean out the source code. S-HTTP code was all over and removing all traces of it was an error-prone, tedious, and time-consuming job. Obsolete code due to S-HTTP was taking a toll on performance in several major ways. First, there were many occurrences of data members introduced by S-HTTP into various objects. Those members were initialized and destroyed, unnecessarily consuming CPU cycles since their values were essentially dead. Moreover, there were plenty of if then else decision points to separate S-HTTP execution flow from HTTP:

```
if (/* HTTP */) {
    ...
    }
else {  /* S-HTTP */
    ...
    }
```

Those extraneous branch points hurt performance by adding cycles as well as introducing bubbles into the processor's instruction pipeline.

Other minor damages inflicted by obsolete code are increased executable size, memory footprint, and source code. Source code that contains obsolete and dead code is harder to understand, maintain, and extend. For all those reasons, removing dead and obsolete code is highly recommended as routine source code maintenance.

Key Points

- A fundamental tension exists between software performance and flexibility. On the 20% of your software that executes 80% of the time, performance often comes first at the expense of flexibility.

- Caching opportunities may surface in the overall program design as well as in the minute coding details. You can often avoid big blobs of computation by simply stashing away the result of previous computations.

- The use of efficient algorithms and data structures is a necessary but not sufficient condition for software efficiency.

- Some computations may be necessary only on a subset of the overall likely execution scenarios. Those computations should be deferred to those execution paths that must have them. If a computation is performed prematurely, its result may go unused.

- Large-scale software often tends towards chaos. One by-product of chaotic software is the execution of obsolete code: code that once upon a time served a purpose but no longer does. Periodic purges of obsolete code and other useless computations will boost performance as well as overall software hygiene.

15

Scalability

Faced with the task of speeding up a C++ application, you generally have the following options:

- Tune your application. Reduce the application's pathlength by optimizing the code. This has been the focus of our discussion up to this point, speeding up a single thread of execution on a uniprocessor (single CPU) machine.

- Upgrade processing speed. A faster CPU should result in faster execution for CPU-bound workloads.

- Add processors. A multiprocessor machine consists of multiple CPUs. In theory, multiple CPUs should outperform a single CPU of identical speed. This is what scalability is all about.

The scalability challenge facing an application code is to keep up with the additional processing power. When you move an application from a uniprocessor to a 2-way multiprocessor, it would be nice if you could double execution speed. Would your application run four times as fast on a 4-way multiprocessor? eight times as fast on an 8-way multiprocessor? This is the scalability challenge. Most applications will not exhibit such perfect linear scaling, but the goal is to get as close as you can.

To understand the software performance issues on a multiprocessor, we have to establish a rudimentary grasp of the underlying architecture. Since multiprocessors evolved out of uniprocessors, let's step back and start with the world's quickest overview of the uniprocessor computer architecture. The mainstream uniprocessor architecture consists of a single CPU and a single main memory module. Program data and instructions reside in main memory. Since CPU speed is at least an order of magnitude faster than memory, we also have an additional (very) fast memory inserted between the processor (= CPU) and main memory. This fast memory is also known as the cache. The cache provides faster access to program data and instructions. The cache may be split into two physical units, one for data and another for instructions. We'll ignore that distinction and refer to it as a single logical entity. The processor needs at least one memory access per instruction in order to retrieve the instruction itself. On most instructions it may need additional memory references for data. When the processor needs memory access, it looks in the cache first. Since cache hit-ratios are upwards of 90%, slow trips to main memory are infrequent. This whole story is summarized in Figure 15.1.

An application is a single process or a set of cooperating processes. Each process consists of one or more threads. The scheduling entity on modern operating systems is a thread. The operating system does not execute a process, it executes a thread. Threads that are ready to execute are placed on the system's Run Queue. The thread on top of the queue is next in line for execution (Figure 15.2).

Modern uniprocessor machines are controlled by preemptive multitasking operating systems. An operating system of that type creates the illusion of concurrent program execution. From the user's point of view, it seems like multiple programs are executing simultaneously. As you know, this is not the case. At the hardware level, there's

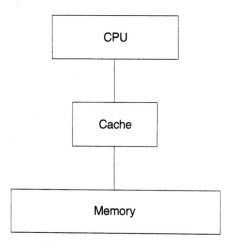

Figure 15.1. Single processor architecture.

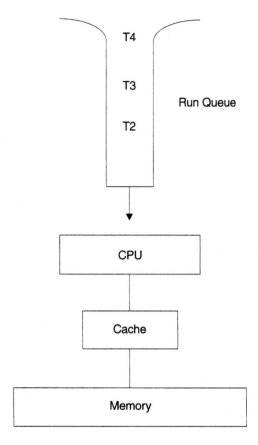

Figure 15.2. Threads are the scheduling entities.

only one CPU and only one thread of execution at any one time. Multitasking on a uniprocessor is accomplished by having threads take turns using the CPU.

With this picture of a uniprocessor architecture tucked away, we are now ready to move on to multiprocessors. Faithful to our 80-20 principle, we will focus the discussion on the dominant multiprocessor architecture, the Symmetric MultiProcessor (SMP).

The SMP Architecture

The name SMP already gives it away:

- It is MP, as in multiprocessor. The system consists of multiple identical CPUs.

- It is symmetric. All processors have an identical view of the system. They all have the same capabilities. For example, they have identical access to any location in memory as well as to any I/O device.

- Everything else is single. It has a single memory system, a single copy of the operating system, a single Run Queue.

Figure 15.3 captures the SMP story.

Unless your application code bends over backwards, threads have no affinity to any particular CPU. The same thread may execute on CPU_1 in one particular time-slice and CPU_2 on the next time-slice. Another lesson driven by Figure 15.3 is that multiple

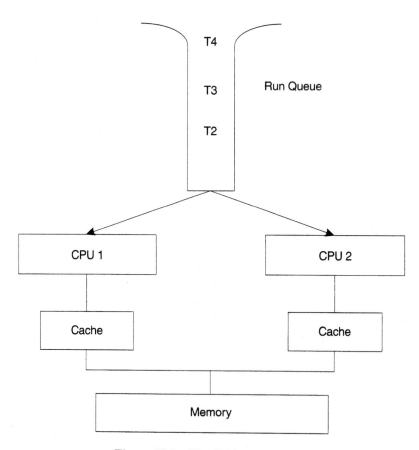

Figure 15.3. The SMP Architecture.

threads really do execute simultaneously. While thread T1 executes on CPU_1, thread T2 may very well execute on CPU_2. Since the scheduling entity is a thread, there's nothing preventing threads T1 and T2 from belonging to the same process. In this case it is very likely that they will access the same memory locations on a regular basis. Which brings us to the next issue: There is only one bus connecting the processors to the memory system. The bus is the major bottleneck in SMP systems and the chief reason why 256-way SMP machines are not commonplace—because bus contention will bring them to a grinding halt.

The solution to bus contention is large caches, one per processor. A large cache will make bus trips infrequent, but raises a new problem: What if two distinct caches both have a copy of a variable, x, and one of the processors updates its private copy? The other cache might have a stale, incorrect value for x, and we hate when that happens. This is the *cache consistency* problem. The SMP architecture provides a hardware solution for it. The details are not terribly important; all we need to know is that when variable x gets updated, all of its other cache copies get updated as does the main memory master copy. The *cache consistency* hardware solution is completely invisible to the application software.

The SMP architecture offers potential scalability. Obviously, the number of processors presents an easy upper bound. You cannot get more than 8x speedup on an 8-way SMP. The practical scalability limit may be even tighter than that. We explore that practical limit next.

Amdahl's Law

Amdahl's Law quantifies the fact that the sequential portion of an application will put a lid on its potential scalability. This is best illustrated by an example such as matrix multiplication. It consists of three stages:

- Initialization: read in the matrices data values.

- Multiplication: multiply the two matrices.

- Presentation: present the resulting matrix.

Let's assume further that the whole computation takes 10 ms, broken down as follows (these numbers are completely fictitious but help illustrate the point):

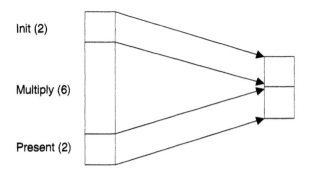

Figure 15.4. Potential speedup is limited.

- Initialization: 2 ms

- Multiplication: 6 ms

- Presentation: 2 ms

Over the years, many clever parallel algorithms have been developed to exploit multiprocessor architectures to speed up the matrix multiplication phase. Not so with the Initialization and Presentation phase. Practically, these two stages in the computation are fundamentally sequential. In the ideal world, an unlimited number of parallel processors could, in theory, reduce the multiplication stage to 0 ms. But they would not help at all with the other two sequential stages, as shown by Figure 15.4.

An unlimited number of parallel processors has only reduced a 10 ms computation to 4 ms. Looks like 2.5x is the speedup limit for this particular application on any SMP system regardless of the number of processors.

This matrix example exhibits a response-time limit. The same idea also applies to throughput. Consider the original design of our Web server, a 3-stage pipeline (Figure 15.5).

Let's assume that the whole pipeline consumes 10 ms as follows (again, the numbers are fictitious):

- Accept: 2 ms

- Service: 6 ms

- Log: 2 ms

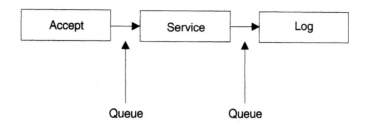

Figure 15.5. A specific design of one Web server.

At 10 ms, we can serve 100 requests-per-second on a uniprocessor. Our server was designed to have a single thread perform the Accept stage. It then queued accepted connections to the Service stage. A pool of available threads consumed requests off of that queue to perform the Service stage. Upon completion of the Service stage, a log record was queued to the Log stage. The Log stage, like the Accept stage, was performed by a single thread. It follows that only the Service stage could benefit from an SMP. The Accept and Log stages were inherently sequential, as they were single-threaded.

Regardless of the number of parallel processors, we only have a single thread accepting new connections. Since each new connection takes 2 ms to establish, this thread cannot accept more than 500 connections-per-second. This puts a 5x scaling limit on our Web server design even if we move it from a uniprocessor to a 12-way SMP.

Sequential (single-threaded) computations are the major roadblock on the way to scalability. In the following sections we will enumerate ways to eliminate or at least minimize sequential computations. Before we go there, we briefly need to clarify some terminology.

Multithreaded and Synchronization Terminology

This is not the first time in this book that we have run into synchronization terminology. We have already used terms such as synchronization, serialization, critical sections, race condition, and locks. We never really explained them, and it is time to step back and clarify the terminology.[1] The first issue is presenting the problem: What is the problem that all that terminology is trying to address?

---

[1] It does not help at all that Java has overloaded the term "serialization" to mean something entirely different and unrelated to synchronization.

Take a simple code statement such as

```
x = x + 1;
```

If two threads execute this statement, we expect the resulting value stored in x to be x+2. Any other value would be incorrect. The problem with this code statement is that it is not executed atomically. It is actually broken into a small number of assembler instructions:

```
load  x, r5    // load the value of x into register r5
add   r5, 1    // add 1 to register r5
store r5, x    // store the value of register r5 into x
```

If two threads execute this code at roughly the same time, their instruction execution could interleave in a way that would result in x+1 stored as the new value of x instead of x+2. That unfortunate interleaving of thread execution is called a race condition. The solution to this race condition is to guarantee that this block of assembler statements executes atomically. We call that block a critical section. Once a thread enters a critical section, no other thread can enter until the first one leaves. In that case we say that the two threads are synchronized (or serialized) and that the critical section is mutually exclusive. Since the variable x is accessed by more than a single thread it is considered shared data. Critical sections always revolve around access to shared data. To guarantee safe access to shared data (and correct execution) we use a lock—a flag (bit or int) associated with shared data. A thread must check the state of the lock prior to entering the critical section. If the lock is off, no other thread currently is executing in the critical section. Consequently, access permission is granted and the state of the lock status is changed to reflect it. (Testing and setting the lock are guaranteed to be atomic by the hardware.) If the lock is on, the thread must wait until the lock status is turned off by the thread currently executing in the critical section. When a critical section is protected by a lock, we often say that its execution is sequential. Multiple threads wanting to enter the critical section have to line up and enter one at a time.

With this terminology out of the way, we move on to discuss ways to alleviate the scalability bottlenecks inherent in sequential execution.

Break Up a Task into Multiple Subtasks

To unleash potential scalability, your application must divide its computational task into multiple subtasks that could be executed in parallel. The Web server is a good example. The computational task is to service multiple client requests as they arrive on a designated HTTP port. If your Web server is single-threaded, it can perform only one request at a time; all other requests have to wait on a queue. To enable scalability we must break up the service task. The task of servicing all the requests on the queue is split into smaller tasks of serving a single request. By unleashing multiple threads on the smaller subtasks, we can achieve true parallelism and scalability. Breaking up the Web service into parallel subtasks improves several performance indicators:

- Response-time of an individual request

- Server throughput in requests-per-second

- Better server CPU utilization

A Web server performs frequent blocking I/O operations. If the server consists of a single thread, no work is performed while waiting on I/O completion. A multi-threaded server would just switch over to perform other tasks and keep the processors humming. The result is better throughput and higher CPU utilization. One thing that makes customers sick is seeing their 12-way SMP server at 25% CPU utilization.

There are some commercial Web servers that are single-threaded by design. These vendors have intentionally ignored the high volume Web sites that typically require SMP servers. Instead, single-threaded servers are targeted at the low-volume Web sites running on low-end uniprocessor servers.

Cache Shared Data

Anytime you can skip a visit to a critical section, you are looking at a scalability gain. The simplest application of this idea is by caching shared data and reusing it in future access without needing to lock and unlock a shared resource. This was actually the single biggest scalability optimization that we made to our original Web server design and implementation. Initially, not only did it not scale, it had actually exhibited fractional scaling—throughput was slashed in half when we moved from a uniprocessor to a 4-way SMP. Something was seriously wrong.

We have already described the overall design of our Web server earlier in this chapter. We had a 1-1 mapping between threads and requests. A pool of available threads had consumed requests off the connection queue. Once a request was assigned to a particular thread, it remained confined to that thread for the duration of request handling. There were many objects pertaining to the request that were manipulated throughout the lifetime of a request. We needed to make those objects available to those routines that needed them. We could have passed them on the stack as function call arguments, but that would force us to pass 10–15 object references to hundreds of deeply nested calls. Not only would this be ugly, it would raise the overhead of function and procedure calls.

A more elegant choice was made to package all the relevant data in a single data structure. A skeleton of it is shown here:

```
class ThreadSpecificData {
    HTRequest    *reqPtr;     // Attributes of current HTTP request
    StreamSocket socket;      // Socket used by current HTTP connection
    ...
};
```

The ThreadSpecificData object contained all the data necessary for the various procedure calls invoked by the thread during request lifetime. Now we needed to make this data private to a particular thread. The pthreads library provides the machinery to do that. The pthread_setspecific() function creates the association between the calling thread and the data pointer:

```
void initThread(...)
{
    ...
    ThreadSpecificData *tsd = new ThreadSpecificData;
    pthread_setspecific(global_key, tsd);
    ...
}
```

When a thread needs access to its private data it used the pthread_getspecific() call to get a pointer to its private data:

```
ThreadSpecificData *HTInitRequest (StreamSocket sock)
{
    ...
    ThreadSpecificData *tsd = pthread_getspecific(global_key);
    tsd->socket = sock;
    tsd->reqPtr = new HTRequest;
    ...
    return tsd;
}
```

The handling of a single HTTP request necessitated invocations of many functions and procedure calls. The vast majority of those calls needed access to the request information stored in the `ThreadSpecificData` object. Our code was, therefore, littered with hundreds of calls to `pthread_getspecific()` and about 100 such calls were invoked by each thread during the service of a single request.

Somewhere, somehow, the `pthreads` library is maintaining an association between threads and their private data. Since threads may come and go in and out of existence, this association is dynamic and must be protected by a lock. When you go looking for an association, you want to guarantee that it does not disappear from underneath your feet. What we ended up with is a situation in which multiple threads working on distinct requests were going after the same lock, 100 times per request. As you can imagine, threads spent most of their time spinning idle waiting their turn to grab a hot lock.

This hotly contended lock creates another severe problem on an SMP architecture. The lock word is likely to have a copy on each and every processor cache. Since it is frequently updated (when the lock is acquired and released), it will trigger a *cache consistency* storm as the SMP hardware tries to invalidate stale copies of the lock on all but one of the caches. *Cache consistency* storms are bad. They hit the SMP architecture at its most vulnerable scalabilty factor—the bus connecting the processors to the memory subsystem and to one another.

To unleash the scalability potential of our Web server, we had to ditch the frequent calls to `pthread_getspecific()`. We had to find an alternate way of passing thread data around. The alternative was pretty simple; although the thread data was frequently updated, the pointer to it was constant for the life of the thread. It was essentially a read-only pointer, which automatically suggests caching. We get the pointer via a single `pthread_getspecific()` call at the beginning of the request and subsequently pass it around on the stack as a function (or procedure) call argument. That way, we reduced 100 `pthread_getspecific()` calls down to one and practically eliminated the contention for its internal lock.

```
void HTHandleRequest (StreamSocket sock)
{
    ...
    ThreadSpecificData *tsd = HTInitRequest(sock);

    readRequest(tsd);
    mapURLToFilename(tsd);
```

```
            authenticate(tsd);
            authorize(tsd);
            sendData(tsd);
            log(tsd);
            cleanup(tsd);
            ...
    }
```

By passing the data pointer on the stack, we have eliminated frequent access to the pthreads container maintaining the thread-to-data associations. We effectively have reduced the sharing frequency of this container among the various threads. The reduction in sharing is a recurrent theme in most scalabilty optimizations.

Share Nothing

Reduction in sharing is good, but nothing beats eliminating contention altogether. Instead of sharing a resource, you can sometimes eliminate sharing completely by giving each thread its own private resource. Recall from the previous section that each Web server worker thread (in our implementation) maintained a pointer to its private data object of type ThreadSpecificData:

```
class ThreadSpecificData {
    HTRequest *reqPtr;    // Attributes of current HTTP request
    ...
};
```

The reqPtr member was a pointer to an HTRequest object containing information about the current HTTP request. At the beginning of each request, the worker thread created a brand new object of type HTRequest:

```
ThreadSpecificData *HTInitRequest(StreamSocket sock)
{
    ...
    tsd->reqPtr = new HTRequest;
    ...
}
```

The HTRequest object was destroyed during request cleanup stage:

```
void cleanup (ThreadSpecificData *tsd)
{
    delete tsd->reqPtr;
    ...
}
```

It may not look like it on the surface but there is some thread friction going on here by calling new() and delete(). Using the global new() and delete() created contention among the worker threads. These calls manage memory in the process scope that is shared by all the threads of the process. Access to the internal data structures manipulated by new() and delete() must be protected for mutual exclusion. There are parts of their implementation that are sequential by nature.

The solution in this case is fairly simple. The HTRequest object should not be allocated from the heap on every request. It should be embedded in the ThreadSpecificData object belonging to the thread and recycled for subsequent requests:

```
class ThreadSpecificData {
    HTRequest req;   // An object, not a pointer to one
    ...
};
```

Now, instead of allocating and deallocating HTRequest object we simply recycle the one we have:

```
ThreadSpecificData *HTInitRequest(StreamSocket sock)
{
    ...
    tsd->req.init();
    ...
}
```

The HTRequest object was recycled during cleanup:

```
void cleanup (ThreadSpecificData *tsd)
{
    tsd->req.reset();
    ...
}
```

Now, HTRequest::init() and HTRequest::reset() don't have any serialized code whatsoever since they work on an object privately owned by the thread.

Shared resource pools are a must when you cannot tell in advance how many instances of the resource you may need. If you do know, however, that you are going to need only a fixed number of instances, you can go ahead and make them private.

In our case all we needed was a single instance of HTrequest, per request. We have completely eliminated the sharing of a resource (in this case, memory management data structures) by making the HTRequest object thread-private.

Partial Sharing

We have previously encountered the two opposite extremes of resource sharing: the publicly shared resource pool and the thread-private instance of a resource. Between these two extremes lie the sharing middleground of the partial-sharing resource pool.

When each thread requires a single instance of a resource, you can easily eliminate contention by making it thread-private. If the required number of instances cannot be determined in advance, you need to use a resource pool that is shared among all threads. Such shared resources often become a contention hot spot among threads, which severely degrades performance and scalability. Threads spend significant cycles spinning idle. Partial-sharing of resource pools offers a way out of a hotly contended resource.

Originally, we started with a single resource pool serving all threads, as shown in Figure 15.6. Our goal was to reduce thread contention by reducing the number of threads

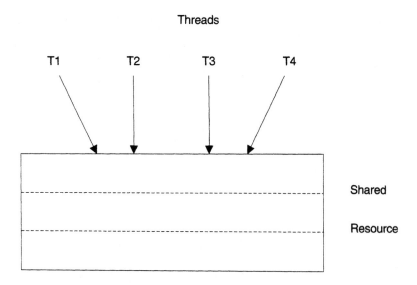

Figure 15.6. A single shared resource.

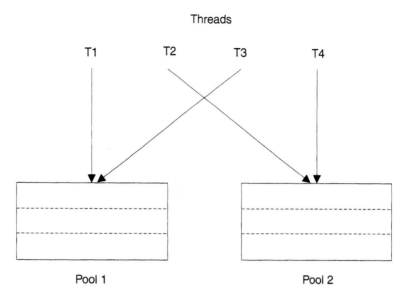

Figure 15.7. Breaking up a single shared resource.

competing for a resource. Towards that goal we converted the single resource pool into multiple identical subpools. We prefered two pools with half the contention, or four pools with one fourth contention over a single pool that draws all the fire (Figure 15.7).

The threads that formerly all ganged up on a single pool have gotten distributed over multiple subpools. Distributing the thread requests to separate pools could be achieved by generating a random number, hashing on the thread ID, or any other trick for fast random distribution. Each subpool must still be protected for mutual exclusion, but the thread contention has been reduced to a fraction of its previous levels.

As you increase the number of subpools, contention among threads decreases. Eventually, you may end up reaching the extreme where the number of pools roughly equals the number of threads. In that case, it is almost like having a thread-private resource with no contention.

We speculate that in most practical scenarios, splitting a single pool into two, four or even eight subpools will suffice to reduce contention into negligible levels. There's a point where going beyond will provide only diminishing returns. The ultimate judge is empirical data, which is application dependent.

Lock Granularity

Most reasonable implementations of a Web server will make some rudimentary statistics available to the Web master. For example, our implementation kept track of the number of HTTP and HTTPS (SSL) requests:

```
class HTStats {
    int httpReqs;
    int sslReqs;
    pthread_mutex_t lock;
    ...
};
```

Since multiple threads may try to manipulate the statistics concurrently, we had to protect it with a mutex lock:

```
void HTStats::addHttpReq()// Increment the counter for HTTP requests.
{
    pthread_mutex_lock(&lock);
    httpReqs++;
    pthread_mutex_unlock(&lock);
}

void HTStats::addSslReq()// Increment the counter for HTTPS requests.
{
    pthread_mutex_lock(&lock);
    sslReqs++;
    pthread_mutex_unlock(&lock);
}
```

As you can tell from this code, the HTStats class uses a single lock to protect the manipulation of all of its counters. Fusing multiple unrelated shared resources under the umbrella of a single lock is normally a bad idea. It widens the scope of the critical sections and creates friction among otherwise independent threads. The only possible exception to this rule is when the following two conditions are satisfied:

- All of the shared resources are always manipulated together.

- None of the manipulations of the shared resources consume significant CPU cycles.

Although shared counters satisfy the second condition (updates are fast), in the case of counting HTTP and SSL requests, the first condition was broken: A thread that updated one counter did not access the other. An SSL thread would update the SSL counter but have no interest in the state of the HTTP counter. Just like breaking a single resource pool into multiple subpools, we prefer two distinct locks protecting two counters so that the contention for each lock is reduced by half.

```
class HTStats {
    int httpReqs;
    pthread_mutex_t lockHttp;

    char smpDmz[CACHE_LINE_SIZE];    // Will explain this one later

    int sslReqs;
    pthread_mutex_t lockSsl;
    ...
};
```

The updates for HTTP and SSL counters will now use distinct locks:

```
void HTStats::addHttpReq()// Increment the counter for HTTP requests.
{
    pthread_mutex_lock(&lockHttp);
    httpReqs++;
    pthread_mutex_unlock(&lockHttp);
}
void HTStats::addSslReq()// Increment the counter for HTTPS requests.
{
    pthread_mutex_lock(&lockSsl);
    sslReqs++;
    pthread_mutex_unlock(&lockSsl);
}
```

This implementation increases scalability and prevents the sets of SSL and HTTP threads from getting in each other's way. Conversely, we can use HTStats to show an example where lock-fusion actually makes sense. Suppose we also keep track of the cumulative number of bytes served on each protocol:

```
class HTStats {
    int httpReqs;
    int httpBytes;          // Add this
    pthread_mutex_t lockHttp;

    char smpDmz[CACHE_LINE_SIZE];

    int sslReqs;
    int sslBytes;           // Add this
```

```
        pthread_mutex_t lockSsl;
        ...
};
```

An HTTP thread that updated the number of HTTP requests will always update the number of bytes sent as well. These two counters are updated together and involve fast operations such as integer addition. For those reasons we chose to fuse them under the same lock:

```
void HTStats::updateHttpCounters(int nBytes)// Increment HTTP
counters.
{
    pthread_mutex_lock(&lockHttp);
    httpReqs++;
    httpBytes += nBytes;
    pthread_mutex_unlock(&lockHttp);
}
```

By separating the SSL and HTTP statistics, we reduced contention for the respective lock. The original design having a single lock created artificial contention among SSL and HTTP threads. On the other hand, we did choose to fuse the updates to two related HTTP statistics. Otherwise, we would have to waste a pair of calls to lock and unlock each counter.

So far so good, but what is that smpDmz character array doing in the middle of our HTStats class definition? This is our SMP demilitarized zone. It has to do with false sharing, which we discuss next.

False Sharing

The atomic unit of a cache is a line. A typical cache line may hold a large number of bytes. A 128-byte cache line is typical. When a 4-byte integer is loaded from main memory, it is not loaded in isolation. The whole line containing it is loaded into the cache at once. Similarly, when that integer value is invalidated by another cache (running on a different processor), the whole cache line is invalidated. It follows that the physical memory layout of variables can play a role in SMP scalability.

Take the HTStats class discussed earlier. If you eliminate the smpDmz character array, you will end up with the two locks close to one another as in:

```
class HTStats {
    int httpReqs;
    int httpBytes;
    pthread_mutex_t lockHttp;

    int sslReqs;            // 4 bytes
    int sslBytes;           // 4 bytes
    pthread_mutex_t lockSsl;
    ...
};
```

The two locks (lockHttp and lockSsl) are only eight bytes apart. They are very likely to end up residing on the same cache line. Suppose that we have an SMP system where thread T1 is executing an HTTP request on processor P1 and thread T2 is executing an SSL request on P2. When T1 acquires the HTTP lock (lockHttp), it modifies the value of that lock variable on the P1 cache. That same cache line on P2 is now invalid. When T2 tries to acquire lockSsl, it takes a cache miss because that line has been invalidated.

You can imagine how this scenario progresses: Threads running on P1 and P2 will continuously invalidate each other's cache line where these two locks reside. Keep in mind that our threads are not colliding on an application shared resource. They are colliding on a cache line, which is an artifact of the class memory layout combined with hardware architecture issues such as *cache consistency*. The resulting *cache consistency* storm can seriously degrade performance and scalability by lowering the cache hit rate below 90%.

In the case of HTStats, we inserted the smpDmz character array to guarantee that the two hot locks will not share a cache line. Ideally, a lock should be placed in close proximity to the shared data that it protects.

Thundering Herd

When a thread fails to acquire a busy lock, it can proceed in one of two ways:

- Spin in a tight loop trying to grab the lock on each iteration. This is effective only for short-lived locks. Spin-locks that are held for long periods of time will cause threads to tie up the CPUs while spinning idle waiting on the shared resource to become available.

- Go to sleep and await notification. When the lock is freed, waiting threads are awakened. We'll call this type a simple-lock to distinguish it from the spin-lock.

When a large number of threads concurrently contend for a simple-lock, all but one are put to sleep. What happens when the lock finally becomes available? Again, there are two scenarios:

- Only a single thread on the waiting list is awakened. Typically, this will be the highest priority thread on the waiting list.

- All the waiting threads are awakened. This triggers the Thundering Herd [Cam91].

The problem with awakening all waiting threads is that all but one are going to lose and go back to sleep. Given that thread context switches are not cheap, we are looking at a substantial performance and scalablity loss. The Thundering Herd event is not an esoteric one. It is a real threat to many commercial server implementations. We have encountered it ourselves during the design and implementation of our Web server.

When we described our three-stage pipeline of accept-serve-log, you might have wondered why we limited the accept stage to a single thread. This decision was a direct result of trying to avoid a Thundering Herd.

When a server thread intends to accept a new TCP/IP connection, it must perform an `accept()` call. The `accept()` tells TCP/IP that the calling thread would like to accept the next available connection on a given TCP/IP port.

For each port, TCP/IP maintains a queue of incoming connections and a queue of threads waiting to accept new connections. Connections are handed over to accepting threads in order of arrival. If no threads are waiting, connections are queued. If no connections are available, waiting threads are queued.

Now picture this: A large number of threads perform an `accept()` on a port (say, port 80) while the connection queue is empty. All threads are added to the waiting list. Internally, all these threads are put to sleep waiting on a signal. Sometime later a connection is established. On most platforms all waiting threads are signalled to wake up, which then causes a mad dash to grab the CPU (hence the name "Thundering Herd"). One lucky thread is going to seize the CPU first and accept the only available connection on the port. The rest of the threads are going to waste a context switch only to find that the connection queue for this port is empty again. All but one thread are going back to sleep on the waiting list. If we had 100 threads on the waiting list, only one was going to grab the new connection. The other 99 were going to waste a costly context switch without performing any useful work. This CPU thrashing can bring a server to its knees and seriously damage throughput. What most system administrators tend to do when throughput is degraded is to increase the number of server threads, which only aggravates the problem. When a Thundering Herd is in effect, more threads mean less performance.

Our Web server implementation ran on many different platforms, which was one of our claims to fame. Initially, all but one of those platforms suffered from the `accept()` Thundering Herd problem. On those platforms we had to use a single thread to accept new connections. A prototype that used multiple threads had exhibited worse performance than a single-threaded `accept()`. This is one of those scenarios where you can have too many threads.

The Thundering Herd is not limited to TCP/IP. It may happen any time a large number of threads compete for too few resources. The place where you are most likely to run into it is locking. The lock itself is a single resource for which many threads contend. The solution here is to learn the characteristics of the locking schemes available on your platform.

Some platforms provide both type of simple-locks—the type that wakes up all waiting threads as well as the type that wakes up only one. If you have that choice, you ought to use the single-thread wakeup locking scheme.

Reader/Writer Locks

Another way to ease the pain of synchronization is to relax the requirement that one and only one thread may have exclusive access to shared data. The need to serialize access to shared data stems from the fact that the shared data may be modified by one of the threads accessing it. It follows that we must give exclusive access only to those threads aiming to modify shared data (writers). Conversely, threads that are merely interested in reading shared data (readers) could access shared data concurrently.

Reader/writer locks are those that allow multiple readers to access shared data instead of waiting for exclusive access. A thread trying to get read access to shared data will be granted read access in one of two cases:

- No other thread was granted access.

- The only threads granted access are readers.

If a writer thread has been granted access, all readers must wait for the writer thread to leave the critical section. A writer thread is granted access if and only if no other thread has been granted access to the shared resource.

Many platforms provide reader/writer locks. If such locks are not available for a specific platform, you can build your own from the available synchronization primitive building blocks. See [NBF96] for one such implementation.

If all your threads try to modify a shared resource, then reader/writer locks would not help. In fact, they would hurt performance as their implementation is by nature more complex and therefore slower than plain locks. If, however, your shared data is read-mostly, reader/writer locks will improve scalability by eliminating contention among reader threads.

Key Points

- SMP is currently the dominant MP architecture. It consists of multiple symmetric processors connected via a single bus to a single memory system. The bus is the scalability weak link in the SMP architecture. Large caches, one per processor, are meant to keep bus contention under control.

- Amdahl's Law puts an upper limit on the potential scalability of an application. The scalability is limited by portions of the computation that are serialized.

The trick to scalability is to reduce and, if possible, eliminate serialized code. Following are some steps you can take towards that goal:

- Split a monolithic task into multiple subtasks that are conducive to parallel execution by concurrent threads.

- Code motion. Critical sections should contain critical code and nothing else. Code that does not directly manipulate shared resources should not reside in the critical section.

- Cache. At times, it may be possible to eliminate execution visits to a critical section by caching the result of an earlier visit.

- Share nothing. If you only need a small, fixed number of resource instances, you should avoid the use of public resource pools. Make those instances thread-private and recycle them.

- Partial-sharing. It is better to have two identical pools with half the contention.

- Lock granularity. Don't fuse resources under the protection of the same lock unless they are always updated together.

- False sharing. Don't place two hot locks in close proximity in the class definition. You don't want them to share the same cache line and trigger *cache consistency* storms.

- Thundering Herd. Investigate the characteristics of your locking calls. When the lock is freed, does it wake up all waiting threads or just one? Those that wake up all threads threaten the scalability of an application.

- System and library calls. Investigate the characteristics of their implementation. Some of them are hiding significant portions of serialized code.

- Reader/writer locks. Shared data that is read-mostly will benefit from these locks. They eliminate contention among reader threads.

16

System Architecture Dependencies

We have tried to avoid waving our hands at performance problems because we wanted to provide as much practical information as possible. Most of the foregoing performance discussion has been fairly self-contained. If you know how to program in C++ then hopefully it made sense. Now we are entering an area that is deeply rooted in nonprogramming concepts. Hardware dependency is based on how the hardware works. Unfortunately, unless you have a reasonable background in hardware architecture, some of it may not be easy to understand.

Computer science increasingly has become a software science in which the vagaries of how the hardware actually functions has been left to the train drivers (engineers). This shift away from deep-seated knowledge of hardware functionality has not, in general, hurt most programmers. However, optimal software performance cannot be obtained without the ability to intellectually translate high-level software structures into low-level hardware sequences. The sort of information required is not the type of thing that you pick up by reading a chapter in a book. It is the type of thing you start to understand by studying things like the Hennessy and Patterson [HP97] and Patterson and Hennessy [PH96] tomes.

This chapter contains lots of information, but it is largely of the "look out!" and "remember" sort. We considered abandoning the discussion altogether, but we decided that the discussion may benefit those with the requisite background, and at least it may open the door to ultimate performance for those that have not yet delved into the hardware side of the performance equation.

Memory Hierarchies

Any discussion of performance must, in the end, center on memory usage and memory usage patterns. Frequently the most significant aspects of algorithmic complexity are centered on the number and type of memory accesses an algorithm requires. It has never been more true than it is now that calculation is fast and access is slow.

There are now typically at least five levels in the memory hierarchy of the average computer. Some of the main levels of the memory hierarchy sometimes contain sublevels. The memory hierarchy, from its fastest (lowest access time) to its slowest (highest access time) consists of registers, L1 (level one) on-chip cache, L2 (level two) off-chip cache, main memory (semiconductor dynamic random access memory in all its varieties: DRAM, SRDAM, RAMBUS, SyncLink, etc.), and disk storage. Some of the newer processors carry two levels of cache on-chip, which we would have considered to be logically a single L1 cache, which itself is made up of a smaller extremely fast store and a larger very fast store. Most hard disks now carry their own local caches, and the storage hierarchy of systems with such disks can be thought of as consisting of two subsystems: a relatively fast, small store, and a relatively slow, huge store.

There is a strong tendency to look at memory access simply in terms of access times and cycle rates. This view ignores the interaction between latency and bandwidth. Access time is a latency issue: How long does it take to start getting data? Bus width and burst length are bandwidth issues: How much data can I get once it starts arriving? This is akin to the notion of a fire hose: How long does it take to open the valve, once it is open how much water does the hose deliver per second, and how much water is in the trunk?

Latency is not improving at the same rate that bandwidth is, or, we can move blocks of data with good average access times, but accessing individual bytes of memory is increasingly slow. For example, in the last five years (circa 1999) processor speeds have gone from 90MHz to 500MHz, but main memory access times have only gone from 120ns to 50ns (even the best 8ns SDRAM requires six cycles for the first access). This means that processors are more than five times faster than they were, but memory is only two and a half times as fast. Conversely, memory bandwidth performance has done a better job of keeping pace with processor performance. In the last five years, memory busses have doubled in width and the current burst characteristics of DRAM significantly increases the effective memory bandwidth. The story about disk performance is similar. Access times have not kept pace, but bandwidth has not suffered to the same degree.

A perusal of main memory access characteristics for a computer may look something like "6-1-1-1-2-1-1-1." This means six bus cycles for the initial access and then one bus cycle for each of the next three accesses, followed by two bus cycles for the next access and then three more single-cycle accesses. When you consider that a bus cycle is now typically four processor cycles, this means that a processor is idled for 24 cycles every time it goes out to main memory, and the entire cache line read will take almost 60 instruction cycles. This is not always the case; some sophisticated architectures support multiple outstanding memory requests, and they request data before it is actually needed, but the general principal still generally holds—we hurry up and wait.

In terms of current technology (circa 1999) the access latencies for each level of the memory hierarchy are shown in Table 16-1.

From these numbers it may seem that the registers and cache have roughly the same performance, but this is not at all the case. Computation requires both latency and bandwidth. A register set typically can handle three operands per clock cycle. An L1 cache can really supply only about half of an operand per cycle because a cache access requires a register access or two to create the effective address that will be used to access the cache. Thus a register set has roughly six times the bandwidth of an L1 cache. So while an L1 cache can have good latency characteristics, its bandwidth is not particularly good.[1]

Table 16.1. Memory Access Speed

Memory Level	Latency
Disk	10ms
DRAM	50ns
L2 Cache	4-8ns
L1 Cache	2ns
Registers	2ns

[1] This discussion is a general one and probably not exactly true of any specific hardware, though generally true of most hardwares. Super-pipelined and super-scalar architectures bias the effective speed of registers and caches in different ways, but in general registers tend to provide much more bandwidth than the cache no matter what type of processor you are using.

Registers: Kings of Memory

Registers are the lowest latency, highest bandwidth, lowest specification overhead entities in the memory hierarchy. As already indicated, they are effectively at least twice as fast as an L1 cache. Typically, register sets are at least triple ported; that is, a register set typically can read two operands and write one operand every clock cycle. This means that a simple 600MHz, 64-bit RISC architecture would have a maximum register bandwidth of approximately 14.4 gigabytes per second. This is three to six times greater than a respectable L1 cache's bandwidth and more than 30 times the effective bandwidth of a 64-bit wide, 100MHz external DRAM interface.

Registers are directly addressed within machine code statements. Five bits within an instruction format can access one operand (a 5-bit register specifier can address one of 32 registers). This means that a three-operand, 32-bit instruction has an effective register bandwidth of three operands per 32-bit instruction, or a three-to-one ratio of operands to instructions. All other levels of the memory hierarchy are based on virtual or physical addresses or on indices within an operating-system-managed storage system (file system). To obtain a memory-based operand, at least one full address of bits are necessary to load it, plus another instruction may be needed at some point to store the value. On a RISC processor with 32-bit instructions and 32-bit data addresses, this would mean that 64 bits would be required to perform any meaningful operation on a single operand. Thus registers have six times less operational overhead, three-to-six times more bandwidth, and half the latency of an L1 cache. The advantage of registers vis-à-vis the other succeeding levels of the memory hierarchy are proportionally greater.

So, registers are great. Let's just put all our data in the registers and be done with the rest of the memory hierarchy. This solution will work fine if your program has less than a couple dozen atomic variables, but any program of even modest size will find the confines of the register set far too restrictive. Many processors now sport 32 general purpose registers and there are architectures soon to be released that have in excess of 100 registers. But even if a "magic" huge register set could be designed (one that did not need to pay any homage to the laws of physics) the direct addressing characteristic of registers makes them a difficult medium for large-scale memory mapping. Direct addressing provides registers with much of their speed, but it also makes it impossible to embed arrays into registers and dynamically index them (without resorting to self-modifying code, a compelling capability in this instance, but one fraught with difficulties). It is extremely difficult to create a pointer to a register-based variable. Variable-to-register mapping is context insensitive; that is, register 3 is always register 3, independent of how deep we might be in a call tree (this is actually only mostly true; architectures that support overlapping register windows do remap registers).

Registers work great as temporary repositories of atomic data, but there are too few of them and their addressing characteristics are too limited to consider them seriously as the only memory store. They are great for the right type of temporary data, though. Let's examine what the right kind of temporary data is, and let's also look at what compilers can do to help in the variable-to-register mapping department, as well as what we can do to assist the compiler when it fails to make the best decisions.

Compiler writers are as aware of the importance of good register mapping as anyone. They do their best to allocate variables to registers, but they tend to be somewhat conservative and they understand the aliasing issues associated with languages like C++ that allow unrestricted pointer manipulation. Pointers allow variables to be aliased in arcane fashions. Though we believe that there is no imperative to continue to support this type of programming, we also realize that changes in compiler methodology that breaks existing code are viewed as unadvised in many circles.

The `register` reserved word indicates to the compiler that there is no need for a variable ever to be placed in memory, or more accurately, for a variable ever to have a memory address. This is just a suggestion, and just like the `inline` directive, it can be ignored by the compiler. Some compilers completely ignore all register directives. We can only assume that the writers of such compilers believe that their register allocation algorithms will make better decisions than a programmer will, a belief that in some cases is true and in other cases is far from it.

We earlier indicated that in an ideal world, inlining should be done automatically and optimally by the compiler. This is even more the case for register basing of variables. The compiler should be able to do a better job of register allocation, or of making decisions about where variables should be based, than a programmer does. If a compiler were able to take advantage of profiling information, which would give the compiler a reasonable basis for making decisions about the dominant execution path through each method, then a compiler should be able to make optimal decisions about register allocation. This seems to be the direction in which some compiler writers are moving and we applaud them for it. As we indicated earlier, we believe that profile-based compiler optimization offers the greatest possibility of automating the optimization process and will be the most effective technique for freeing the programmer from making explicit, low-level optimization decisions. Programmers should be concerned with class implementation decisions, not spending their time on low-level register basing issues. Unfortunately, many compilers still make far from optimal register basing decisions, and some programmer directed assistance is frequently in order.

Following are three methods, a, b, and c, each of which contain a local variable i, which in method a should be register based, in method *b* should not be register based, and in method c may or may not be a good candidate, based on our understanding of the common execution path for the method.

```cpp
int x::a (int x, int& y)
{
    int i = -x + y;
    y = i -10;
    i = x;
    y -= i;

    return i + 10;    // i used 5 times in 5 instructions with
}                     // no intervening calls

int x::b (int x, int& y)
{
    int i = -x;
    y = test(x);
    y = -y;
    int j = test(y);
    y = -j + 12;
    cout << j << y;

    return i + j;    // i used 2 times in 8 instructions with
}                    // 2 intervening calls between its first
                     // and last usage

int x::c (int x, int& y)
{
    int i = -x + 100;
    if (i < 0) {
       y = test(x) + i;
       }
    y = -y;
    int j = 15;
    if (i <= 0) {
       j = test(y) + x;
       }
    y -= -j + 12;
    return i + j;    // i used 5 times in 9 instructions, but with
}                    // potentially two intervening calls between
                     // its first and its last usage
```

The salient metric for the decision about whether to register base a variable is the number of times the variable will need to be loaded and stored. If a variable is register based, then the register in which it resides typically will need to be stored if the method makes a call and then restored when the called method returns. This amounts to a load and store for each method call that occurs between a variable's first and last usage. If the variable is not register based, then the variable will not need to be loaded and stored every time its defining method makes a call, but it will need to be loaded and stored every time its method uses it. This makes it relatively simple to count the calls and the usage points and make a decision. The compiler can do a relatively good job of this. The only time that the compiler should need help is when there are a significant number of conditionally invoked methods. These instances make profile information very useful, but since most compilers have no automatic feedback loops, the programmer must sometimes supply the appropriate hints to the compiler by specifying that certain variables should be register based.

Proper register basing of a variable can improve the performance of individual methods generated by some compilers by an order of magnitude. In most such instances the compiler should recognize these optimization possibilities and perform register basing itself, but it never hurts to check. Register basing decisions, like inlining decisions, should be profile based. Only code that lies on a program's critical path should be considered for register pragma specification. One relative quality metric of a compiler can be gauged by finding the most likely candidate for register basing, supplying the register pragma, recompiling, and reprofiling. Any improvement in execution speed indicates that either explicit register allocation decisions need to be supplied by the programmer, or that the level of optimization supplied by the compiler needs to be increased. NOTE: Profile data should be gathered with the highest functional level of compiler optimizations enabled. Profiles of unoptimized code can make it look like the compiler was written by performance morons. Most compilers need to be explicitly enabled before they will perform interesting automatic optimizations.

Disk and Memory Structures

File structures are a topic for entire books all by themselves, and it is beyond the scope of this one to go into them in any significant detail. We will, however, discuss some of the more significant reasons why it is important to understand file structures and use appropriate ones when data persistence requires file storage, or when dynamic data size requires extensive use of virtual storage.

B+ trees and b* trees are the canonical file structures associated with the storage of volatile ordered class instances. Simple linear files or indexed files are viable structures for data that has sequential access characteristics or that is infrequently modified. These file structures are often considered more appropriate to persistent storage of data, and they are not typically considered particularly applicative to run-time data management. Run-time management of large data sets requires a storage mechanism more closely aligned with the system's virtual memory mechanism.

Unfortunately, we have met far too many programmers who view virtual memory as a "magic elixir" that makes unrestricted memory consumption both possible and affordable. This view is, in part, responsible for some of the program executable-image bloat that has become so ubiquitous. The tendency to rely on virtual storage to maintain very large run-time data sets has at times been exacerbated by the ability, on newer operating systems, to access persistent data sets (files) by mapping them into the system's virtual address space. This remapping of simple sequentially managed data into the random access memory model makes software easy to write, but it can result in programs that are not particularly efficient or fast. That is not to say that file mapping is an inapropriate strategy. For some types of data, mapping files to virtual storage can yield significant performance gains. We are only warning against an indescriminate reliance on an operating system's virtual memory storage mechanism.

There is nothing magic about virtual memory. The fact that operating system code is responsible for maintaining the memory residence of your data instead of your own code does not necessarily make access to that data any faster. Disk access is roughly as expensive for the system's virtual paging system as it is for explicit memory management code.

It takes an average of about 12–20 ms to access a disk (a number supplied by the disk manufacturers and generally considered overly optimistic, particularly on busy systems). This amounts to about 3 million cycles of processor latency. A typical disk access involves at least two context switches and the execution of a low-level device interface. This amounts to at least a couple thousand instructions of overhead. Disk access latency can be covered by other activities on busy systems, but the cycles consumed by the device interface cannot. Disk access is expensive. Undisciplined reliance on a system's virtual memory system can have very deleterious effects on a program's performance.

When allocating storage, the goal should always be to maintain as much data locality as possible. If data sets are large, this locality should be considered page locality.

Data should be organized such that a minimum number of page accesses are necessary. This is the raison d'être of the aforementioned b+ tree structure.

A binary search is typically the fastest search mechanism on ordered data (let us ignore hashing for the moment) with a search complexity of order log_2N. This means that an element can be found from within an array of 1 billion ordered elements with only 30 comparisons. However, if 20 of those 30 comparisons have a page fault associated with them, then our real efficiency is not particularly good. A solution that required more comparisons, but resulted in fewer page faults would be much better. After all, the computational overhead of a page fault is thousands of instructions and the latency is millions of instructions, whereas comparisons generally require less than half a dozen instructions. You can do a lot of comparisons in the time it takes to process a page fault.

In many cases, natural data locality makes very efficient use of a system's virtual memory capability. In such cases, data shows good temporal and spacial locality. This means that a program may access very large quantities of data, but only a small subset of that data is actively used at one time. This subset of active data, called a program's working set, tends to be only a small fraction of the program's total memory usage, and can prove to be fairly stable (the average tenure of the pages within the working set can be fairly long). A program's working sets may gradually transition pages in and out as new pages are accessed and old pages are no longer accessed. A program's call stack demonstrates exactly this type of locality. Conversely, a program may exhibit a flurry of page faults as a significantly different working set is loaded into memory followed by a period of very infrequent page faults. A shift from one major processing subsystem to another can exhibit this type of behavior.

Some programs have good data locality, whereas other programs can demonstrate sparse data usage, resulting in frequent page faults and poor performance. This is sometimes the result of a failure to manage the storage for a program's dominant classes. Class storage management has already been discussed in a general sense; what we are now interested in is how to manage classes with large storage requirements.

In general, program code will tend to have very good locality, and code storage management will be unnecessary. In instances where the working set size of a program's code becomes problematic, the code may need to be rearranged based on execution profiles to locate commonly associated code within the same file or files. This should only be a problem in extreme instances, and it is, interestingly, a place where C++'s `namespace` capability can become very handy. A very large program may benefit from spacial colocation of its primary methods within a single compilation unit. `Namespace`s have made this a relatively simple operation as each of the colocated methods can carry its own name space identifier. It is not a bad idea to begin to rely increasingly on `namespace`-based partitioning instead of file-location-based partitioning anyway. The next generation of integrated development environments could well make the file concept obsolete and move to automated namespace management convention (a move we heartily support).

Code reorganization for performance reasons is another area where profile feedback into a compiler could provide significant automatic optimization. The code for a method does not care where within an executable module it resides, and there is no reason to necessarily keep the methods for a class together in one area, though you do need to be careful to maintain at least a semblance of maintainability while extracting that last ounce of performance. If you do spray a class' implementation across the filescape, then be sure to note in the header where each method's implementation can be located, and be sure to explain why you did something so strange.

Although code requires placement optimization only occasionally, managing data storage is a common necessity. Though the reuse of OO has tended to be overstated, class storage management is an area that acquits itself quite well in terms of mix-in class and template reuse. A vast selection of very sophisticated storage management algorithms can be reused easily. Some of these solutions leverage very good, general-purpose implementations of multithousand code line data management mechanisms. We need to think very hard about it before purposely choosing to write our own b+ tree when one is readily available via reuse.

Unfortunately, the easy availability of sophisticated storage structures makes it all too easy to use the wrong one. It is always a good idea to understand the underlying concepts behind the structures you plan on using, or at least to have a reasonable idea of the computational efficiency of the storage structures you select. Fortunately, the use of user-defined classes, with their associated constructor/destructor specification mechanism, can make the fundamental storage mechanism for a given class' objects transparent to the class' users. This can make transitioning from one storage management scheme to another fairly painless. Our recommendation is to start simple and employ increasingly sophisticated storage mechanisms as profiled performance metrics dictate.

For example, we may start with a simple array, or an STL `vector` as the storage mechanism for very large ordered lists. If profiling does not expose any flaws in this implementation, then we are done. If profiling indicates that we are spending too much time sorting or searching the array (`vector`), then we may choose to employ a hash table access mechanism. Or perhaps we could adopt a b* tree or an indexed key approach. The availability of these sophisticated management classes, with essentially identical interfaces, allows us to replace one management implementation with another easily. Adoption of increasingly sophisticated management code only when profiling indicates that we need it will allow us to use complexity when necessary and leave simplicity everywhere else. Remember, complexity is the enemy of correctness and maintainability. Employ the simplest solution that solves the problem. Parsimony says that the simplest working solution is the best—keep your software parsimonious.

In all this talk about being careful we failed to note one of the most effective C++ hardware oriented optimizations: *Get more memory* and *a faster processor!* We sometimes find ourselves spinning our optimization wheels trying to extract another 10% performance gain, sometimes at great expense, and we fail to do the obvious: respecify the minimal acceptable hardware requirements for the software. Going from a 200MHz processor with 32 megabytes of RAM to a 500MHz processor with 256 megabytes of RAM can do more to improve code performance than a hundred memory placement optimization tweaks. Hardware is relatively inexpensive; do not be afraid to admit that you are solving a big problem and that big software solutions require access to big hardware platforms.

Cache Effects

A cache provides more than just fast access for previously accessed data; it also provides a small prefetch region around that previously accessed data. Caches fetch and manage lines of data. A typical cache line consists of 32 bytes of data aligned on a 32-byte boundary. Typically caches lack the capability to manage anything other than complete lines. This means that if an instruction accesses a single byte of data at address 100, then the cache will load bytes 96–127 into a line. The initial access to address 100 may well result in a cache miss and cause the processor to stall for dozens of cycles while the desired data is fetched from memory (or half a dozen cycles if it is fetched from another level of the cache), but subsequent accesses to bytes 101, 102, 103, … 127 will probably not fault, unless a significant time passes before the neighboring locations are accessed.

This automatic cache blocking should be taken into consideration when building code. Consider the following two implementations of class 11a that encapsulate an array of linked lists into which 11a objects can be linked based on a priority argument. The first implementation uses two independent arrays of first and last pointers to maintain the priority list:

```
class 11a
{
public:
    ...
    void insert ();

private:
    ...
    int priority;
    11a *next;

    static 11a *first[1024];
    static 11a *last[1024];
}

void 11a::insert ()
{
    if (first[priority]) last[priority]->next = this;
    else first[priority] = this;
    last[priority] = this;
}
```

The second implementation uses a single array of first/last pairs:

```
class 11a {
public:
    ...
    void insert ();

private:
    ...
    int priority;
    11a *next;

    struct pairs {
        11a *first;
        11a *last;
    };
    static pairs ptrs[1024];
}
```

```
void lla::insert ()
{
    if (ptrs[priority].first) ptrs[priority].last->next = this;
    else ptrs[priority].first = this;
    ptrs[priority].last = this;
}
```

The second implementation may seem somewhat less obvious in its operation, but consider the cache effects of the two implementations. In the first implementation, the test of first[priority] will have no effect on the loading of last[priority]. A cache miss on the first access of first[priority] will not affect the likelihood that last[priority] will be present. In the second implementation, the first and last pairs are allocated in adjacent memory words. If the pairs array is properly aligned in memory, then the initial access to a first[priority] will guarantee that the associated last[priority] is present in the cache.

The entreaty to keep related data together does not only manifest itself in the cache. It is also possible that the initial access could page fault. In this example, the first and last arrays in the first implementation are each reasonably large, and it would not necessarily be the case that a page fault on first[priority] would also bring last[priority] into memory. Although any significant level of structure usage would tend to keep both arrays in memory and insignificant levels of usage will tend to have little impact on performance, it is still best to do things right the first time.

Cache Thrash

One of the interesting effects of having a cache in a multiprocessor system is the effect of cache coherency protocols on cache performance. A cache coherency protocol is a mechanism employed by memory/cache controllers that maintains a coherent view of memory across a number of what would otherwise be unassociated caches. The problem is simple: processor A wants to write to memory location 100 and processor B wants to read from memory location 100. If B has previously read from location 100 and has a copy of it in its cache then another read will not go out onto the system bus to refetch it. This is the behavior you want if the processor is to go fast. However, if processor A has written a new value to location 100 between the time B read that location the first time and the time B read it for the second time, then without a coherency protocol, processor B will read the stale (old, incorrect) contents of location 100, not the fresh (new, correct) content.

Cache coherency protocols are based on notions of memory ownership and explicit invalidation of peer cache entries on reads. This basically amounts to a protocol that allows multiple caches to share a copy of a single data item, but only one cache to have write privileges for the data item at a time. If the owner (the one with write access) is not actively updating the data, then other caches can have their own copy of the cache line, but every time the owner of the cache line modifies the line, it tells all other caches to invalidate their copy. Invalidating the other copies will force the other caches to get another copy before they read it again. This will allow the owning cache to supply its peer caches with what is now the only correct value for the cache line. At some point the cache line will be flushed out to memory, maintaining the overall consistency of the memory system.

Cache coherency protocols can require direct communication between caches. Significant amounts of such communication can slow system performance. This is because the path between the caches is a shared system resource. Such communication must be serialized between caches. This can force a cache to wait if the memory bus is already busy with another cache transaction. This waiting for cache update access is referred to as *cache thrash*. Cache thrash is typically the result of multiprocessor systems that do not maintain any processor affinity for its processes. Processor affinity amounts to keeping track of which processor a process ran on last time it executed, and trying to increase the likelihood that it will execute on that same processor the next time it executes.

Consider the effect of an affinity free process queue on a 2-way SMP system. The likelihood that a process will execute on the same processor it ran on previously is 50%. If a process is swapped out 10 times between invocation and termination, the likelihood that it will run on the same processor the entire time is one in one thousand. With increased processor scaling, the cache effect becomes worse. A 16-way SMP system only has a 1 in 16 chance of continuing a process on the same processor and a one in a trillion chance of executing on the same processor across 10 context switches.

As already discussed, maintaining a process' working set in a cache is the key to good performance, and cache misses idle the processor for dozens of cycles. Cache thrash is an antiscaling artifact that must be dealt with to obtain high performance in large-scale SMP systems. Some SMP systems are starting to provide affinity mechanisms for processor assignment. Though this is perhaps a very advanced hardware concept, it is also one that must be addressed for high performance software on multiprocessor systems. This is not a C++ issue. It is purely an operating system issue.

There is some disagreement about its importance, but we believe that when the dust settles, maintaining processor affinity for some high priority threads will have significant performance advantages, particularly on the next generation of multithreaded processors. If processor affinity characteristics ever filter down into the multithreading or multiprocessing programming interfaces, it is important to understand the implications of the capability the API is making available.

Avoid Branching

Modern processors tend not to be particularly branch friendly. In the "good old days" one processor instruction would finish before the next instruction was issued. This meant that if one instruction calculated the target for a branch or set a condition code on which a branch decision was dependent, the result of this instruction was available for immediate use by the next instruction. This made for a simple processor architecture, though generally not a particularly fast one.

Almost all modern processors are now pipelined. A pipelined processor breaks up instruction execution into a number of stages. A simple pipeline might have five stages: instruction fetch, instruction decode, operand fetch, operation execution, and result store. This five-stage pipe would, in general, mean that while one instruction was storing its result into a register, the next instruction would be using the ALU to calculate something, and the instruction after that would be fetching its operands from the registers, and the instruction after that one would be decoded, and still the next instruction would be fetched. During any given clock cycle the processor is engaged in five concurrent activities (the execution of five sequential instructions).

Pipelining makes for fast processing; ideally one instruction could finish per cycle, and the basic clock cycle for the processor could possibly be decreased by a factor of five relative to its nonpipelined predecessors (overly simplistic analysis, but hopefully you get the idea). This substantially improves performance when the pipeline can be kept filled. Unfortunately branches, particularly conditional branches, tend to stall the pipeline. A pipeline stall occurs when an instruction is prevented from entering the pipeline because its entry is contingent on an as yet unknown value. For example, suppose you had the following two assembly level statements:

```
CMP  r1,  r2 // compare r1 to r2 and set the condition codes
BLT  x       // branch if the condition codes indicate that the
             // result was less than zero.
```

The compare instruction might enter the pipeline during clock cycle 100, and the branch instruction would then enter at clock cycle 101. At clock cycle 102 we would ideally start loading the next instruction, but the condition in the branch requires that the compare instruction complete its subtraction and set the condition codes, which does not complete until cycle 104. This results in a two-cycle stall while we wait to decide whether we will branch or not. These two lost cycles could have been used to do some useful work if we had not branched.

Although this discussion of pipelining is admittedly overly simplistic, it does get at the core of the branch problem in pipelined processors. Sophisticated processors use branch prediction, out of order execution, and/or branch delay slots to decrease the cost of branching. Conversely, such processors also tend to have deeper pipelines (more stages between operation completion and instruction fetch), and short of a multithreaded processor approach (that sacrifices latency for bandwidth and is still a very new technology), small branching will remain an uncomfortable expense.

One place where branching seems to be much in evidence is argument sanity checking. We have seen numerous instances of functions that are 90% argument checking and 10% calculation. Unfortunately most of this argument checking is conditional testing. Given that conditional testing has negative performance repercussions, it is best to try to keep overly defensive programming out of the critical code path. We have seen numerous instances in which a value is passed down through three or four levels of function calls and the same range check is applied to it at every level. This repetitive application of conditional branching gobbles cycles without a commensurate benefit.

The fastest code is straight line code: no conditional tests, no loops, no calls, no returns. In general, the more the critical path of a program looks like a straight line, the faster it will execute. Remember: Short code sequences with lots of branches will frequently take longer to execute than longer code sequences with no branches.

Prefer Simple Calculations to Small Branches

As previously discussed, branching can be expensive in performance terms. Frequently, branching cannot be avoided, but sometimes branching is used in place of calculation. This can be a critical performance mistake. Take, for example, the following code sequence:

```
const int X_MAX = 16;
...
++x;
if (x >= X_MAX) {
    x = 0;
    }
```

It is really just a bit mask operation and can just as easily be done with the following code sequence:

```
const int X_MASK = 15;
...
x = (x + 1) & X_MASK;
```

In the first case there is a load, an increment, a store, a conditional test, and another store. Even on a machine with a short pipeline, the conditional test will cost at least three cycles, and thus the effective cost of the conditional solution is roughly the same as executing seven machine code instructions. The unconditional version has a load, an increment, possibly one or two instruction mask creation sequences (something to get the value 15 into a register or immediate field), a bit-wise AND operation, and a store. In the worst case this is six instructions, in the general case this is only four instructions; almost twice as fast as the conditional version. On a deeply pipelined machine the calculated version will be proportionally faster.

Notice that these code sequences are essentially equivalent, but not exactly so. The first solution is more flexible than the second one. There is no power-of-two alignment requirement for X_MAX, but there is one for X_MASK. Thus, for the values in the example they provide the same function, although the faster solution is more restrictive than the first. In general, if performance is of primary importance, we should expect to trade some flexibility for fast calculations that avoid the necessity to branch.

Threading Effects

Multiprocessing and multithreading are two closely related, but different, types of concurrent programming. Although both concepts exist in a larger context, we will limit our discussion to their impact on the creation of a monolithic software system, not on the interaction of multiple essentially independent software systems within an operating system environment.

Multiprocessing is an old concept. Multiprocessing allows multiple, largely independent processes to communicate with each other. Processes used to be the schedulable entities that existed in an operating system. Historically, multiprocessing was the only mechanism available to system designers who wanted to be able to perform multiple, pseudoconcurrent, asynchronous activities. InterProcess Communication (IPC), typically a socket library, was used to facilitate communication between processes. `fork()` and `exec()` were used to create new processes and process termination was used to join processes. Processes cooperated via socket calls, pipes, shared memory, and semaphores. None of these were particularly easy to use, and each was very operating system specific.

Multithreading is a more recent concept. Threads are subprocesses. They are pieces of a larger process, but they are also independently schedulable. Threading, in perhaps overly simplistic terms, is just multiprocessing, in which a group of lightweight processes can all access a shared memory region. Each lightweight process in the group of processes that share a memory region would be a thread, and the group as a whole would be referred to as a process or task. Threads are the schedulable entities within a task. Most operating systems treat threads as their only schedulable entity; that is, a task cannot be scheduled, only the threads within the task can be scheduled. Most threading systems treat tasks as memory management structures and threads as scheduling structures. A much more involved discussion of task scheduling can be found in almost any operating systems text.

Any discussion of multitasking from an application's viewpoint will need to include a discussion of blocking. There are typically two different flavors of most I/O requests: blocking and nonblocking, or synchronous and asynchronous. Synchronous I/O waits for the requested I/O to complete before it allows its processing context to continue; that is, it blocks, waiting for its I/O request to be fully satisfied. Asynchronous I/O performs as much of the requested I/O transaction as is immediately satisfiable, and returns to its processing context the amount of progress it has made, but it does not block no matter how little of the requested transaction was completed. Typically, there is also an intermediate I/O request capability, one that acts synchronously for a specific amount of time and them becomes asynchronous. Although this middle ground between synchronous and asynchronous operation provides interesting operational capabilities to tasks, from a performance viewpoint it is essentially synchronous in its operation.

A thread blocks when it synchronously requests a resource or some data that is unavailable. The requesting thread must then wait for the system to satisfy the request, which typically requires the completion of an I/O operation. While a thread is waiting for the completion of its associated I/O operation it is swapped out of the processor, and other threads that are not blocked are allowed to run. After the requested I/O completes, the thread once again becomes schedulable and it will eventually be swapped back into the processor. A blocked, very high priority thread will typically resume processing as soon as its I/O request completes.

A typical program is synchronously single threaded, and as such, it can only do one thing at a time. Any time a request is made that cannot be fulfilled immediately, the entire program becomes blocked waiting for the operating system to complete the request. Conversely, some sophisticated programs are written with multiple logically concurrent physical or logical processing streams. This allows multiple, relatively independent aspects of a program to execute without regard to whether one of them may, at some particular time, be unable to completely satisfy an I/O request. For example, a multithreaded program that contains ten threads could still make forward progress even if nine of its ten threads were blocked. A program that relied on asynchronous I/O could continue to execute even if an I/O request did not return all the desired data. Writing software that supports the concept of concurrent execution, though more complicated, can provide much better performance, particularly in terms of its latency characteristics, than simple synchronous single-threaded solutions. This performance advantage of multithreading becomes even more pronounced on multiprocessor systems that can really perform multiple operations in parallel.

Multithreading is a very valuable capability, and on the right systems it can yield tremendous performance advantages, but misapplication of the threading concept can cause significant performance problems. Multithreading implies context switches and context switches can consume thousands of processing cycles. Multithreading also frequently requires locks around shared memory regions. Locks can also consume a significant number of processing cycles without making any progress towards program completion. Although multithreading is now relatively easy to do, we have found that it seems to be hard to do right. Far too often programs are broken up into threads that lack the necessary level of independence from each other to make threading effective. We have seen numerous examples of threaded programs that had so many locks and serialization semaphores that the net result was serialized thread execution (more than one simultaneously runable threads was the exception rather than the rule). When the overhead of context switching was added into the mix, some of these programs ran faster as asynchronously polled monolithic programs, than as synchronous multithreaded programs. One of the keys to understanding the cost equation for multithreading is to understand the performance impact of context switching.

Context Switching

What is a context switch and why is it so expensive? A context switch is moving one process (thread) out of a processor and another process into the processor. This involves saving the process' and the processor's state. The process' state needs to be saved so that an accurate record of the process' execution point is maintained. The processor's state needs to be saved so that the processor can be put back into that state when the associated process continues its execution. Processor state is a component of a process' state, but not the whole story.

A process context is an operating system construct, and as such is very OS dependent. It is managed by a structure in the OS that contains the relevant aspects of a process' state, such as allocated memory range, page map table, open file pointers, child processes, processor state variables (registers, program counter, possibly translation-lookaside buffer (TLB)), and process state variables like priority, owner, invocation time, and current state (runable, blocked, running). The bulk of a process' state is located in memory and is accessed only occasionally, but the processor state portion of a process context is used constantly by the processor and must be resident in the processor for a process to execute. The process-dependent portion of a processor's state must migrate from the processor to memory every time a process is swapped out, and it must be loaded back into the processor every time a process is swapped back in.

There are three primary cost aspects to a context switch: processor context migration, cache and TLB loss, and scheduler overhead. Let us address each in order. A processor context is the portion of a processor's state that is specific to a process. This typically includes the entire register set, including the program counter and stack pointer when they are not included in the register set proper; any conditional status flags, typically included in a processor status word or two; page table pointers, valid address range indices; and possibly a portion of the TLB, a structure that caches page table entries. Page tables are used to manage the individual pages that make up a process' linear virtual address space. Saving a process' state typically requires the writing to memory of between 20 and 50 words of data. This is the explicit cost of a context switch, and in some cases its least expensive aspect, with a cost of sometimes as little as 100 cycles, though it should be remembered that it is at least 100 cycles to save one context and then at least another 100 to load another. Machines with more registers and/or more processor resident process contexts would see proportionally more context switch overhead.

The interaction between context switches and caches often has the most pernicious impact on a program's performance. The structure and type of cache will have a significant impact on this characteristic of system performance. Caches can be partitioned into two classes based on the type of address with which they are accessed. Virtually addressed caches are accessed with addresses from the process' virtual address space. Virtual addresses are not process specific. That is, every process in a system may be using virtual address 100, but the physical resolution of virtual address 100 will be possibly hundreds of different physical addresses. A cache that relied purely on virtual addresses would need to be flushed/invalidated on each context switch. This would mean that after every context switch, a process would need to rebuild its cache content.

Suppose a process' working set is made up of 200 cache lines. This would mean that rebuilding the working set from scratch after a context switch would entail 200 cache misses. At a dozen cycles per miss, this is 1,200 cycles of additional context switch overhead. This is perhaps one of the reasons that there are very few systems that rely on virtually addressed caches. There are mechanisms that can decrease these types of cache effects. For example, a process identification field can be added to the cache line's address tag. This would allow multiple instances of the same virtual address to exist in the cache (each would have a different process ID), and it would remove the necessity of flushing the cache on a context switch. This would allow a cache to handle multiple processes efficiently, and cold cache start (using a logically empty cache) penalties would be decreased.

The other type of cache, physically addressed caches, are essentially the same as virtual caches with ID tags. The difference is that instead of relying on the ID/address pair in the tag, they force the system to translate virtual addresses into physical addresses before they are submitted to the cache. The reality is that because of the mechanism used for page mapping, the bottom 9–14 bits of the address can be sent immediately and only the remaining upper bits of an address actually require translation. This turns out to be very handy in terms of cache latency. Physical caches also make it easier to eject lines from the cache. Their memory location is specified in the line's tag and is independent of process-specific page mapping. Most processors use physically mapped caches. This makes context switching transparent to the cache; that is, a context switch need not invalidate cache lines. Physically mapped caches can have better context switching characteristics than virtual ones, but even with a physically mapped cache there is still a capacity problem. The cache can hold only so much data. Take, for example, a processor with a 32K-byte L1 cache with a 32-byte line size. Such a cache has 1,024 cache lines. If a machine with this sort of cache were multiprocessing on a set of 10 processes, then the relative processor residence characteristics of each of these processes would determine the amount of warm data the cache holds when a process is switched into the processor.

Suppose process A is swapped out and process B is swapped in, but B only executes momentarily and is then swapped out, and A is swapped back in. In this case you can reasonably expect that the 1,024 cache lines will still contain a reasonably good set of A's context. Conversely, suppose A is switched out because of a page fault. It could be a million cycles before A is runnable again. The other nine processes will probably walk all over the cache in that time and when A makes it back into the processor it is unlikely that any of A's context will still be cache resident. A significant amount of the motivation for the currently spiraling L2 cache sizes is an attempt to build caches large enough to provide a modicum of transcendence to process cache context.

The data and instruction cache(s) are only one form of cache in most modern processors. Translation-look-aside buffers (TLBs), caches for a process' page map tables, are another type of cache. TLBs are very variable in size, sometimes as small as eight entries and sometimes more than hundreds of entries. TLBs are as system dependent as register sets. Some TLBs are process identification tagged and can transcend a context switch, and others are not and need to be invalidated on a context switch. Hit rates for TLB tend to be fairly high, and a single TLB entry can map a significant amount of data. Conversely, TLB misses can be much more expensive—two to five times more expensive—than cache misses. Cold starts on TLBs are another significant aspect of the performance cost of context switches. The cost of dynamically recovering a dozen TLB entries can easily run into the 500-cycle range.

The last major context switch cost is scheduler execution. The scheduler typically is executed as the last phase of most interrupts. The scheduler will decide whether to continue running the interrupted process, or whether to load a different process back into the processor. A scheduler is part of an operating system's core functionality; in fact, the micro-kernel type operating systems have a kernel that is little more than a scheduler. Although scheduling is relatively straightforward and need not consume a significant number of operating cycles, there are complications, like process aging and dynamic priority assignment, that consume something between 50 and 500 cycles.

Thus the first order, explicit cost of a context switch (processor state migration and scheduler execution) consumes somewhere between 250 and 1000 cycles. Second order, context switch costs (cache and TLB misses) can consume thousands of additional cycles more. This makes context switches moderately expensive, and not an event that a high-performance program would invite without good reason.

Kernel Crossing

Asynchronous polling can be a reasonable alternative to synchronous multithreading. Although not as simple a software technique, it can, on some systems, offer significant performance advantages. The issue surrounds the cost of kernel crossings relative to context switches. We have already discussed context switching, so let us now delve into the notion of a kernel crossing.

A kernel crossing occurs when a program explicitly calls a service routine that requires kernel privilege to execute. When this happens, one of two things happens: a fat system call or a thin system call; depending on the mechanism employed by the operating system and depending on the type of service requested.

Fat system calls are, in their worst cases, full context switches into the kernel. The process requesting service is swapped out and the kernel service routine is swapped in. The scheduler typically is executed after the service routine to determine which process will run next. If the service request was satisfied, the requesting process is still runnable, the process has not consumed all of its execution quantum (maximum amount of time a process may continuously occupy the processor), and there is no other process with higher priority waiting, then the process that requested the service will be swapped back into the processor. Thus servicing the fat system call required almost two full context switches (the scheduler was run only once).

Some kernel service requests can be satisfied without performing a full context switch. A thin system call need only save a few registers and change the processing priority and level of the system. Such calls can perform their work with relatively little impact on performance and return to the calling routine with something that looks like little more than a very expensive method call. The processor vendors are increasingly cognizant of the cost of kernel crossings and are starting to build special purpose kernel entry and exit capabilities into the hardware. Such systems can be in and out of the kernel in a few hundred cycles, roughly an order of magnitude less overhead than a fat kernel crossing.

On systems with efficient kernel entry mechanisms, a dozen asynchronous I/O operations can consume less time than a single synchronous one. This can make the adoption of a multithreading approach (based on internally managed I/O vectors within a single monolithic process) an interesting alternative to systems-managed multithreading. Polling (asynchronous reading and writing) the significant I/O vectors allows a single program to avoid the locking and serialization frequently necessary in system-managed multithreading and obviates the need for context switches between threads. If a quick perusal of the I/O vectors yields no processable data, then a synchronous "select" style I/O call can be employed to put the process to sleep until additional data arrives. Conversely, if an I/O vector is polled a dozen times without any change in state, then a context switch would probably have been faster.

Threading Choices

There are three primary threading approaches: monolithic, small-scale, and large-scale. Monolithic threading, in its simplest incarnation, is just a typical simple program that has only one thread of control. However, in its more sophisticated forms, monolithically threaded programs can use asynchronous I/O to perform logically concurrent and independent activities. The monolithic, asynchronous model relies on structures internal to the program to monitor the state of the program's constituent pieces, and it relies on polling to test the availability of I/O within those pieces. Using asynchronous I/O guarantees: one, that no subtask will block the entire task because some I/O request is not immediately satisfied; and two, that the control element of the program will be able to determine when to relinquish control of the processor and when to continue processing. Such systems tend to be built around a central control loop that serially executes each subsystem. This tends to be a very complicated approach, but one that can offer better performance than its multithreaded peers in some environments. It is also an approach that, when misapplied, can become lost in fruitless polling cycles that make no progress. Software built on this asynchronous model allows logically multithreaded structures to be layered on top of operating systems that do not support multithreading. It can also ease multiplatform porting concerns by removing any reliance on what may turn out to be divergent, platform-specific, threading characteristics.

Large-scale threading is a mechanism that treats processing requests as independent processing entities. This can be thought of as the one thread per significant object methodology. Significant objects are, at birth, allocated their own thread whose sole purpose is to journey with the object from birth to death. This mechanism can be very effective, but it can also suffer from context switch fever. This approach is perhaps the simplest conceptually, treating core objects as semi-independent synchronous programs. Unfortunately, the semi-independence can sometimes be illusory if the threaded objects rely too much on shared resources. The serialization semaphores necessary to prevent concurrent access to critical code sections can result in threads burning cycles spinning on locks, on wake-up storms (the system waking up a group of threads when a resource becomes available only to have all but one of the newly awakened threads go right back to sleep after consuming a context switch), or both.

Small-scale threading is a mechanism that mixes elements of monolithic threading with elements of large-scale threading. Small-scale threading tends to be centered more around completion of subtasks than around the entire completion of individual processing requests. In small-scale threaded environments objects tend to migrate from thread to thread as they journey from birth to death. Small-scale multithreading tends to be more complicated than large-scale multithreading, but it is less likely to suffer from thread serialization problems, it decreases context switch overhead relative to large-scale threading, and it tends to provide better scalability than monolithic threading.

Take, for example, a simple program that starts by spawning three threads, one thread to manage input, one thread to perform the program's primary function, and one thread to manage output. Suppose the threads communicate via pipes. This is a very respectable model for program execution, but it can be an expensive paradigm in the wrong situation. Suppose the program is interested primarily in character-based input, and that the input thread collects characters, performs some simple input filtering and editing, and passes what it receives on to the central function thread. If input rates are low, this could mean that the program performs a context switch between the input thread and the central process thread every time a character arrives. A context switch can cost a thousand instructions. The question must be asked: Would asynchronously polling the input stream of a monolithic program consume fewer cycles than constant context switching?

There is no fixed answer. Sometimes the context switching is more expensive and sometimes the asynchronous polling is more expensive. The right answer for a particular application is wrapped up in a number of issues. Does processing new input have immediate processing requirements? Is the expected rate of input high or low? How much input processing can be done in the input thread? On what type of hardware will I be running? Application of the wrong threading model can significantly impact system performance, and of course picking the right model can significantly improve performance. Unfortunately, a program's threading model is not easily changed as part of a post implementation performance optimization.

Possibly the most significant aspect of the threading decision will be the hardware base upon which the program is expected to run. Are you writing for a desktop system on which response latency is probably the most important performance requirement, or are you writing server software, where latency may not be as critical as throughput, and where resource usage may be more constrained? Does your intended hardware platform have any specific features that make context switching less expensive? Are you targeted at multiprocessor systems?

Applications that require minimal response latency are typically better served by synchronous multithreaded solutions than by asynchronous polled solutions. This is because asynchronous programs rely on control loops and lack a mechanism to alert themselves when input arrives. The main problem here is that asynchronously polling a device is not free. It costs cycles. The more you do it and find that there was nothing there, the poorer the program's performance. The less you look for input, the less performance the polling loop consumes, but the poorer the program's response latency. If latency is not a concern, then an asynchronous polled solution may offer the best performance; if latency is a concern, then multithreading is probably the right direction.

Busy servers are frequently resource constrained. A server may not welcome your program's 1,000 preallocated service threads. Conversely, servers are increasingly multiprocessor systems. Monolithic software cannot spread itself out across multiple processors like the other models. This can result in idle processors even when the program is swamped with data.

A new series of processor architectures that will significantly change the effective costs of multithreading is currently under development. Multithreaded architectures have the capability of performing essentially zero overhead context switches. This makes it unadvised, in the long term, to accept the complication and expense of managing a logically synchronous threading model by managing it yourself within an asynchronous model. In the shorter term, a serious design decision must be made with regard to whether to use a synchronous model or an asynchronous one. Sadly this is not the type of decision that can be delayed until after a system is built and then "fixed" as part of the system's profile-based optimization. It is nontrivial to change a system's threading model, and virtually impossible to alter it conditionally along a program's critical path. Thread models are very good candidates for prototyping early in the design phase.

Key Points

- The farther the memory you want to use is from the processor, the longer it takes to access. The resource closest to the processor, registers, are limited in their capability, but extremely fast. Their optimization can be very valuable.

- Virtual memory is not free. Indiscriminate reliance on system maintained virtual structures can have very significant performance ramifications, typically negative ones.

- Context switches are expensive; avoid them.

- Lastly, though we are aware that internally managed asynchronous I/O has its place, we also feel that the coming shift in processor architecture will significantly disadvantage monolithic threading approaches.

Bibliography

[ALG95] J. Alger. *Secrets of the C++ Masters*. AP Professional, Chestnut Hill, MA (1995).

[AHU74] A. Aho, J. Hopcroft, and J. Ullman. *The Design and Analysis of Computer Algorithms*. Addison-Wesley, Reading, MA (1974).

[Ben82] J. L. Bentley. *Writing Efficient Programs*. Prentice-Hall, Englewood Cliffs, NJ (1982).

[BM97] B. Meyer. *Object-Oriented Software Construction, Second Edition*. Prentice-Hall PTR, Englewood Cliffs, NJ (1997).

[BR95] A. Binstock and J. Rex. *Practical Algorithms for Programmers*. Addison-Wesley, Reading, MA (1995).

[BR97] R. Booth. *Inner Loops*. Addison-Wesley, Reading, MA (1997).

[BW97] J. Beveridge and R. Wiener. *Multithreading Applications in Win32*. Addison-Wesley, Reading, MA (1997).

[Cam91] M. Campbell *et al*. "The Parallelization of UNIX System V Release 4.0," *Proceedings of the Winter 1991 USENIX Conference*.

[Car92] T. Cargill. *C++ Programming Style*. Addison-Wesley, Reading, MA (1992).

[CE95]   M. Carroll and M. Ellis. *Designing and Coding Reusable C++*. Addison-Wesley, Reading, MA (1995).

[CL95]   M. P. Cline and G. A. Lomow. *C++ FAQs: Frequently Asked Questions*. Addison-Wesley, Reading, MA (1995).

[CL99]   M. Cline, G. Lomow, and M. Girou. *C++ FAQs, Second Edition*. Addison-Wesley, Reading, MA, (1999).

[ES90]   M. A. Ellis and B. Stroustrup. *The Annotated C++ Reference Manual*. Addison-Wesley, Reading, MA (1990).

[GH95]   E. Gamma, R. Helm, R. Johnson, and J. Vlissides. *Design Patterns: Elements of Reusable Object-Oriented Software*. Addison-Wesley, Reading, MA (1995).

[HP96]   J. Hennessy and D. Patterson. *Computer Architecture: A Quantitative Approach*. Morgan Kaufmann, San Francisco, CA, (1996).

[KP74]   B. W. Kernighan and P. J. Plauger. *The Elements of Programming Style*. McGraw-Hill, New York, NY (1974).

[KR88]   B. W. Kernighan and D. M. Ritchie. *The C Programming Language, Second Edition*. Prentice-Hall, Englewood Cliffs, NJ (1988).

[Knu97] D. E. Knuth. *The Art of Computer Programming: Fundamental Algorithms, Volume 1, Third Edition*. Addison-Wesley, Reading, MA (1997).

[Knu97] D. E. Knuth. *The Art of Computer Programming: Seminumerical Algorithms, Volume 2, Third Edition*. Addison-Wesley, Reading, MA (1998).

[Knu97] D. E. Knuth. *The Art of Computer Programming: Sorting and Searching, Volume 3, Second Edition*. Addison-Wesley, Reading, MA (1998).

[Lak96] J. Lakos. *Large-Scale C++ Software Design*. Addison-Wesley, Reading, MA (1996).

[Lew1]   T. Lewis. "The Next 10,000 Years: Part 1," *IEEE Computer*. April 1996.

[Lew2]   T. Lewis. "The Next 10,000 Years: Part 1," *IEEE Computer.* May 1996.

[Lip91]   S. B. Lippman and J. Lajoie. *C++ Primer, Third Edition.* Addison-Wesley, Reading, MA (1998).

[Lip96C] S. B. Lippman, Editor. *C++ Gems.* SIGS Books and Multimedia (1996).

[Lip96I]   S. B. Lippman. *Inside the C++ Object Model.* Addison-Wesley, Reading, MA (1996).

[McC93] S. McConnell. *Code Complete.* Microsoft Press, Redmond, WA (1993).

[Mey96] S. Meyers. *More Effective C++.* Addison-Wesley, Reading, MA (1996).

[Mey97] S. Meyers. *Effective C++, Second Edition.* Addison-Wesley, Reading, MA (1998).

[MS96]   D. R. Musser and A. Saini. *STL Tutorial and Reference Guide.* Addison-Wesley, Reading, MA (1996).

[Mur93] R. B. Murray. *C++ Strategies and Tactics.* Addison-Wesley, Reading, MA (1993).

[NBF96] B. Nichols, D. Buttlar, and J. P. Farrell. *Pthreads Programming.* O'Reilly & Associates, Inc., Cambridge, MA (1996).

[O98]   J. M. Orost. "The Bench++ Benchmark Suite,*" Dr. Dobbs Journal,* October 1998.

[Pat]   D. A. Patterson. "Microprocessors in 2020," *Scientific American,* September 1995.

[PH97]   D. Patterson and J. Hennessy. *Computer Organization and Design: The Hardware/Software Interface.* Morgan Kaufmann, San Francisco, CA (1997).

[Str97]   B. Stroustrup. *The C++ Programming Language, Third Edition.* Addison-Wesley, Reading, MA (1997).

Index

Register
Your Book

at www.awprofessional.com/register

You may be eligible to receive:

- Advance notice of forthcoming editions of the book
- Related book recommendations
- Chapter excerpts and supplements of forthcoming titles
- Information about special contests and promotions throughout the year
- Notices and reminders about author appearances, tradeshows, and online chats with special guests

Contact us

If you are interested in writing a book or reviewing manuscripts prior to publication, please write to us at:

Editorial Department
Addison-Wesley Professional
75 Arlington Street, Suite 300
Boston, MA 02116 USA
Email: AWPro@aw.com

Addison-Wesley

Visit us on the Web: http://www.awprofessional.com